Tl   g Nineteenth Century, 1750–1914

The Long Nineteenth Century, 1750–1914

Crucible of Modernity

Trevor R. Getz

BLOOMSBURY ACADEMIC
LONDON • NEW YORK • OXFORD • NEW DELHI • SYDNEY

BLOOMSBURY ACADEMIC
Bloomsbury Publishing Plc
50 Bedford Square, London, WC1B 3DP, UK
1385 Broadway, New York, NY 10018, USA

BLOOMSBURY, BLOOMSBURY ACADEMIC and the Diana logo are trademarks of
Bloomsbury Publishing Plc

First published in Great Britain 2018

Cover design: Adriana Brioso
Cover image: "Saruwaka Cho, Yoru Shibai," 1856 (1925). Saruwaka Street, Yedo, with theatres, in
light of the full moon. A print from The Colour Prints of Hiroshige by Edward F. Strange, by Cassell
and Company Limited, 1925. (© The Print Collector/Getty Images)

Bloomsbury Publishing Plc does not have any control over, or responsibility for, any third-party
websites referred to or in this book. All internet addresses given in this book were correct at the
time of going to press. The author and publisher regret any inconvenience caused if addresses
have changed or sites have ceased to exist, but can accept no responsibility for any such changes.

A catalogue record for this book is available from the British Library.

A catalog record for this book is available from the Library of Congress.

ISBN: HB: 978-1-4742-7053-3
PB: 978-1-4742-7052-6
ePDF: 978-1-4742-7055-7
eBook: 978-1-4742-7054-0

Series: The Making of the Modern World

Typeset by Newgen KnowledgeWorks Pvt. Ltd., Chennai, India
Printed and bound in Great Britain

To find out more about our authors and books visit www.bloomsbury.com
and sign up for our newsletters.

Contents

List of Illustrations

Series Introduction

The Making of the Modern World

This world history series comprises a unique, three-volume, set of books for use in the classroom or for those wishing to understand world history since 1500.

It consists of three separate volumes:

The Early Modern World, 1450–1750: Seeds of Modernity (forthcoming)
John C. Corbally, Trevor R. Getz, and Jacob Whittaker

The Long Nineteenth Century, 1750–1914: Crucible of Modernity (2018)
Trevor R. Getz

The Twentieth-Century World, 1914 to the Present: State of Modernity (2018)
John C. Corbally

The series is unconventional in its approach to understanding the world since 1500 through popular perspectives and experiences: those of common, ordinary people; of peasants, women, workers, slaves, serfs, and outsiders rather than of kings, generals, or politicians. In doing so, it aims to understand humanity's past by transcending the traditional emphasis on nations, empires, masculinity, war, or acquisition.

The authors intend for a diverse array of learners to appreciate just how connected our globalized world has been since 1500, instead of assuming separate peoples lived in separate nations with separate histories. They reveal rather than hide the complex and unappealing sides of history, outlining the history as it is understood, whether pleasing or not.

The series is purposely written in a nonacademic style, to invite students and general readers to enjoy the story while learning the broad outlines of world history. It is clearly organized, with short segments providing the opportunity for the reader to absorb one section at a time. Each chapter in each volume has a clear thesis, making a historical point supported by the sources, exploring a distinct period of the modern past through five different lenses: environmental, political, economic, intellectual, and technological history. Framed around social experience and cultural perspective, each chapter in each volume explores the development and contested construction of modernity. Together, the series forms an interpretation of the modern past that will help readers both understand and question the development of the world in which we live.

What Is This Book?

This book is a history of the world during the long nineteenth century, c.1750–1914, a period of great transformation in global affairs and human experience. Its subtitle, *The Crucible of Modernity*, is meant to reflect the interpretation that it was during this period that the world entered a new phase—the modern era. The chapters of this book introduce many of the critical themes of this era on a global scale. Moreover, this is a textbook, and as such it was designed to be a framework for exploring themes and episodes more deeply in a classroom setting.

The Long Nineteenth Century: The Crucible of Modernity is structured around seven themes. This was a period in which the world was truly being knit together and therefore an era in which a number of themes can be usefully employed to tie together important stories about changes and continuities that were experienced across continents and oceans. The seven chapters of this book reflect these useful categories—political (empire and nation), economic, intellectual and religious, technological, and environmental (demographic and scientific). The approach I take to is to focus on continuity and change in individual and collective human experiences. From these stories, I seek to say something important about how individuals and groups of people lived their lives and sought to manage and understand the changes going on around them. I also try to share the vision of history as an element of our everyday lives. Not only do the events of the past have an impact on how we live today, but they are also things that people strive to understand through nostalgia, traditions, memories, heritage projects, and popular culture. I try to dig a bit deeper into those connections in three interludes between the chapters of this book. These interludes explore ways that people in our own time have interacted with the events and experiences of the period 1750–1914.

One final note. Some teachers believe that the purpose of history classes is to simplify the past and make it easier to understand. While I agree that it's important to write and teach histories that are understandable, I also want to help students understand how messy the real human past is, and thus to leave them with questions that can stimulate an intellectual curiosity that takes them far beyond the book. I hope both instructors and students find this book useful in that regard.

Trevor Getz

Introduction: The Construction of Modernity

The Xhosa Cattle Killing

On a bright day in April, 1856, a young woman of about 15 and a girl of about 10 were watching the maize grow on the banks of the Gharxa River in South Africa. The woman was named Nongqawuse, and her sister was named Nombanda, and they were members of the Xhosa people. Their job that day was to scare birds away from their crops. Food was scarce in the Xhosa kingdom that year. The arrival of corn (maize) from the Americas two centuries earlier had helped to increase the population of this region, which enjoyed a pleasant climate perfect for growing Mediterranean grains such as wheat and American crops such as corn (maize) brought by Europeans in the seventeenth century. However, those Europeans—first the Dutch in 1652 and later the British—had brought not only new crops but also diseases such as smallpox, and they were equipped with horses and firearms. Together, disease and weaponry, over a period of 200 years, pushed the Xhosa into smaller and smaller territories. European settlers who occupied their land turned it into vast ranches on which sheep were raised to supply wool to the voracious textile factories of industrial Britain.

As European-owned ranches and farms spread across the countryside, the territories that still belonged to the Xhosa became more and more crowded with refugees. Then, in the early 1850s, the Xhosa were hit by an imported disease called rinderpest that killed off many of their cattle. Finally, a series of droughts in the same years deeply affected the production of grain. These tragedies, and especially the death of many cows and bulls, had a severe impact on Xhosa society. In Xhosa tradition, cattle ownership helped to indicate status and mark the authority of chiefs. It was also a symbol of adulthood for men, and the ritual payment of cattle from a man's family to a woman's was one part of the process by which a couple set up their own household. As fewer men could afford cattle, marriages decreased and incidents of nonconsensual sex increased, deeply affecting women's sexual security just as it affected men's ability to achieve status. As the cattle died off, both authority on a grand scale and domestic tranquility were disturbed, and Xhosa society entered a period of turmoil.

Figure 0.1 Xhosa combatants after a fight with the British. Their wounded comrades are carried on the backs of cattle, whom the Xhosa prized highly.

It was in the midst of this turmoil that Nongqawuse and Nombanda were sitting by the edge of the river, guarding their crops from the birds. On this morning, however, they heard a rustle in the bushes, and a voice said to them:

Legend
voice of
their
chiefs
(ore-that)

You are to tell the people that the whole community is to rise again from the dead. Then go on to say to them that all the cattle living now must be slaughtered, for they are reared with defiled hands, as the people handle witchcraft. Say to them there must be no ploughing of land, rather must the people dig deep pits (granaries), erect new huts, set up wide, strongly built cattlefolds, make milksacks, and weave doors from buka roots. The people must give up witchcraft on their own, not waiting until they are exposed by the witchdoctors. You are to tell them that these are the words of their chiefs—the words of Napakade [the forever man] and Sifubasibanzi [the broad-chested one].[1]

The instructions of these two ancestor-spirits, Napakade and Sifubasibanzi, were clear. If the Xhosa would kill their cattle, burn their crops, and foreswear "witchcraft," their ancestors would return with great hordes of cattle and stores of grain. These reinforcements would help them defeat and drive off the British settlers. The result would be a return of the better days of the past about which the elders reminisced.

In the months that followed, tens of thousands of Xhosa followed these instructions, destroying their cattle and crops and building houses and enclosures for the ancestors and their cattle soon to return. When the ancestors failed to appear, many Xhosa were left destitute. Some starved to death, while others had to travel to British territory to seek help; a few managed to get food from European missionaries. The British governor of Cape Colony, however, ordered that no Xhosa receive help unless he or she agreed to become workers on settler's ranches or for the government. He hoped in this way he could not only provide cheap labor for European ranchers but also put the Xhosa into a subservient position that he believed was appropriate for black Africans. Consequently, he gained new territory for the British Empire and considerable prestige for himself.

In the following years, the last independent Xhosa territory was swallowed up by the European settlers, who annexed it to the Cape Colony. Most Xhosa men became workers on sheep farms and in mines, producing raw materials for British factories. Xhosa social rules fell apart, and the chiefs—who had once ruled through community consultation and by the power of their own wealth and authority—became instead poorly paid officials carrying out the laws and edicts of the colonial government.

The creation of the modern world

The Xhosa "cattle killing" episode, as it is known, was just one incident in the creation of the modern world. It is an episode that highlights the process by which a particular system and lifestyle changed dramatically through the confluence of several nineteenth-century global trends. One of these was the rise of capitalism and the industrial economy, by which factories in Britain and a few other industrialized countries began to demand raw materials like wool from not only the southern tip of Africa but also distant Australia, as well as Canada. A linked phenomenon was the spread of colonialism to many corners of the world, partly to gain possession of land and resources. By 1914, when this book concludes, most of Africa, South and Southeast Asia, Oceania, and the Pacific had become colonies of transcontinental empires based in Europe, Japan, and North America. The Xhosa kingdom had merely been one victim of this empire-building.

These economic and political trends resulted in major social and cultural transformations. The spread of evangelical Christianity by missionaries was one of these. This transformation is evident in Nongqawuse's story. The two "ancestors," Sifubasibanzi and Napakade, were likely based at least partly on Jesus Christ and the Christian God, and the cattle killing was very much influenced by the notions of the apocalypse taught by Christian missionaries. The spread of Christianity was tied in his era to the "civilizing mission," a set of ideas based on the concept that "modern," industrial European civilization was superior to that of the others, and that Europeans had the responsibility to bring the advantages of their own society to others. This set of ideas coexisted uneasily within colonialism with scientific racism, which held that inferior societies would naturally dwindle away or take on a subservient role, and should not be protected or helped. These racialist ideas were present in the response of the British governor of Cape Colony to the cattle killing when he refused to give aid to the Xhosa refugees.

Another cultural tension within modernity in this period was the struggle over women's power and status in the world. This was represented in Xhosa society by the loss of protection for women's sexual rights as cattle disappeared and women like Nongqawuse tried to fix the situation.

This book discusses transformations like these that were experienced in common, but in unique ways, by societies in many parts of around the world in this period. Together, this pattern of changes can be described as the coming of **modernity**. For our purposes, modernity can be defined as a set of experiences and perspectives, many of them rooted in an earlier period described in Volume 1 of this series, *The Seeds of Modernity, 1492–1750*, but maturing and spreading around the world during the period 1750–1914. The components of modernity may be said to include a number of features:

- political ideas like nationalism and imperialism and the structures of the nation-state and empire that they supported
- the technological and social transformation of the Industrial Revolution
- capitalist global economy and social organization that underpinned industrial production and the socialist critique aimed against it
- urbanization, population growth, and the increasing diversity of communities as migrants and travelers moved more easily around the world
- the development of a modern mentality focused on order and predictability but also extolling progress as a virtue
- the creation of modern sciences, especially evolutionary biology but also the earth, physical, and life sciences.
- the systematization of "liberal" secular and religious values that were based on ideas of ideas of the rights of the individual to equality and liberty, but that ironically also made room for colonialism, paternalism, and scientific racism.

- the uniform working day, time standardization and measurement, the nuclear family, and other ways of acting and being that were aligned with liberalism, capitalism, and industrialization.
- the sense that all of these transformations were leading society upwards in progressive stages toward a better world.

Multiple modernities, or one?

The spread of these elements of modernity is a common lens through which to view the period from 1750 to 1914. However, there is an intrinsic problem with constructing a global history with this theme at its center. For a long time, modernity was understood to be a uniform pattern that emerged in the "West," and whose spread around the world was purely directed and imposed by Europeans and Euro-Americans. Indeed, some scholars have come to label the set of ideas and processes that includes the doctrine of progress, the secular outlook, individualism, and industrial capitalism as *Euromodernity*. In doing so, they mark the fact that it was Europeans, and colonizers and settlers of European extract, who seemingly drove and who unevenly benefitted from this process. Whether you are a fan of this kind of modernity or not, they argue, the inescapable fact is that it was through a type of "Westernization," that modern ideas and power spread to or were imposed on the "East" and "South."

Yet some scholars argue that the scholarly investigation of the historical pattern of modernity actually reveals a landscape of difference. While there was perhaps a broad set of shared components of modernity across the world, the ways that it was actually expressed actually varied widely across regions and societies. This variability has led to many scholars, especially sociologists, to argue that the world was—and is—characterized by multiple modernities, or alternative modernities, and not just one. Perhaps we should see the nineteenth century less as an era in which a single "modern" vision of the world was slowly imposed than as one in which the question of quite what "modern" means was being interpreted differently in different parts of the world.

Whether we should speak of one modernity or many, a couple of principles do emerge from the evidence of world history in the long nineteenth century. Two of these are perhaps the most significant for our purposes.

- The first is that during this era people around the world understood they were undergoing "**modernization**—the process of becoming modern—and were struggling to shape and control what modernity means to them.
- The second, related principle, is that that people around the world were actors and participants in the development of modernity, and not just passive recipients and victims. Although modernity was at the time (and remains) identified with the "West," it was in fact created through the interaction

of many people in different parts of the world and the relationships they created with each other.

The cattle killing described above is a somewhat extreme case of modernization in that the Xhosa people encountered a modernity over which they seemingly had no control or authority. British settlers and colonizers brought modern weapons, an industrialized economy, and a philosophy of superiority to bear upon the Xhosa for much of the nineteenth century. However, the Xhosa were seeking ways to deal with modernity, partly by fusing their own religion with ideas brought by missionaries, partly by fighting back against settler encroachment. In the end, it was probably a series of droughts and diseases that caused them to turn to the millennial, dramatic response of the cattle killing. This movement combined a call to ancestry and tradition with the innovation of a new religious prophecy. Thus it combined two strategies for dealing with the dramatic changes brought by modernization—adaptation and rejection. These strategies were part of a wider toolkit that societies brought to the rapid changes ushered in by nineteenth century, in which they not only sought to shape their own pathways to modernity but also contested the very nature of what is modern.

Throughout this book, we will see moments at which the order and meaning of modernity was contested. The question of how to modernize was embedded in Egypt's state-guided attempts to industrialize on its own terms, Japanese artists' ambivalence toward Western "fine arts," and Bengali intellectual engagement with the Enlightenment. It formed an important strand of intertwined religious movements among indigenous Americans, enslaved Africans, and Protestant revivalists in North America. It helped to define both capitalism and its socialist critique around the world. In each case, people experienced pressures and drivers to both conform to a powerful ideal of modernity, and to redefine that modernity to fit their own situation.

So, the emergence of a global modernity is the organizing theme of this book, but because modernity has many flavors there is lots of room to explore difference within each chapter. As you will see in each chapter, various groups of people around the world all sought to shape their worlds to their own needs and conceptions. By 1914, there were more than 1.7 billion people in the world, which means 1.7 billion different experiences and perspectives, and growing. Their stories prove that the form of modernity we have today was not predictable, but rather emerged from a variety of different models and experiments because of the choices people made, the challenges they faced, and the very contingent realities of their interactions.

Key terms

In each chapter, I present a number of key terms that help students to understand the themes and elements of the material presented within that chapter. For the introduction, there are only two key terms. Other terms used in this section are introduced in later chapters:

modernity [xvi]
modernization [xvii]

Further readings

At the end of each chapter, I recommend some additional texts for readers who are interested enough to pursue a theme or topic further. For this introduction, I would like to recommend three histories of the long nineteenth century. These are three books that were written by historians who are broadly admired, and each is a masterpiece in its own way. I have learned a great deal from each of these volumes, and in writing this book I have thought deeply about each one and often drawn upon them, although I do not entirely agree with any of their authors.

Eric Hobsbawm is a British historian whose epic work covers this era in three volumes, *The Age of Revolution: 1789–1848* (London: Weidenfeld & Nicolson, 1962), *The Age of Capital: 1848–1875* (London: Weidenfeld and Nicolson, 1976), and *The Age of Empire 1875–1914* (London: Abacus, 1987). Although economics and class take center stage in Hobsbawm's account of the era, this epic work embodies a analysis of culture as well.

C. A. Bayly's much more recent *The Birth of the Modern World 1780–1914* (Blackwell: Oxford, 2004) is a truly global text. The author benefits from the increasing depth and breadth of scholarship available about the history of Asian societies, especially. Rather than being strictly organized, Bayly's account follows the flow of ideas—especially those surrounding the nation, imperialism, and religion— throughout this period and around the world. If you are interested in the notion of multiple versions of modernity, you could read the essays in Dilip P. Gaonkar's *Alternative Modernities* (Durham: Duke University Press, 2001). This edited volume includes chapters by a group of scholars covering a range of regions and cities where, they argue, the question of modernity was being reinterpreted or disputed during the nineteenth and twentieth centuries.

Jurgen Osterhamel's *The Transformation of the World: A Global History of the Nineteenth Century* (Princeton: Princeton University Press, 2014) was originally written for a German audience, and its author focuses somewhat on Europe while nevertheless effectively tying together events and trends in different parts of the world. It is a massive tome, divided into chapters that explore pervasive themes, vast trends, and even philosophical issues.

If you are interested in the notion of multiple versions of modernity, you could read the essays in Dilip P. Gaonkar's *Alternative Modernities* (Durham: Duke University Press, 2001). This edited volume includes chapters by a group of scholars covering a range of regions and cities where, they argue, the question of modernity was being reinterpreted or disputed during the nineteenth and twentieth centuries.

1

Empire and Imperialism

Chapter introduction

One of the lessons we learn from studying history is the interrelatedness of all things. Admittedly, in order to understand the past, we have to chop it up, dividing historical events into categories such as economics, culture, social organization, intellectual trends, and politics. However, in the real lived experience of people everywhere, these categories overlap in a mishmash of daily activities and personal identities.

In the first two chapters of this book, we will look at two broad and seemingly unrelated categories of experiences—first empire, and then intellectual and spiritual trends. In part, these themes are placed first in the book because transformations in both areas were foundational to many of the other topics we will be discussing. However, it turns out also that the three "E's" of these early chapters—Empire, Enlightenment, and Evangelism—were closely tied together in the way they operated in the real world. Many of modernity's intellectual and religious features are in fact products of empire, while the experience of empire were deeply influenced by intellectual and religious change. We will begin to tell the story of this relationship in the next two chapters.

We start with empire in this chapter partly because looking at nineteenth century empires will help give us a geographic shape for this world and partly because empire was so influential to the emergence of modernity. For example, we cannot look at the vital role played by peoples of the Americas in formulating modern nationalism without framing it as a response to imperial rule over these continents. Similarly, we cannot understand modern geopolitics and global inequities without comprehending the development and impact of the Atlantic slaving system or the ways in which imperial states and their colonies emerged in unequal relationships. Such fundamental ideas as "race" and "civilization" are inextricably tied to the imperialism of this period.

Along the way, we will encounter key terms that describe empire, the first of these being **empire** itself. As we will see, empires in this period were generally made up of **colonies** that were in a subordinated relationship with dominant states, or **metropoles**. The metropoles each had particular, if somewhat shared, **cultures of imperialism** that lobbied for and supported empire. Over the course of the long nineteenth century, different types of imperial relationships emerged, including both **informal imperialism** of mid-century and the so-called **new imperialism** of the 1880s and 1890s. We will also look at the **civilizing mission** as a vehicle for promoting the empire and at **indirect rule** as a tool for managing colonies. Together, these terms describe the enduring but also changing political frame of empire as a thread running through this period. We will revisit this thread in later chapters that focus on the experience of both colonizers and the colonized through other themes.

By the end of this chapter, you should be able to:

- Explain the origins of modern forms of imperialism in this period.
- Describe how cultures of imperialism developed during this period.
- Compare the different expressions of imperial politics in metropole and colony in the late nineteenth century.

Edité par la CHOCOLATERIE D'AIGUEBELLE, Monastère de la Trappe (Drôme)

LE MYRE DE VILERS, PLÉNIPOTENTIAIRE ; A MADAGASCAR.

Figure 1.1 Charles le Myre de Vilers, resident general of Madagascar. The building of empires connected politics with commerce and culture. Here the French governor of Madagascar appears on a chocolate tin, celebrating France's conquest of this island state.

- Interpret individual expressions of support for or opposition to empire through writing, art, and other forms of expression.

Empire at the beginning of the long nineteenth century

The long nineteenth century was an age of empires. An **empire** is a kind of state in which country or one group of people claim authority or exert significant control over other people. In an empire, different populations are considered to be politically separate, are not equal, and do not enjoy the same rights. The dominant country or state in an empire is known as the **metropole**. The subordinated countries or states are often called **colonies**. The population of the metropole generally espouse a set of ideas known as **imperialism** that support the building and maintenance of empire. The way that they rule or subordinate the colonies is usually known as **colonialism**.

The legacy of early modern Eurasian empires

The empires of the long nineteenth century grew out of the fertile soil of imperialism handed down from an earlier age—the long "early modern" period that can be said to stretch from about 1500 to 1750. Many of these early modern empires had themselves developed from the ruins of an even earlier empire—the Mongol Khanate that had controlled much of Asia until about the 1350s, when it collapsed under the weight of the Black Death plague. The Qing Dynasty in China, the Romanov Tsars of Russia, the sultans of the Ottoman Empire, and the Mughal emperors of India and Afghanistan were all headquartered in territory that had once been part of the Mongol domains. Of the great early modern empires that emerged in Europe and Asia around the fifteenth and sixteenth centuries, only the Habsburgs in Europe were exclusively outside of former Mongol territory.

These vast empires all already existed in 1750, and their rule was sustained by a series of technologies that helped set the stage for the modern state. One of these was gunpowder weaponry. The technology of the gun and the cannon tended to be most useful for large, highly organized states that sought to dominate rebels and regional rulers. The cannon could reduce the walls of castles and forts, making it difficult for regional lords to hide in their fortresses and wait for attackers to go away. Yet they were so expensive that only the wealthiest—great kings and emperors—could afford them. As a result, large states and empires that could afford cannon developed a military advantage over small, regional rulers, warlords, and communities seeking political autonomy.

The hand-wielded gun had a similar effect. Early guns could be effective against the best armor but could be used by peasants with only basic training, meaning that a king could equip poor soldiers to fight regional aristocrats and knights. But guns too were expensive, and only monarchs could generally afford the large numbers needed to equip an army. Together, these two forms of firearm tended to favor the growth of large empires that could afford them, and the states that use these two forms of weaponry have thus been described as "gunpowder empires."

Another technology that underpinned the development of the modern empire was organizational. The large states of the early modern era increasingly needed large bureaucracies staffed by civil servants, of which some of the most startling are the vast system of scholars that ran the Qing state in China after the sixteenth century and the professional clerks and lawyers who came to dominate the state of France in the eighteenth century. These bureaucrats were especially efficient at collecting taxes to pay for large-scale projects. Closely controlled by the emperor or ruler from his or her capital, they centralized power in the hands of the imperial court. They also provided much of the organization and logistics needed for a state to expand. For example, Tsar Mikhail Romanov spread Russian rule south to the Caucasus Mountains and eastward into Central Asia in the mid-seventeenth

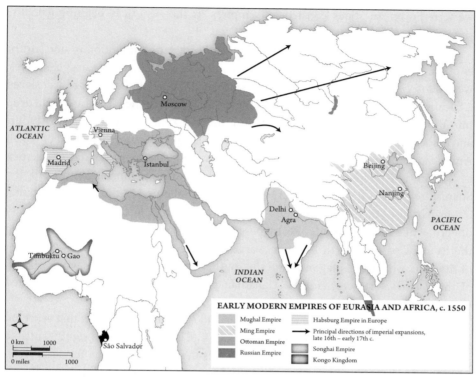

Figure 1.2 The expanding gunpowder empires of Eurasia, c.1550–1750.

century through the work of a veritable army of bureaucratic clerks, soldiers, priests, and artisans.

By 1750, much of Eurasia and North Africa was in the hands of these vast empires, who continued to compete to expand into remaining independent territory in Central Asia, North Africa, and the Balkan Peninsula of Europe.

European empires in the Americas

Unlike the large empires to their east, the states of western Europe had little chance to expand, for they were on the far edge of the great Eurasian landmass. For that reason, these states—such as Spain, Portugal, France, and England—were forced to look for new territory and new trade revenues by turning to the ocean. Some of their state-sponsored overseas voyages turned southward, to Africa and from there around the Cape of Good Hope to Asia. Others pushed westward, across the Atlantic Ocean to the Americas. Along with their advanced ships and weapons, they brought with them waves of Eurasian diseases such as cholera and smallpox that decimated the local populations of North and South America and the Caribbean, and caused the collapse of major states and small societies alike. On the ruins of these societies, western European states constructed empires in the Americas beginning in the sixteenth century.

By 1750, much of the Americas were under European domination of one sort or another. The Caribbean Islands, under the control of a vast array of European states, were densely populated and intensively cultivated, largely by the labor of enslaved Africans and indigenous Americans. In the far north, the French Empire spread deep into the interior from a few urban bases into a vast claimed frontier of fur-traders and associated Native American communities. Along the Eastern Seaboard of North America, British settler colonies slowly spread westward from coastal cities such as Boston, Philadelphia, and Savanna. From the Florida peninsula southward, the Spanish reigned as the Vice-Royalty of New Spain anchored in their colonial capital of Mexico City. Much of South America was also claimed by Spain as the Vice-Royalty of Peru, while Brazil fell under Portuguese rule. Even Russia had made inroads along the Pacific Coast of North America. Large areas were still independent—the basin of the Amazon River, Patagonia, and the southern tip of the landmass, great regions of the Pacific Northwest and the Canadian plains. But European rule dominated most of the two American continents.

These European colonies in the Americas had a number of features that set them apart from older, imperial possessions in Eurasia. The first was the significant role played by corporations or chartered companies in alliance with the imperial state. Massive merchant companies managed the fur trade in the north, the Transatlantic slave trade, and gold and silver mining, and even promoted settlement of new areas.

The separation between ruler and ruled was also unique in these colonies. Eurasian Empires like those of the Mughal and Ottoman sultans may have depicted the inhabitants of the territories they seized as foreign, but to a large degree they recognized them as fellow humans and sought to assimilate them. The Russian Tsars, Orthodox in religion, nevertheless sponsored Muslim mosques in their Central Asian possessions. The Muslim Mughal rulers generally promoted Hindu participation in governance. The Ottoman sultans recognized Christians and Jews as people falling somewhat under their own laws, even if they had to pay additional taxes for the right.

By contrast, most Europeans of the early modern era accepted the conviction that both indigenous Americans and the Africans brought to the Americas as laborers were inferior: barbarians, heathens, or even animals. The Spanish monk Juan Ginés de Sepulveda famously argued that Native Americans were "natural slaves." The French termed them *sauvages*, or wild people. Englishmen Sir George Peckham referred to them as "wild, degenerate men." The enslavement of nearly 12 million Africans to serve as labor in the Americas was justified by arguments that Africans were inferior, accursed by God, and would fare better under a "kind European master" than "their own despotic governments."

Through such arguments, colonizers sought to cover the savageness and terror of the plantation and mining economy of the American colonies. This regime is covered in Chapter 4, on economics, but it bears pointing out here that these American colonies, more than any previous, were created to export profits to the metropoles in Europe rather than profiting themselves. This continued to be true despite the growth over time of a very large number of European settlers. The movement of Europeans to the Americas had, by 1750, created the largest colonial settler movement in world history. But the settlers created a unique problem for the European empires. Settlers were by definition members of the metropolitan society, superior to the indigenous and enslaved African population. However they also had needs and priorities that were different from those of the men sent on short-term assignment from Europe to rule them. Most of all, the settlers wanted to develop and create profits for the colony in which they lived, more so than for the imperial metropole back in Europe.

Imperial shifts, 1750–1820

In 1750, empire was a widely experienced the global political situation. Between them, the land-based gunpowder empires in Eurasia and the somewhat younger European maritime empires claimed almost a third of the world's landmass. Yet the 1770s would prove to be the high-tide mark for empire for the next century. Already the Mughal Empire in South Asia was beginning to fragment, partly under the pressure of European interference. The Ottoman Empire would also begin to recede in the decades that followed. Perhaps more dramatically, European empires in the Americas were being challenged both by local populations and by the very settlers whom they expected to hold their colonies for them.

The end of European empires in the Americas

European-based empires faced a number of problems in their American colonies in the late eighteenth century. One challenge was resistance from indigenous populations who tried to halt encroachment on their land. Diseases such as smallpox and influenza, brought by Europeans who were somewhat resistant to them, had decimated many indigenous American populations in the sixteenth and seventeenth centuries. However, recovering indigenous populations continued to resist at the edges of the expanding European empires in places like the Mississippi river basin and Patagonia. Moreover, a number of revolts broke out in the late eighteenth century among even those populations deemed to have been conquered, including in the Yucatan Peninsula of Spanish Mexico. Added to these were revolts by enslaved Africans and maroons—former slaves who had escaped to establish their own communities outside of imperial control. A number of resistance movements even brought together indigenous peoples and maroon communities in alliance.

Another challenge was what to do with problem created by groups of people who considered themselves to be citizens of the metropole, despite the fact that they had never lived there and were not considered to have political rights by the authorities. One example were the *gens de colour* (free people of color) in the French Caribbean. The descendants of enslaved Africans, French settlers, and the indigenous people of the islands, many of them spoke French and embraced French culture to such a degree that, in 1789, they sent a list of grievances to the French National Assembly that was considering the new political path for the metropole itself.

Large groups of people of mixed racial heritage were, in fact, a major legacy of colonialism in this era. So, too, was a vast population of non-Europeans. Between 1500 and 1800, for example, only about 700,000 Spaniards moved into the vast Spanish American empire that stretched from southern Argentina to Florida and California. This population was quite a bit smaller than the number of enslaved Africans brought during the same period. As a result, most of the population of this empire was not European but rather indigenous people or Africans, or people of mixed European, African, and indigenous descent. Many of these communities nevertheless identified somewhat with Spain. They converted to Catholicism, spoke Spanish, and to some degree adopted European dress and lifestyle. Claiming a Spanish heritage provided some material benefits such as access to better jobs and social standing and even more favorable laws. It was also a cultural choice based on their self-identification. However, very often the colonial administration sent over from Europe did not accept these claims, and instead limited or segregated this population. People of mixed heritage were divided into *castas*, or racial classes, with corresponding limitations on their rights and privileges. As a result, they were often highly frustrated by the colonial government. This was especially true in the Spanish and Portuguese Empires, but also elsewhere.

European setters themselves also constituted a particular problem for the metropole. Although they spoke the same language and generally shared a culture with their countrypeople back in the metropole, their interests didn't always coincide. In particular, the imperial government sought to control trade and impose taxes to make the colonies pay for themselves and contribute to the imperial treasury. Settlers, by contrast, looked for ways to avoid paying these taxes, or to trade with whomever they wanted.

Differences between settlers—called *creoles* in Spanish—and administrators sent from Europe grew in the late eighteenth century. These problems coupled with the difficulty in suppressing resistance and revolts by indigenous and enslaved populations increased the cost of empire significantly. Most imperial governments sought to cover these costs by imposing more taxes, which only worsened resentment by the settler communities. This resentment ultimately caused settlers to break from their allegiance to the metropole. Thus between 1776 and 1820, most of the colonial possessions in the Americas fought for their independence from European metropoles. We will look at this story more closely in Chapter 2, beginning with the War of Independence that created the United States in 1776 and continuing into the Haitian and Latin American revolutions around the turn of the century. For now it is important to note that by the 1840s most of the formerly colonized regions of the Americas were independent, with the noted exceptions of the sparsely populated area that would become British Canada as well as some Caribbean islands.

Franco-British rivalry

One of the contributing factors in these successful revolutions in the Americas was competition between the major European empires. In the late eighteenth and nineteenth centuries, the most important of these was the rivalry between Britain and France. These two states shared a number of characteristics that helped them to become leading European powers in this period. They both had large cities with extensive commercial establishments that contributed taxes to the state. These urban zones were complemented by large rural regions that contributed both food and populations who could serve in large armies and navies. Both Britain and France, in this period, had established a national identity and were relatively well integrated politically. Both had good access to the Atlantic Ocean and far-flung colonies. By contrast, the Netherlands did not have a large rural population, Spain had few cities, and the Habsburg Empire was politically fragmented.

Franco-British rivalry was a key factor in the struggle for independence in the Americas. The Seven Years War of 1756–1763, in many ways the catalyst for the independence struggles that would create the United States and Haiti, was largely caused by conflict over territory and resources in North America, which resulted in the British conquest of French Canada. In response, France gave significant support to English-speaking settlers rebelling against Britain during the American War of Independence (1776–1783). However, the costs of this conflict helped to bankrupt the French monarchy, creating the conditions for the French Revolution (1789), and also for a slave-led uprising in French-occupied Haiti. Britain opposed the revolutionaries in France, and became the enduring opponents of the new French Republic. What followed was a series of conflicts as French troops under the leadership of Napoleon Bonaparte conquered much of Europe despite the opposition of Britain and a shifting alliance of other powers. In these Napoleonic Wars (1803–1815), France came to dominate the European continent but Britain used its navy to win victories around the world.

These wars in turn created the conditions under which Spanish American colonies could win their independence. Not only were the revolutionaries in these countries influenced by French Republican sentiment, but they were helped by a British blockade of Spain once that country came under French rule. Thus while the defeat of Napoleon Bonaparte in 1815 left Britain as the major European power on the global stage, it also marked the decline of European empires in the Americas.

Imperial shift in Asia

Of course, this decline did not lead to the end of European maritime empires. Rather, European attention was already shifting from the Americas to Asia. In the 1770s, Britain, the Netherlands, and France had located lucrative opportunities in South and Southeast Asia, while during this same period the Russian Romanov Dynasty was building an empire of more than 150 million people stretching east across the Asian continent to Siberia. In Central Asia, the Russians found themselves competing with the Chinese Qing Dynasty and the Ottoman Empire, both of which had staked claims in this region centuries before. Thus by 1800, large stretches of Asia were contested zones between competing empires.

Probably the most important imperial shift in Asia during this period was the transfer of control in South Asia from the Muslim-ruled Mughal Empire to a British chartered company and, later, the British Crown. This transition was partly a result of Mughal weakness. Sultan Aurangzeb's policies of military extension and intolerance toward non-Muslims in the seventeenth century had threatened the agreements and rituals that bound together the various religious communities of his empire. A series of eighteenth-century rebellions and the rise of strong opponents like the Hindu Marathas weakened the Mughal state dramatically. By the 1750s, European companies that traded in South Asia found they could take advantage of this weakness, engaging in smuggling and forcing Mughal merchants to lower their prices. They formed alliances with some Mughal administrators who were willing to make mutually beneficial deals that kept money from reaching the Mughal court. In other cases, however, Mughal officials opposed European corporations. One such conflict emerged as early as the 1750s between the British East India Company (BEIC) and the administrator, or Nawab, of the wealthy Mughal province of Bengal. During the Seven Years War, the Nawab tried to eliminate the BEIC by allying with the French. However a series of victories by the British and their local allies led to the defeat of the Nawab and the occupation Bengal with the reluctant assent of the Mughal emperor. Soon after, the BEIC began to expand its territory, gradually taking over much of the vast subcontinent of India and ensuring British domination of the area until 1947.

The shift of British attention from the west (Atlantic) to the east (South Asia) had important repercussions for how Britons thought about empire. Previously, most of their empire had been made up of settlers' colonies, with British citizens and other Europeans moving to the new lands and forming much of their population. Even though many Britons at home looked down on settlers in North America, Australia, and the Caribbean, they still generally saw them as culturally similar, members of an extended family, and potential equals. To be sure, there was widespread sentiment that saw enslaved Africans in these colonies as "different," but this wasn't yet the focus of imperial thought. With the shift to South Asia and the extension of British authority over large populations of Asians, however, many Britons began to distinguish more between British "citizens" and colonial "subjects." They began to increasingly write about the inhabitants of the colonies as being inherently different in culture and being both biologically and culturally inferior. This set of ideas formed an important strand in the weaving of the ideas of race that would help to define the dominant form of modernity in years to come.

British hegemony, 1820–1880s

Despite the loss of many of its North American colonies, Britain in the early nineteenth century was quickly becoming the leading power on the planet and spreading its influence globally with confidence bordering on arrogance. Victory over its main European rivals in the Napoleonic Wars had left Britain in the possession of the world's greatest naval fleet and colonies around the world. The British military now controlled vital ports at the world's key geographic choke points—Gibraltar at the western opening of the Mediterranean, Cape Town in southern Africa, and Aden on the Red Sea. When combined with Britain's growing industrial might, this small country had become world's leading maritime power. As a result, the British Empire was able to grow rapidly in territory in this period, particularly in South Asia, where by 1860 almost the entire subcontinent plus the island of Ceylon were in British hands. In North America, British settlers and troops spread westward across the continent until Canada assumed its shape in 1871 as a British colony. Similarly, Australia and New Zealand became massive British colonies in this period. New territory was also added in southern Africa.

Having learned from their mistakes in North America, the British government allowed Canada, Australia, and New Zealand to form representative governments and to largely rule themselves on a day-to-day basis. These self-managing colonies were called Dominions, and were characterized by large settler populations. Colonies without large European populations were not given such rights, and when South Africa was given similar status in the early twentieth century, voting was largely restricted to the population of European descent. In all cases, the British government retained veto rights and exercised authority over the Dominions in matters such as defense and foreign policy.

Informal empire and the emergence of "race"

Outside of the Dominions, India, and a few small colonies, Britain's power in this period was marked by a more subtle form of control usually labeled **informal**

Figure 1.3 The British Empire in 1837. Map of the world with British possessions shown in black and underlined.

imperialism. Through this type of imperialism, the British government was able to exercise economic and political control or influence over many foreign nations without actually conquering or annexing them. The key combination that made informal imperialism possible was the British navy, industry, and diplomatic corps, all of which were unparalleled in their size. For example, as British exports to Latin America tripled between 1840 and 1860, British companies and investors came to own much of the infrastructure and production in these countries. This was especially true in Uruguay and Argentina. When local governments made decisions that negatively affected these companies and investors, their directors could call in the British fleet to blockade or even bombard these states. In 1845, for example, a British blockade of Buenos Aires forced the Argentine government to accede to the demands of several large corporations.

The British also exercised a great deal of influence over the Ottoman Empire in the Middle East. British investors made money from loans to the Ottoman government and from trade, and the British embassy was extremely influential in the Ottoman capital, Istanbul. In 1854, the British even joined the Ottomans in the Crimean War against Russia with the aim of protecting their commercial investments in the Ottoman Empire. Informal empire was also extensive in China, where British investors made huge amounts of money beginning in the 1820s by selling opium that was grown, conveniently, in their Indian colony, in Bengal. Of course, the imperial Qing government of China tried to stop this massive drug trade in 1839. In response, British opium traders called upon their nation's military, which between 1839 and 1842 defeated the Chinese in the so-called First Opium War. In the aftermath, Britain was able to take control of several Chinese ports and flout Chinese law at will. They were soon followed in this pathway by other industrial powers such as France, Japan, and the United States. This interference by foreign powers contributed considerably the fall of the Qing Dynasty in 1911.

The great success of British industry and military power contributed to the trend toward a rigid sense of difference not only between Britons and others, but also between Europeans in general and other people of the world. As a result of this culture of difference, the imperial administration that was emerging in this period began to experiment with the idea of a strict segregation between British citizens and colonial subjects. Of course, the colonial idea of "difference" had existed before the nineteenth century, justifying both atrocities against Native Americans and the enslavement of Africans. But in this era these ideas reached a new level. In Britain itself, scientific theorists and cultural leaders wrote about the superiority of British society and hence British people over others, drawing partly on rising nationalist sentiment and partly on the evidence of their control of large portions of the globe. They were supported in these ideas by growing numbers of officials, missionaries, and other Britons overseas who wanted to protect their power by excluding Indians, Oceanians, Native Americans, southern Africans, and other subjects from positions

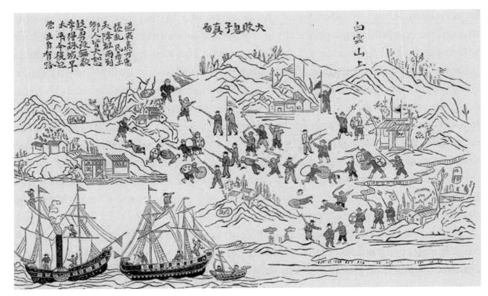

Figure 1.4 Second Opium War, 1856–1858. Chinese depiction of the engagement between the British and Chinese at Fatsham Creek on Canton river. British wood engraving. This Chinese woodcut of the First Opium War makes clear the technological disparities between European and Chinese forces.

of authority or wealth. As a result, British literature and writing began to promote the idea that "races" were truly different from each other and that one—white Europeans—were superior to the others. Nor were they the only ones—by the last decades of the nineteenth century, other Europeans were also beginning to talk about race in a new and more rigid sense than before.

The political impact of the Atlantic slaving system on Africa

European notions of race were increasingly important in the context of Africa, which was suffering through a process of political fragmentation and disintegration directly caused by the Atlantic slave trade. This commerce in enslaved Africans had been an economic backbone of European empires in the Americas before the nineteenth century, and it also prepared the ground for European imperial rule in Africa by gradually destroying long-standing African political institutions in many parts of the continent. As the trade in enslaved Africans persisted well into the nineteenth century—despite attempts to criminalize it—these effects compounded in many regions.

The most obvious factor in the breakdown of African political systems were the increasing numbers of wars whose objectives were the capture of humans for sale to Atlantic slave traders. As early as the sixteenth and seventeenth centuries, under the pressure of these conflicts, large states such as the Jollof Confederation of Sengambia and the Kingdom of Kongo had broken down into smaller units or even decayed into chaos and anarchy. A less obvious political impact of the Atlantic slaving system was the increasing stress on the networks and relationships of governance that occurred even in states that survived this era. Again, the underlying cause of this stress was violence associated with the slave trade. The Europeans who arrived in Africa seeking captives for the slave plantations of the Americas brought with them guns and (in some cases) horses. While some Africans refused to deal with them, they found some individuals and groups who were willing to trade. These Africans were able, through the sale of enslaved people, to acquire new weapons from their European partners. They used these weapons to become armed warrior elites. By contrast, those communities who resisted or refused to participate in the trade were unable to acquire these weapons and became victimized. The only protection was to cluster around a warlord who could protect a community, usually by trading in slaves himself. In many regions, this meant that authoritarian chiefs and warlords took over from long-standing and more egalitarian styles of government.

A few African rulers were able to benefit politically from the Atlantic slave trade. Dahomey and Asante were vast West African countries that emerged in this era partly through their dominance of the trade in slaves in their respective regions. In some places, states became completely reoriented toward the slave trade, neglecting economic growth or development in any other areas. These "vampire" states devastated entire regions. As the trade in enslaved Africans expanded to East Africa, for example, a slave trader named Tippu Tip built an enormous state whose economy was devoted entirely to raiding surrounding communities for slaves, who were then sold to merchants on the coast.

Only a minority of African societies were able to avoid the political upheavals caused by the slave trade. Those that were well into the interior and protected by mountain ranges or other geographic barriers, such as Buganda and Bunyoro, were generally safe. A few states, like the Rovzi of Southeast Africa, sought to ban Europeans from their territory. In general, however, the slave trade caused massive political dislocation and upheaval along the West and East African coasts and well into the interior by the early nineteenth century.

The new imperialism, c.1880–1914

The political chaos caused by the Atlantic slave system weakened African societies at a critical moment in world history. Beginning around 1880, a scramble for new colonies in Asia, Africa, and the Pacific began. This voraciousness for formal colonies was partly a result of increased competition in Europe. Britain's preeminence was coming to an end. Italy and Germany, newly fledged nation-states without colonies of their own, rushed to create empires. They were joined by France, the United States, Japan, and smaller European states like Belgium and the Netherlands. The British government, of course, had to respond by switching from a policy of informal imperialism to a strategy of actively acquiring colonies in these regions as well.

Over the next few decades, these imperial states together occupied more than nine million square miles of new territory in the Caribbean, Africa, the Pacific Ocean islands, and Southeast Asia. Germany moved early, claiming scattered new colonies in Africa and the Pacific in the first years of the 1880s. France responded by expanding its hold on much of northern Africa and also built a vast empire in West Africa and Southeast Asia. The United States completed its expansion across the North American continent, and then seized territory in the Caribbean and the Philippine Islands. Belgium's king claimed a vast area of the trunk of Africa as the so-called "Congo Free State." Japan annexed Korea, parts of China, and a number of Pacific Islands. Britain grabbed several slices of West Africa including the 15 million inhabitants of Nigeria, as well as most of southern and eastern Africa. In mainland Southeast Asia, the British Empire expanded to include Burma and Malaya. The Netherlands expanded their grip on the islands of Southeast Asia.

Core ideas of the new imperialism

This era of expansion is often known formally as the **new imperialism**, a term that applies not only to the acquisition of new colonies, but to the set of ideas and transformations that justified and enabled this sudden surge of imperial activity.

Aside from competition among industrialized states, several factors contributed to the new imperialism. One of these factors was the emergence of new technologies. The growing difference in firepower between the imperial, industrial powers and the rest of the world made conquest easier. Other technologies such as the telegraph and railroad made faster communication possible and thus contributed to the ability of imperial administrations to run vast areas. New medicines, such as quinine for malaria, made it possible for Europeans, North Americans, and Japanese to live in areas where they previously succumbed to local diseases.

Capitalism and the need to find large markets and resources for industrial economies also helped to stimulate the new empires. Industrial economies demanded large amounts of raw materials, and these could be found in abundance in many colonies. Equally importantly, the colonies were seen as markets for the sale of goods produced in the factories of the metropole. Finally, they were places where investors could make vast profits building railroads, ports, and other infrastructure to turn the colonies into markets and providers of raw materials.

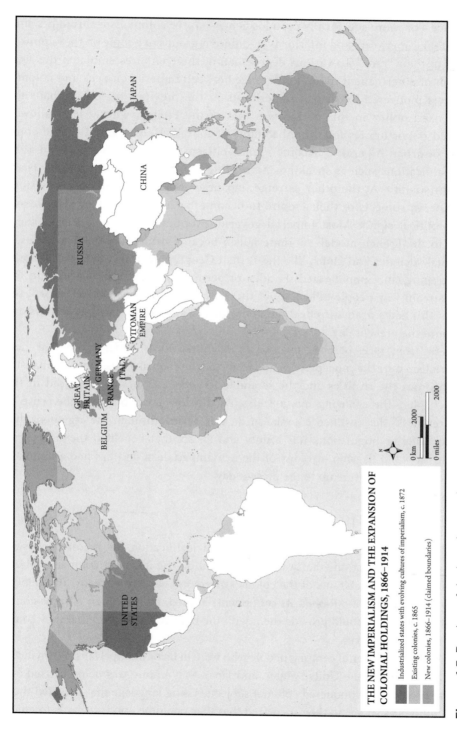

Figure 1.5 Empires of the late nineteenth century.

New ideas also contributed to the rush to claim colonies in these regions. Science—or more specifically pseudoscience—drove colonialism through claims about the superiority and inferiority of different groups of people on the supposed basis of their "race." To various degrees, all of these empires emulated the rigid notion of a permanent natural difference between imperial citizens and colonial subjects pioneered by British imperialists in the previous period. Perhaps the least fixed policy in this period was that of the French, who at least allowed limited opportunities for the inhabitants of four West African cities and some parts of urban Algeria to become French citizens so long as they fulfilled a list of qualifications such as speaking and reading French and following either Islam or Christianity. At the other extreme, Japanese authorities made no provisions for Korean subjects of their empire to become Japanese citizens or achieve any real political rights. Most imperial governments hewed closer to the Japanese than to the French model. As imperialism became firmly ingrained in politics, colonial societies and clubs, like the British Geographic and American National Geographic club, popularized the idea of permanent racial differentness in the mainstream way people talked about the world and their society. As we will see below, this had a dramatic effect on literature, art, and culture, with repercussions well into the present day.

Aside from race, perhaps the two foundational ideas underpinning the new imperialism were the concepts of nationalism and the civilizing mission. Nationalism, which drove the rivalries and the scramble for new colonies, is discussed in the next chapter. The civilizing mission, discussed below, contributed to the sense of "differentness" that justified colonialism in this period through the argument that ruling "inferior populations was a duty and an act that benefited the conquered people." It was a flagship ideology of the new imperialism and has had a dramatic impact on global culture up to the present day.

The "civilizing mission"

The ideology of the **civilizing mission** was a justification for holding overseas territory and populations that was largely based on the idea that colonial subjects (the indigenous inhabitants of the colonies) were not capable or ready for political freedoms and equality. Rather, its proponents argued, metropolitan citizens could help teach them or could provide them with the political leadership that they could not provide themselves.

In the late nineteenth century, people who were in favor of imperialism convinced citizens in Europe, the United States, and Japan that empire was being carried out for the good of the conquered colonial subjects. Using language that depicted their own cultures as superior, they suggested that they could be good stewards to guide supposedly inferior cultures toward political maturity. Consider, for example, the

Figure 1.6 A political cartoon from the *Chicago Tribune,* titled "What the United States Has Fought For," by John T. McCutcheon, 1914. This pro-empire cartoon shows the justification of empire through the "civilizing" of the people of Philippines, Cuba, and elsewhere.

words of the pro-empire writer Rudyard Kipling in his poem *The White Man's Burden,* which was written in 1899 to celebrate the U.S. occupation of the Philippines:

> Take up the White Man's burden—
> Send forth the best ye breed—
> Go bind your sons to exile
> To serve your captives' need;

To wait in heavy harness,
On fluttered folk and wild—
Your new-caught, sullen peoples,
Half-devil and half-child.

To a European and U.S. audience, the meaning was clear. Kipling was depicting the U.S. troops and administrators as doing a service to the Filipinos, whom he depicted as "fluttered folk and wild" and "half-devil and half-child." The occupiers, in his view, were in fact civilizers. A similar message can be seen in the cartoon below, from the same time.

Governing empire and colony

The empires of the new imperial age made efficient use of the increasing sophistication of political organization in this age. Within each empire, colonies were generally officially run by a ministry of the central government—the British Colonial Office, for example, or the French ministry that was in charge of the navy and colonies. These ministries were generally separate from offices of Foreign Affairs, which were charged with dealing with foreign countries, and also from the office of the Interior, which was normally charged with domestic governance within the metropole. Thus the colonies occupied a separate space in government and received their own special instructions that were different from the laws that governed citizens of the metropole—instructions that were often shaped by ideas of race and the civilizing mission.

Although periodic directives and orders went out from these ministries to the colonies, the distance between the metropole and the colonies and the need for on-the-ground knowledge meant that most were governed day-to-day by a governor who was appointed by the metropole and was resident in the colony. This government official was given huge and often autocratic power, generally much more than a governor in the metropole would have held. While parliaments and constitutions might have limited the power of executive officials over citizens in Britain, France, or the United States, a colonial governor had few or no such restrictions. He (governors were almost always men) might have an advisory council, but in this period, at least, colonies did not have legislative branches and the governor could make decisions that affected the lives of hundreds of thousands or millions of people without their input.

The governor and other colonial officials appointed under him were in charge of all of the elements of a colonial government, including the health and welfare of the population of the colony, the building and maintaining of infrastructure to facilitate trade and governance, as well as the military and police. This organization structure in some ways looked like the metropolitan state. But it was different in a number of ways, some of which gave it the potential to be much more oppressive. For example, while charged with "civilizing" the people of the colonies, colonial governments also had to maintain the superior position of Europeans (or U.S. or Japanese) citizens. Thus in reality, government policy frequently supported segregation of living spaces, entertainment, transportation, and daily life. Also, because the populations of the colonies weren't citizens, the colonial state was freer to force their labor and to use violence against them if they protested or refused to serve.

At the same time, colonialism could not survive if its only tools were violence and oppression. In most colonies, there were relatively few officials and soldiers from the metropole. Moreover, the government back home wanted the colonies to be run cheaply, and both war and police actions were expensive. Thus colonial administrations searched for other strategies for getting local populations to cooperate with them. By 1900, most had begun to settle on some form of **indirect rule.** This was a strategy by which the government co-opted local leaders to support them or work with the colonial state. Many of these leaders were chiefs, princes, or kings of conquered states. They were often paired with a colonial official who became both their partner and their superior. In this system, local rulers implemented the laws and policies of colonialism and were usually paid a salary in return. If a society didn't have a chief or prince, the colonial state created the post and imposed it over them. In this way, the colonies were divided into "tribes" and "provinces" with their own ruler, no matter what had existed before.

Indirect rule was designed partly because it was cheaper to pay local rulers than colonial administrators and partly because these chiefs and princes were better able to understand and administer their own people than outside officials. It worked because it gave at least some colonial subjects access to the government. Chiefs and princes in Asia, Africa, and the Pacific could use the indirect rule system to try to negotiate with the governor, to advise against laws that they thought were unfair or would cause problems, and even to protest some actions taken by the administration. This does not mean that they were seen as equals or that colonial subjects were being given political rights, but it did give them some influence over politics in their colony.

The metropolitan experience of the new imperialism

What was it like living in a political environment of imperialism? Imperialism was one of the most important cultural political forces in the industrialized, expansionist states in the long nineteenth century. Of course it also had a significant impact on the regions that were annexed and turned into colonies. We will explore the colonial experience at length in subsequent chapters, but in this section we will look at the transformations wrought by imperialism in the world's imperial metropoles, because in many ways these were core to dominant model of modern thinking.

Imperial organizations and institutions

In the era of the new imperialism, empire was seen as a way to provide money, pride, and opportunities for a nation's citizens, militaries, and businesses. Thus it is no surprise that many political institutions in imperial metropoles became pro-empire in this period. In the German-speaking principalities, for example, the nationalist "King and Fatherland" and "Catholic Pius" Associations that had been formed in the 1860s to agitate for a unified Germany quickly became proponents for a German overseas empire to match that of Britain and France. Similarly, the National Geographic Society of the United States and the Royal Geographic Society of Britain started by mapping their own countries but quickly moved to sponsor exploration and empire-building abroad in the 1880s and 1890s.

These organizations helped to build support for empire within many different segments of society and social classes. They were often financially supported by industrialists and financiers, many of whom who benefitted financially from trade within the empire. Such business leaders had the motivation to convince workers and consumers that jobs and low prices for imported goods depended on empire, and they used their economic power to lobby for pro-empire policies. But they were not alone. Another important powerful sponsor of empire in many regions were religious groups, especially Christian evangelical missionary societies. Throughout the nineteenth century, such societies grew rapidly in Britain, the United States, and continental western Europe. They sent missionaries to Africa, Asia, and the Pacific in order to convert the local populations. They often agitated for the expansion of empire because they believed that ruling an overseas region would make it easier to convert its people. Their pro-empire messages made their way into hymnals and religious books for adults and children. The Christian London Missionary Society, for example, published an article in 1860 that told British children that "it is very wonderful when you think how these different nations conquered, or tried very hard to conquer [India], that God should have taken it from the Tartars, the Hindoos, and the Mahommedans; kept it from the Greeks, the Portuguese, the Dutch, and the French, and given it to the English."

Schoolbooks and educational materials in schools also tended to be staunchly pro-empire. In post-1870s Britain, schools were usually overtly imperialist—every classroom featured a map of the empire for children to gaze upon hour by hour, day by day. In 1872, a directive was given to schools to "excite interest in the colonial and Foreign Possessions of the British Crown." Nongovernmental pro-empire groups such as the Royal Colonial Institute sent out lecturers and lantern-slide shows on the benefits of empire after 1910. Special children's periodicals, for example, the *Boys'*

Own Paper and *Girls Own Paper*, discussed the roles not only of men as humanitarian crusaders for empire and conquerors of the world and of women as imperial pioneers, but also of mothers and wives willing to let their husbands and sons go to war.

Consumption and the empire

Empire was present in the food and everyday consumables of late nineteenth-century Europeans and U.S. citizens as well. For example, by the 1880s, Britain had begun to import large amounts of tinned meat from Australia. Britons already consumed massive amounts of chocolate, most of which was made from cocoa grown in British West Africa. Moreover, approximately 15 percent of the total calories consumed in Britain around 1900 were from sugar, none of which was grown in Britain. The iconic British drink was tea, over 93 percent of which came from imperial possessions in South Asia.

Nor was such an imperial connection restricted to Britain. In the United States of 1900, fruit grown in possessions and informal colonies dressed dinner tables across the country. Advertisements in newspapers from the period promoted the consumption of exotic goods like silk lingerie from the Philippines and sugar from Cuba. Unfamiliar foods like the banana and chilies made their way from colonies and possessions to become part of the American diet. Advertising was also pro-empire in many cases. In 1910, a *Good Housekeeping* advertisement promoted peppers as a product of the American conquests, while another trumpeted that "Uncle Sam is literally ransacking every corner of the globe for dainty and novel foods." In newspapers across Europe, as well, carved African and Afro-Caribbean figures were used to advertise tobacco, Indian figures to sell textiles, and Chinese faces and figures to advertise tea.

Special events like imperial exhibitions and regional fairs also contributed significantly to national pride in empire. Whereas food from empire satisfied the tastes of metropolitan citizens, the symbolism and imagery of empire found at fairs and exhibitions promoted national pride through sight, performance, and experience. The model for these kinds of exhibits was the British Great Exhibition of 1885, held at a specially constructed series of glasshouses called Crystal Palace. This event was in many ways the first example of modern mass tourism, as companies for the first time offered special trips designed to bring everyday people from around Britain via train to stay and view the exhibit for several days.

The Crystal Palace exhibition displayed the empire to the over six million Britons who visited. Visitors could see, among other things, 520 colonial exhibits portraying the products and cultures of Britain's imperial possessions. The largest colonial pavilion featured India and displayed crops, rare jewels, and weapons, as well as handicrafts. Over the following decades, similar fairs sprang up in every country that saw itself as a great power—France, Italy, Japan, the United States, even Argentina!

Figure 1.7 Displaying the nation and the empire at Crystal Palace. Here the British Queen Victoria is opening the exhibition.

Music, film, and literature

The populations of the imperial metropoles also encountered empire in popular music and books of the day. The bands at dance halls, an important entertainment venue for the working class, played songs that jingoistically proclaimed the superiority of Britons including "Britain's Sons shall Rule the World" and the martial hit "We're marching to Pretoria," memorializing the conquest of the Transvaal Republic in South Africa. Children and adults followed leading imperial figures like modern stars in newspapers and books. These heroic figures included General Charles Gordon, the so-called defender of Khartoum against

Sudanese rebels. In reality, it was the Sudanese who were defending against British encroachment led by Gordon, but this perspective would have seemed absurd to a Briton of the time.

Empire figured prominently in British literature as well. One of the most commonly owned books in this period was Robinson Crusoe, actually written in the eighteenth century, but which was popular partly because of its imperial themes including Crusoe's mentorship of his African sidekick and man's conquest of nature. Even the newly emerging film industry focused on empire. In Britain, the first newsreels were about the 1899–1902 war in South Africa. In the United States, many of the early films were about the Spanish-American war and the conquest of Cuba. The first film shown at the White House namely the overtly racist *Birth of a Nation* was premised upon the superiority of white Americans over other peoples both within and outside of the now imperialist United States.

Empire was also often represented as a great adventure, a theme that appealed to millions of workers and children drained by the onslaught of life in a factory or spent sitting in schools. Popular books in the United States and France followed explorers such as Henry Morton Stanley and Rene-Auguste Caillié, who were the celebrities of their day. In Japan, one immensely popular song from 1892 was "The Future of Empire," which promised "Should the entire enemy be struck down and the glorious flag of the rising Sun wave o'er the Himalayan peaks, What fun! What joy!"

Popular sources also featured the civilizing mission and the supposed "duty" of imperial powers to conquer and colonize. This theme featured especially in the series of romantic books and artistic productions known as the Orientalist school. Orientalists in Europe and the United States were both intrigued and unsettled by the colonies and the Islamic world. They tended to speak of other parts of the world as being very different from or even opposite to their own countries. Whereas they saw their own societies "modern," they depicted other parts of the world as being "traditional" or "backward." Whereas they were "dynamic," other parts of the world as "stagnant" and "unchanging." These themes were used to justify the imposition of empire, whether formal or informal, on people all over the world.

Of course, not all Europeans (or Japanese or U.S. citizens) were in favor of empire. Some, like leading socialists such as Vladimir Lenin whom we will meet in later chapters, rejected the economic exploitation of colonial subjects, who they saw as fellow members of the global working class. A number of critics also believed that empire was simply economically disadvantageous for the citizens of the imperial metropole. Most notable was the British economist John Hobson, who argued that Britain should remain a small country focused on its citizens' welfare rather than on developing an empire. Other liberals, like Henry Labouchère, criticized the racism and violence inherent in the new imperialism. He expressed this argument in his

Figure 1.8 *Carpets for Sale,* by Lorenzo Delleani. This painting demonstrates the depiction of Muslim societies as "stagnant" and "indolent" that characterized European Orientalism in this late nineteenth century.

poem "The Brown Man's Burden," in which he responded to Kipling's "The White Man's Burden":

> Pile on the brown man's burden,
> compel him to be free;
> Let all your manifestoes
> Reek with philanthropy.
> And if with heathen folly

He dares your will dispute,
Then, in the name of freedom,
Don't hesitate to shoot.

Labouchère, Lenin, and Hobson were, however, in the minority. Politically, economically, and culturally, empire was a defining force of the long nineteenth century, and its impact would be felt long after.

Key terms

civilizing mission [18]
colonialism [3]
colony [3]
cultures of imperialism [2]
empire [3]
imperialism [3]
indirect rule [21]
informal imperialism [11]
metropole [3]
new imperialism [16]

Further readings

There are several recent surveys on modern empire. One that covers the period from about 1450 to the present is Heather Streets-Salter and Trevor R. Getz, *Empires and Colonies in the Modern World* (New York: Oxford University Press, 2015).

Alice Conklin and Ian Christian Fletcher edited an incredibly rich set of documents emerging from nineteenth-century empires in *European Imperialism: 1830 to 1930* (Boston: Wadsworth, 1998).

Daniel Headrick's *The Tools of Empire: Technology and European Imperialism in the Nineteenth Century* (New York: Oxford University Press, 1981) is a classic history of the kinds of technologies that made possible the conquest and rule of vast areas of Africa, Asia, and the Pacific by European powers.

The great Palestinian intellectual Edward Said gives a richly-textured view of literature, art, and empire in *Culture and Imperialism* (New York: Vintage, 1994).

2

Faith and Question

What tools and ways of thinking did people develop over the long nineteenth century to explain the changing world around them? How did they build worldviews to encompass the transformations they saw? How did these phenomena lead to changes in the way people conceived of the world? In this chapter, we delve deeply into changing ideas and values of the modern era from around the world. This exploration culminates in a global-scope discussion of the Enlightenment and evangelical Protestantism, two intellectual and religious worldviews that disordinately shaped modernity, but we will also look at trends from many regions that helped to create the multiplicity of modernities in the world today.

Enlightenment thought and religious innovations like evangelical Protestantism are, on one level, very different approaches to understanding the world. Yet they were closely linked in the creation and operation of a dominant frame of modernity that characterized the long nineteenth century. Not least, as this chapter details, people around the world encountered both together in the form of imperialism and in the model of the world brought by colonizers. Thus they are best considered together rather than separately.

In exploring changes within human thought and social values, this chapter will need to briefly introduce concepts that are more comprehensively covered in later chapters, such as industrialization, nationalism, and capitalism. However, the key terms in this chapter all revolve around intellectual, religious, and cultural ideas. We explore changes in religious thought and practice in many parts of the world, but especially focus on **evangelism**, and look at the **missionary** project that brought Protestant evangelicals to many parts of the world. We will try to view this encounter

Figure 2.1 G. McCulloch, a German Protestant missionary and Indian townspeople discuss philosophy, c.1860.

partly through the eyes of local communities and the ways in which they took **syncretic** approaches to the missionary's teachings, using both **inculturation** and **acculturation** strategies and resisted these teachings through **millenarian** and other resistance ideologies. We similarly look at a variety of responses to the **Enlightenment** in different parts of the world, including **reformism, nihilism, primitivism**, and **agnosticism**. We introduce gender into this process by exploring **paternalism** and **first-wave feminism**. Finally, we look at particular intellectual products of this period, such as **social science** and the **travelogue**.

By the end of this chapter you should be able to:

- Construct a model of global origins and contributions to Enlightenment thought.
- Situate the rise of evangelical Christianity within other global religious and intellectual movements of the late eighteenth and early nineteenth century.
- Analyze the tensions and overlaps between two rapidly expanding worldviews of modernity in this period—the Enlightenment and evangelical Christianity.
- Describe the ways in which religious and intellectual thought was connected to the emerging classification of the world into "civilizations."
- Explain some of the limits of Enlightenment inclusivity.
- Categorize strategies of resistance and syncretism to Enlightenment ideology and evangelical Christian missionism.

Shifting grounds

The world in 1750 was composed of many different intellectual and religious traditions, each changing in its own way. To be sure, these far-flung societies were linked more closely than ever before by fast ships and trade routes that helped to spread ideas rapidly from one region to another. Yet the diversity of their thought systems was still enormous.

This is an important point for two reasons. First, most world histories focus on changes in Europe, including the Enlightenment, as the principal intellectual and religions story of this era. As we will see, this is an important narrative indeed. Yet there were many other developments about which it is important to learn if we are to begin to construct an accurate picture of this period. The second reason to begin this chapter by talking about global dynamism is that many histories depict modernity as a process by which Europeans alone introduced or imposed new ideas on "traditional" societies, giving the impression that much of the world had previously experienced only stagnant and unchanging intellectual and religious systems. In this section, we show that these ideas are misconceptions by more accurately situating the Enlightenment and evangelism in the context of broader global trends.

Of course, we cannot ignore the fact that just imperialism took hold in many parts of the world in the nineteenth century, the particular values and worldviews of Europeans and their models of the world came along for the ride. Yet the extent of this trend should not be overstated. In the first place, as we will see, these ideals took on different flavors in different regions, in many cases incorporating local religious and intellectual patterns. In the second place, societies outside of Europe and often reacted vigorously to the imposition of these values and ideas. Even within Europe and its settler colonies, in fact, some inhabitants resisted and mutated these ideas to suit themselves.

Mid-eighteenth-century trends in Africa and Eurasia

The Islamic world was one realm of intense intellectual and religious debate around 1750. In central Asia and the Arabian peninsula, the decline of the power of the Ottoman and Safavid states in this era was hastened by emerging reformist movements, many of which hoped to revitalize Islam by returning to worldviews and religious practices closer to those of the Prophet Muhammad. Among the most important of these movements was the Wahhabi reformation, based on the work of the religious philosopher Muhammad ibn Abd al-Wahhab. Wahhab called for a strict religious orthodoxy, rejecting peasant innovations as well as the art and culture of the Ottoman court. His followers were told to reject the common practice of venerating holy people as saints and not to pray to God for individual aid. They also declared Muslims who did not follow these rules, including the Ottoman sultans, to be infidels. This set up a confrontation over Islamic values and worldviews that soon broke into open warfare.

In the interior of West Africa, as well, a slew of eighteenth-century Islamic intellectuals also critiqued rulers whom they saw as corrupt despots. They generally did so through their own formulation of Islam that was reformist like Wahhabism but also quite unique. Among the most important of these reformers were the Torodbe, or "seekers," who emerged along the Senegal River in the 1760s. These men criticized their rulers for failing to promote Islam among nonbelievers and for exploiting Muslim herders and peasants to enrich the ruling classes, rather than helping to improve their lives and religious faith. The Torodbe promoted literacy, especially the reading of the Quran in Arabic, as well as an egalitarian sense of brotherhood among male members of their communities. Unlike the Wahhabi, some Torodbe embraced the notion of holy individuals whose graves were shrines to be visited. Some argued that the implementation of Sharia—Islamic law—could end corruption and bring enlightenment to political rule, but others disagreed with these strict rules. In some places, the reformers managed to build coalitions that succeeded in gaining control

Ibrahim s'élance contre les partis ennemis et les disperse.

Figure 2.2 Ibrahim Pasha and Ottoman troops in battle against the Wahhabis, early nineteenth century. Jean Adolphe Beauce, 1847.

of government, as in the Sokoto Caliphate in the region of modern northern Nigeria. In other parts of West Africa, however, their intellectual differences kept them from uniting.

Across much of East Asia, east of the Islamic world, cultural change during this period frequently involved scuffles over the continued regional dominance of established Chinese ideas and moral codes such as Confucianism. In southern Vietnam, a struggle emerged between the Nguyen rulers and rebels known as the Tayson. In some respects, although this conflict was one between rival districts and powerful lords, there was also a cultural and spiritual contest. The Nguyen were seen as conservative, Confucianist rulers who enforced a strict hierarchical social code. The rebels, by contrast, offered a number of new ideas. They gained support by sponsoring a kind of Vietnamese national identity, one that opposed Confucian ideas of obedience with a call to social revolution and the redistribution of wealth to rural farmers. The Tayson family managed to conquer much of Vietnam, and although their rule was short-lived the contest over Vietnam's national values continued after their decline.

In Korea, meanwhile, the debate over Confucian values in the late eighteenth century took place partly in new forms of cultural expression such as novels. Many of these, like the famous *The Story of Ch'unhyang*, were written in Korean script for consumption by a growing literate community and had as their moral the victory of peasants over greedy aristocrats. Other, more satirical, stories also commented on the antics of the ruling class and their conservative Confucian values. For example, the allegorical story *The Story of a Male Pheasant* featured a pheasant hen that refused to submit to her husband. Thus it critiqued Confucian conventions of obedience in marriage. Yet even as these stories became popularized, older forms of poetry and prose, written using Chinese characters and reflecting Confucian values, continued to be available.

Mid-eighteenth-century trends in the Americas

Protestant Europe and the European settle colonies of late eighteenth-century North America, meanwhile, were experiencing a Christian revival that centered around philosophies of personal connection, awe, and obedience to God as well as the quest for personal redemption and salvation from sin, and the duty to teach these ideas to others. These ideas form the framework of modern Christian **evangelism**, a movement with many variations. In Germany, it took the form of the Pietist movement, which stressed individual spirituality and whose followers sought to live pure and holy lives. In Britain, especially England, the movement centered for a while around the messages of Methodism, which similarly stressed personal lifestyle and relationships with Jesus Christ, but also emphasized duty to the whole community of man. But perhaps the greatest area of Christian innovation in this period was not in Europe but rather in the Americas.

For example, in the British North American Colonies—particularly New England—Methodist and other evangelical messages culminated in the First Great Awakening, a mass movement that imparted emotion to Christian practice with similar messages of personal salvation and a call to action to preach to and convert others.

The Great Awakening occurred in the context of a variety of religious changes taking place across the Americas, where the movement of large numbers of people in previous centuries had allowed for the sharing and transformation of religious ideals. For example, in the mid-eighteenth century, large communities of indigenous Americans began to profess Christianity. In Spanish and Portuguese America, these transformations took place first in the setting of the Catholic mission, in which Americans were intensively exposed to Catholicism in an exclusive setting meant to encourage conversion. Soon, however, local communities began to adapt Catholicism outside of its formal, church setting. Eventually, this led to the development of religions like Santeria that drew heavily on Catholic symbols and liturgy but placed them within the frame of indigenous and African thought systems.

Elsewhere, including in English-speaking colonies in North America, a similar if subtler kind of religious synergy took place. Here, different groups of American Indians witnessed ceremonies and listened to or read about the revival of Protestant spiritual awareness in European and European American communities. Various American Indian communities responded to this religiosity in unique ways. Some converted to mainline Protestant denominations. Others helped to grow congregations like the New Light churches that focused on strands of Christianity that embraced personal revelations, ceremonies full of singing and dancing, and divination that seemed like their own shamanism. Still others formed their own congregations that integrated Christian faith and the Bible with visionary spirituality and attempts to use faith to control the natural and spiritual world.

The descendants of Africans—many brought to the Americas as slaves—also engaged with Christianity and in the process transformed it. For some, becoming a Christian was an act of rebellion, because many planters opposed conversion, fearing that the Christian message of spiritual equality and universal salvation as well as the story of the liberation of Jewish slaves in Egypt would prompt rebellion. Many of the enslaved saw conversion as a way to appeal for better treatment or to bond with other enslaved Africans from very different ethnic and religious backgrounds. The new religions that they formed by mixing Christianity with faiths brought from home often included practices of divination and herbalism and belief in a God who was supported by many other gods and supernatural figures. For Native Americans as well as for diasporic Africans, therefore, the important story in this period was less one of conversion than of religious innovation and mixing.

The Enlightenment in global history

Religious and intellectual change was widespread across the world in the mid-eighteenth century. In Europe, as well, conservative values and old institutions were being rapidly challenged. Some of this change came in the form of new flavors of Protestantism, but perhaps the most significant challenge to the status quo here was the ideas of the **Enlightenment**. Probably no other intellectual or religious transformation was as influential to eighteenth- through twentieth-century global history. The Enlightenment was the ideological force that powered the Industrial Revolution, nationalism, industrial capitalism, and the great modern empires. Its ideas were harnessed to justify industrialization as progress, to buttress claims of national identity, and to support capitalism as a rational system. For better or for worse, the Enlightenment brought us both modern paternalism and feminism and both liberal ideas of equality and inclusion as well as contemporary justifications for racism and colonialism. And for a century, historians have told the story of the Enlightenment as a purely European story. But was it?

The global inspirations of Enlightenment thinkers

Reaching critical mass in the late eighteenth century, the Enlightenment was based on a core set of ideals: that reason could be used to explain the world, that all things could be organized into understandable systems, and that through study of these systems humans could progress toward a better world. Enlightenment philosophers also contributed to **secularism**—the separation of thought and action into distinct secular and religious sphere.

It is no surprise that the intellectuals' ideals of the Enlightenment were synthesized in the same region as capitalism, nationalism, and industrialization—northwest Europe and to some degree the European colonies in the Americas—since Enlightenment worldviews underpinned and justified each of these transformations. For example, one of the key intellectual products of the Enlightenment, Diderot's *Encyclopédie* became the reference tool of industrialization. More than just a collection of entries, this book was representative of a new systematization of organization and thought. The entries were carefully ordered alphabetically, so that they would be easy to find. The book's authors also specifically promoted industrial tools and methods as products of *human* innovation, rather than as natural or divine inspiration.

Over the long nineteenth century, the thinkers of the Enlightenment like Diderot drove the political, technological, industrial, scientific, and economic projects of the time. From Paris, François Voltaire's writings about freedom and railing against religious authorities underpinned the nationalist revolutions of the 1770s and 1790s.

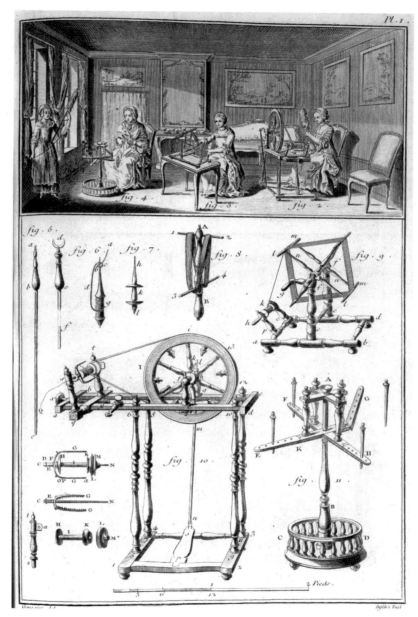

Figure 2.3 Precise depiction of spinning wheels in a cottage industry setting, from Diderot's *Encyclopédie*, 1765.

In Edinburgh, another Enlightenment center of thought, Adam Smith and David Hume developed their capitalist canon as an argument about rational economic organization. Industrialization got a boost from Emilie du Châtelet's scientific experiments and the mathematical models of the world devised by Gottfried Leibnitz and Isaac Newton in the German-speaking state of Hanover and England respectively. John Locke and Thomas Hobbes connected rationalism and reason to nationalism in England. In each case these projects—whether technological, scientific, political, or economic—were built around core Enlightenment principles of rationalism and progress.

Yet the Enlightenment was much more global in its origins and development than this small grouping of countries in northwest Europe would suggest. Indeed, many Enlightenment thinkers developed their views and ideas out of increasingly available information about other regions of the world that were the result of growing trade and diplomatic connections. In 1755, for example, Voltaire adapted Chinese histories of the Mongol Empire to argue that highly organized societies were superior to those that failed to organize individuals. A year later, he mused on the best structure of governance using a fictitious conversation between a Hindu intellectual and a French official. Similarly, the German philosopher Alexander von Humboldt imported evidence from Latin America to help formulate the basis for this thinking about the natural world.

Georg Hegel, the father of modern history, also found inspiration for his historical philosophy in events and trends overseas—in particular the Haitian Revolution. This slave revolution was watched closely by Europeans, especially the French bourgeoisie, some of whom lost a great deal of wealth in the rebellion but others who were sympathetic by the Haitians' claims to freedom. Georg Hegel was one of these observers. In 1807, Hegel published an important analysis of the relationship between master and slave that became one of the most important calls for intellectual, property, and spiritual rights of the Enlightenment. Without a doubt, it was news of Haitian's overturning of the slave system that helped inspire this work.

At the same time, Europeans were digesting comprehensive reports from explorers encountering societies and environments that were very different from their own, and they were trying to understand the implications of these differences. In fact, the **travelogue**, or traveler's account of distant places, was among the most popular and influential form of writing in Europe of this period. Among the most popular were accounts of explorations in the Pacific Ocean by explorers such as the British Captain James Cook and the French Captain Louis Antoine de Bougainville. Their stories of savage cannibals as well as peaceful societies that lacked the restrictive rules of modern bourgeois behavior were devoured by the European reading public. Some Europeans even came to wonder whether Pacific Islands like Tahiti might be more of a paradise of freedom than their own "civilized" but rule-bound European societies.

On the other hand, northwest Europeans frequently used their Enlightenment ideals to describe other regions as backward, uncivilized, or degenerate. For example, French scholar Guillaume Raynal and Dutch intellectual Cornellius de Pauw argued that the indigenous people of Latin America were backward and denied that they had ever possessed great societies, despite the archaeological evidence of massive states and cities in Mexico, Peru, and elsewhere. Whether purposefully misleading or just ignorant, their writing helped to create European's conception of South America as an inferior region.

Global variations and encounters

While the Enlightenment took firm hold in northwest Europe, its ideas were also spreading around the world, carried along trade routes along with capitalist commerce and empire. In the process, thinkers in many different regions began to contribute to the debates on reason, freedom, history, and society that made up the increasingly international discourse of the Enlightenment. In many cases, these philosophers contributed their own regional intellectual and cultural ideals, which they frequently mixed with the ideas emanating from Europe.

Egyptian intellectuals were among those who found ways to integrate Enlightenment ideals with their own intellectual and religious worldviews. Many Egyptians were stimulated to understand European thought by the 1798 French invasion of Egypt, which prompted them to consider their own modernization as a way to ward off future attacks. One leading Egyptian philosopher, Abd al-Rahman al-Jabarti, chronicled the French invasion. He interviewed French soldiers and officials in an attempt to understand French secularism, nationalism and Republican values, and reported these conversations for his fellow Egyptians.

When Muhammad Ali took over the Egyptian government a few years later, the study of Enlightenment ideas got official backing. Ali even sent a number of young Islamic religious leaders, including Rifa'a al-Tahtawi, to study in France. Upon his return, Al-Tahtawi published an account of his visit to France, in which tried to analyze his experiences and determine the usefulness of French Enlightenment thought for his own country. He wrote about the way that the French government mixed monarchy and constitution and how the French attempted to ensure the ethical behavior of their public officials. He also focused his studies on the natural sciences and mathematics, two areas in which he was particularly interested. A trained theologian, Al-Tahtawi argued that these research areas were entirely in keeping with Islam. In fact, he contended (not entirely inaccurately) that European science was a refinement of earlier Islamic (and pre-Islamic Egyptian) models, and thus not really foreign to Egyptians at all. He also argued that science should not be seen as either philosophical or moral, but rather just a tool. Thus it could coexist quite easily with Islam. Al-Tahtawi saw many similarities between the two societies, arguing that conservative Muslim religious officials and French intellectuals were both often entrenched in their beliefs and unwilling to explore different ways of looking at things than what they expected.

In the Spanish-speaking Americas, meanwhile, creole intellectuals fought back against Enlightenment thinkers like Raynal and de Pauw who derided their societies as uncivilized and brutish. They argued that these writers, who had only briefly or never visited the region, were in fact not using reason at all! Rather, they reviewed the works of these European scholars as uninformed and biased. José Ignacio Borunda was one of the Latin American scholars who engaged with European thinkers in the 1790s. He argued that rather than "rationally" looking at artifacts and histories of indigenous societies in Latin America, most Enlightenment scholars had been distorting them to their own purposes. Along with colleagues in Mexico, he wrote a rebellious history of the region that defied the characterization of Spanish-speaking creoles and Native Americans both as lazy, backward, or stagnant. He then published these widely in an attempt to contest these presumptions. Along the way, Borunda helped to invent forms of anthropological studies and linguistics similar to those that would be developed only a century later in Britain and France.

Spanish-speaking creole intellectuals like Borunda didn't reject the Enlightenment, but instead argued that it was being misused. In doing so, they introduced important innovations, like the translation of Mayan and Inca scripts, and began to establish their own universities. In Portuguese-speaking Brazil, as well, academies were opened in the late eighteenth century to study science and logic with an emphasis on the local environment and history. It was through this process that the concept of a "Latin America," with its own thought patterns and shared identity, really began to be formulated.

Enlightenment ideas also received a local twist in Russia, where the Romanov Tsars were searching for ways to modernize the state and economy without infringing on their own authority. Between the 1760s and 1796, Catherine Romanov, known as Catherine the Great, promoted many of the structures that defined Enlightenment society, including a widespread system of schools to teach education in the sciences, history, and mathematics. She also sponsored the production of plays and printing of texts by Voltaire and other French philosophers. Yet Catherine sought to control the Enlightenment in Russia for her own benefit. For example, she emphasized Voltaire's works specifically because he, unlike many of his peers, believed that "enlightened despotism" by a beneficent ruler could be a better form of governance than a Republic. She also tried to promote the teaching of science without endorsing secularism. This was not only because she needed the support of the Russian Orthodox Church but also because she wanted to avoid the raising of questions about state and religious authority, which could threaten her own rule. Of course, Catherine could not entirely control the ways that Enlightenment ideas penetrated Russia, but by sponsoring yet limiting reforms and cultural exploration, she managed the process effectively.

One of the most important figures in Catherine's reforms was an Orthodox Christian priest known as Father Platon. Platon, like many of the other principal intellectuals in Russia at the time, focused his writing and teaching on the question of how to live a good and proper life. Some of his conclusions were quite conservative for the time. For example, he thought a moral, purposeful person should be pious, loyal, respectful to superiors, and honor his or her parents. He wanted all young Russians to have a religious education that stressed these values. Yet Platon also extolled the values of secular education in the sciences for expanding a person's knowledge of the world, which he felt could help people to explore and to grow in knowledge and curiosity. He reconciled these two strands by arguing that science and rationality were useless without honesty and a good conscience, which could only be produced through a fear of God. In this way, he tried to balance Enlightenment secular learning and church teachings.

In South Asia, the ideas of the Enlightenment were perhaps most hotly contested in Bengal, the center of the growing British colonial administration and thus the region where European ideas—both secular and religious—created the greatest challenges and opportunities. In the early nineteenth century, religious and intellectual reformers in Bengal began to formulate secular and religious responses to the challenges of both evangelical missionaries and Enlightenment ideals entering through British colonial

Figure 2.4 Father Platon, painted in the late eighteenth century in a style influenced by French artists of the Enlightenment era. The importation of artistic styles from northwest Europe was one feature of the Russian Enlightenment.

administration. One of the most important figures in this intellectual renaissance was Ram Mohan Roy. Roy's thinking was prompted partly by the restrictions of the unequal society in which he lived. British rule made it difficult for Bengalis to advance in business or politics. Meanwhile, Christian missionaries were trying to push for unpopular changes and Hindu social structures were hardening at the time, partly in response. Roy placed himself in the middle of these issues, calling for reforms in every case. Using Enlightenment language, he called for the modernization of Hinduism including the outlawing of child marriages, the rejection of the hard lines between social and economic classes, or castes, and the abolition of polygamous marriage. He also supported a free press and free speech, which both Hindu authorities and the British East India Company opposed. Some Bengalis saw this as an act of resistance, but it can also be argued that he was arguing a kind of "Westernization" that meant an abandonment of Hindu values. It is no surprise, therefore, that he found himself afoul of both the old and the new authorities. Nevertheless, his work was important to an emerging debate about both Hinduism and British rule.

Encountering the Enlightenment in the Pacific

The broad pattern of the Enlightenment, then, incorporated thinkers and rulers in different parts of the world who saw some value in understanding the core ideals and philosophies Enlightenment, but sought to shape these to their own needs. Yet while there was, to some degree, a global debate about values and worldviews promoted by the Enlightenment, very few people could effectively contribute to this debate. This didn't mean that people excluded from this debate didn't have ways of thinking about new societies, individuals, and ideas that they encountered in this era. But often they found themselves excluded, denigrated, or even threatened by those who wielded the Enlightenment as a weapon.

Polynesian impressions of Captain Cook and other Europeans are a case in point. Like other societies encountering new individuals and ideas, Polynesians tried to fit these visitors into categories that made sense to them. For example, many Polynesians believed that there were people who originated in the sea and others who originated on the land, and cast Europeans as just a different kind of people from the sea, with their own culture but within the conception of the world that Polynesians already possessed.

Eighteenth-century Maori societies in New Zealand produced some particular interpretations of European outsiders, whom they called *Paheka*. Some of their early encounters with Europeans involved violence on both sides—the firing of cannon on the European side, the performance of the *hakka*, a threatening ritualized dance, on the Maori side. Europeans tended not to understand that the *hakka* was a ritual challenge rather than an actual incitement to violence. When Cook arrived in New Zealand, such a similar misunderstanding resulted in Maori deaths. The Maori community in the area then sought to defuse the tension by formally greeting Cook and bringing him within their laws. However, Cook attempted to learn more about the Maori by kidnapping several of them, an act that again resulted in deaths. Cook felt that his actions came from within the "rational," scientific Enlightenment approach to knowledge through studying people and things, but to the Maori community they made no sense at all. The Maori reacted to the kidnapping violently, and Cook felt that this reaction confirmed that they were "savages," and hence outside the reach of the Enlightenment. For many decades after, Europeans would treat the Maori as savages who either had to dramatically change to meet European expectations or face extermination.

Dividing the world

The Maoris found themselves defined as savages within a growing system of classification that was an important feature of the Enlightenment. Among other innovations, Enlightenment philosophers created the **social sciences**—professions that study human societies, their relationships to each other and to the world around them. Like the Enlightenment itself, these disciplines originated in northwest European societies studying their own societies, national histories, and economies. From quite early on, however, they were also turned outward to observe, comment on, and classify the wider world. Embracing the Enlightenment notion of progress, they generally depicted societies as existing along a continuum from the simplest to the most complex, with complexity being the furthest along. They tended to image that all societies moved through stages toward civilization—a term that they argued applied best to their own countries.

These scholars developed complex schematics in which a number of factors were applied to various societies to judge their stage of development. For the most part, these factors were really the values of the Enlightenment—written languages and philosophies, the use of money and banking, technology, ceremonies and manners, types of clothing (and how much of it was worn). In this way, the schematics they developed could do nothing but reinforce their notions of themselves as the most enlightened and civilized people in the world.

By the early nineteenth century, European intellectuals were actively engaged in comparing societies around the world to each other and to placing them in "rational" schematics and hierarchies. One of the new social science disciplines by which industrialized societies measured the world was geography. One 1881 U.S. geography textbook provides an excellent example of the way the social sciences helped to classify people into different groups deserving of different treatment. Its author explained to students the five types of societies in the world: savage, barbarous, half-civilized, civilized, and enlightened:

> The savage state is the lowest stage of existence among the nomadic tribes... The barbarous state is the second stage, a little better than the savage state. Barbarous

tribes, instead of feeding on roots and wild plants, eat the flesh and drink the milk of their flocks and herds... The half-civilized state is a decided progress from the barbarous stage of society. In this state agriculture and the useful arts are cultivated... Civilized and enlightened nations are those which have made the greatest progress in refinement and justice, among whom art is improved and science cultivated.[1]

The author of this book, Augustus Mitchell, went on to fit the societies of the world into the various categories. He deemed most Africans and the indigenous people of Australia to be savages. The "tartars" (Mongols), Arabs, and some Africans were defined as barbarians. South and Central Asians were described as half-civilized, whereas the most enlightened nations are listed as "the United States, England, France, and some other European nations." It is not surprising, of course, that these were the societies from which geography emerged!

Another excellent example of this kind of Enlightenment-influenced classification system comes from a map produced by William Woodbridge in the United States in 1837. Part of the growing field of geography, maps such as this allowed scholars to represent their judgments on the "development" of different parts of the world graphically.

This map is particularly interesting because it represents the division of the world along three criteria. First, Woodbridge adopted the then commonplace categories of savage, barbarous, half-civilized, civilized, and enlightened, which he applied to different parts of the world. At the same time, he also tried to indicate the different forms of government in use in each region. Finally, he indicated the dominant religion (using common language of the time). The result is quite interesting. Almost universally, areas that Woodbridge judged to be enlightened were also Protestant and had Republican or Limited Monarchy forms of government. Catholic areas, at least those outside of Europe, coincided well with areas judged to be merely civilized. Pagan, Islamic (Mahometan) and Greek Orthodox regions (which in his estimation, included China and South Asia) were rarely rated as more than half-civilized. Areas that were ruled by Independent Chiefs were almost always deemed barbarous or savage. Such "coincidences" tell us a lot about Woodbridge's value system, which reflected very well the dominant European and Euro-American ways of judging the world at the time.

Of course, industrialized societies like Britain, France, and the United States were not the first in the history of the world to judge others. Even the words "barbarian" and "savage" are thousands of years old, the first being a Hellenistic Greek term referring to outsiders who did not speak Greek and the latter a Latin term from the Roman Republic referring to people who lived in forests. But the vocabulary of rationality and progress made available by the Enlightenment, together with growing awareness of the wider world, had made it possible for the first time for a society to categorize the entire globe in a single system.

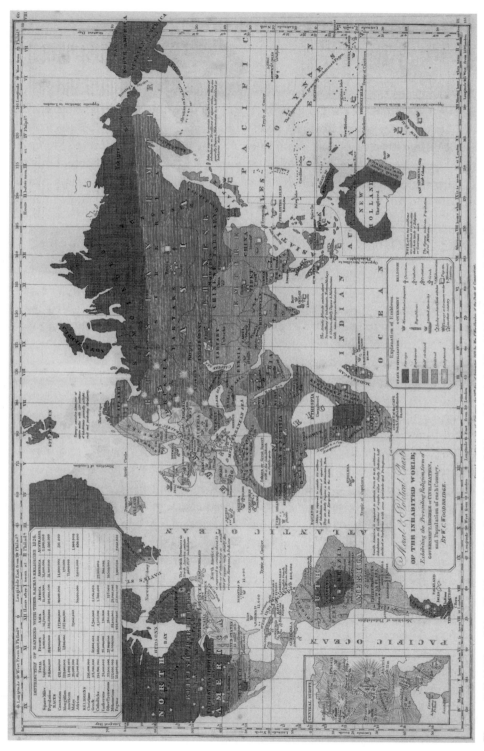

Figure 2.5 William Woodbridge, "Moral and Political Map of the Inhabited World, 1837 ." (Public domain).

Christian evangelism and bourgeois virtue

As Woodbridge's map shows, even in Europe and its North American settler colonies where it was strongest, the Enlightenment did not drive out religion. Rather, just like Al-Tahtawi in Egypt and Roy in Bengal, leading Protestants found ways to reconcile evangelism with the Enlightenment to create a new flavor of modernity. Moreover, this evangelism flowed along many of the same pathways as Enlightenment thought to other regions of the world, where its encounter with local faiths was complicated by trends including the Atlantic slave trade, colonialism, and the spread of nationalism.

The Second Great Awakening

In Britain and the United States, by the 1850s more than half of all churchgoers were members of evangelical denominations such as Baptists and Methodists. These sects identified strongly with being "modern," contrasting themselves from "older" faiths, including the Catholic church and Judaism, that they tended to see as being backward or at least stuck in an earlier time. It was partly because of this belief that they saw their own societies as being the most civilized or advanced.

Yet many evangelical religious leaders of this period also believed that their societies were facing a moral crossroads, not least because of the secularizing influence of the Enlightenment. In the United States, this concern was exacerbated by the fact that many of the rural communities springing up in the west were without a church building or clergy. In response, U.S. evangelicals led a massive reform in the nineteenth century called the Second Great Awakening. Their goal was to revive their churches and to shape the future of their young country. Their proposition began with the belief that God is minutely involved in every event and action on earth. They also called for society to turn away from material things and to focus on obedience and prayer for the deliverance of man by God and Jesus Christ. They spread this message partly through pamphlets and books, but more than anything through huge revival experiences like the 1801 meeting in Cane Ridge, Kentucky, which attracted tens of thousands of people.

The central experience of the Second Great Awakening was the Camp Meeting, or revival. These days-long events first began in the Appalachian region, where there were few large established churches and permanent clergy. Instead, itinerant preachers would call together whole counties to outdoor locations where they would organize emotional sermons business meetings, and informal activities from dawn to dusk. Often, these included a great deal of crying, shouting, and even speaking in tongues. These meeting were very much organized toward the needs of farming communities: they were usually held after harvests had been brought in, and part of

Figure 2.6 Edward Williams Clay, *Camp Meeting,* 1838.

the excitement was the bringing together of isolated families who hardly ever saw each other. Through these experiences, evangelicals were mobilized to work against sin and for morality and society. They organized to call for the prohibition of alcohol, to build hospitals, and especially to promote knowledge and faith in Jesus Christ.

Two visitors from British evangelical churches described a Camp Meeting in the United States with a mix of familiarity and alienation. Well-educated, urban men, they described some of the rural preachers as "plain m[e]n, and without education," and were at first taken aback at the passion they witnessed, reporting that "two or three young women were fainting under the exhaustion and excitement; and one, who was reported to me as a Methodist, was in hysterical ecstasy, raising her hands, rolling her eyes, and smiling and muttering." At the end of the meeting, however, one remarked that "thus closed the most remarkable service I have ever witnessed. It has been my privilege to see more of the solemn and powerful effect of divine truth on large bodies of people than many; but I never saw any thing equal to this; so deep, so overpowering, so universal."[2]

The message of the Second Great Awakening was about both individual and communal sanctity. On the one hand, the preachers and theologians who were its principal proponents called for individual sanctification through personal relationship with Jesus Christ. On the other hand, they argued that this personal faith had to be translated into a duty to eradicate the sins of others and bring about their faith in order to create a better world and perhaps hasten the return of Jesus Christ. Of course, the Great Awakening was not just an abstract statement of faith, but rather also demanded physical action. Believers were exhorted to make a "better" world through their daily behavior. In this way, their mobilization was like many of the great movements in Europe and North America during this era, such as the temperance movement to outlaw alcohol, abolition, and the expansion of education. In fact, evangelicals were leaders in these efforts as well.

The Second Great Awakening was followed by the Holiness movement of the 1860s, which called for holier, less secular living. Centered on the Pentecostal church, these evangelicals taught that individuals could be filled with the Holy Spirit's power, leading them to "speak in tongues," unknown languages that were the word of God. Some evangelicals resisted such beliefs, which they labeled superstition, and this issue helped to promote a split between fundamentalists and denominations that resisted these practices and instead focused on personal expressions of faith.

Missionism

In Britain, the United States, and other Protestant societies in the nineteenth century, evangelism also called upon congregations reaching out to the laboring poor, both to bring to them Biblical teachings and to give instruction for virtuous living in the evangelical model. Indeed, this kind of sharing of the Gospel came to be accepted as a Christian duty. In the late eighteenth century, therefore, many churches formed philanthropic societies with a "mission" to evangelize to the poor. The Baptist Missionary Society was formed in 1792, the multidenominational London Missionary Society three years later. The Methodist Missionary Society, one of the largest, was formally founded in 1818.

Within only a decade or two, the focus of these evangelical groups had grown to include non-Christians around the worlds. Raising money from church congregations in Europe and North America, these evangelical groups began to outfit **missionaries** to preach in Africa, eastern Europe, Asia, and the Pacific. U.S.-based evangelicals at first focused on Native American societies. By the mid-nineteenth century, international missionary societies were highly organized. Before departing, missionaries received instruction in the language of the societies to which they were being sent as well as blueprints for their activities. They were provided with religious and theological materials as well as supplies for daily life. Once in a foreign country, they not only devised religious lessons but also "civilizing" programs to teach their own concepts of hygiene and lifestyle, their languages, and formal education. Meanwhile, they wrote letters and published accounts for consumption in their home societies, where they were often widely read.

Missionism was a logical outgrowth of evangelical Protestantism, with its emphasis on personal faith, proper living, and spreading the gospel. These were values that were generally shared by missionaries, although the many records they have left behind show that they differed from each other in other ways. For example, while some missionaries saw the populations in which they were working as perpetually inferior and primitive, others actually viewed them as actually "purer" and naturally closer to

God than to their own modern communities. For example, many of the nineteenth-century British missionaries working among the Tswana of southern Africa believed that they were more likely to create a holy, faithful community there than in the industrialized, urban cities of Scotland and England from which they came.

Individuals and communities who came into contact with evangelical Christians for the first time in the late nineteenth century reacted to them in many different ways. Some embraced their foreign concepts and faith quite readily, although in general this happened only after a process of translation of both the words and the ideas of Christianity into local cultural and linguistic vocabularies. More frequently, evangelical Christian ideas were mixed with local beliefs in a process known as **syncretism**. Some of this syncretism took the form of **inculturation**, in which Christian ideas were absorbed into local belief systems and rituals. Other mixing looked more like **acculturation**, in which local populations came to identify with Christianity, but mixed some of their own practices into the new faith. Both these processes were selective, meaning that the local populations generally made decisions as to what they would accept and embrace, what they would reject, and how the mixing would occur.

The process of syncretism occurred in different ways in each area. For example, Akan-speaking people of West Africa already possessed the concept of a singular divine creator figure—Nyame. A popular proverb expressed the belief that "nobody saw the beginning of the universe and nobody will see the end, except Nyame." Yet Nyame coexisted with many different minor gods, natural spirits, personal demi-gods, and ancestors. When missionism exploded in the region in the late nineteenth century, many Akan-speakers found it quite easy to assimilate the Christian God into this belief system as Nyame, but resisted missionary attempts to separate them from their additional community and personal gods.

Attitudes toward missionaries were also contingent on local political and economic situations. For example, Tswana leaders reacted to the first missionaries to arrive in their region in the 1820s by asking for gifts of industrial products from Europe in order to increase their own status. However, when the missionaries sought to resist important political rituals like rain-making, in the 1830s, most opposed them. Their position switched again a decade later, when the missionaries began to help the Tswana in their struggle to keep European settlers and miners out of their chiefdoms.

Virtue and the abolition of the Atlantic slave trade

It is tempting to see the evangelism and missionism described in the previous section as being very different from—indeed, contradictory to—the Enlightenment with its emphasis on secularization and rationality. In fact, religion and intellectualism merely provided middle-class Europeans and North Americans with alternate approaches to a shared set of values. If some supporters argued that these values were rational, and others that they were virtuous in a religious sense, then this did not stop them from sharing them. Together, and tied to capitalism and liberal nationalism, they constituted a sort of moral modernity that spread with empire to far reaches of the world.

This moral modernity encouraged a number of actions and beliefs. Men and women were encouraged to settle down as husband and wife, to raise children. The roles of the genders in these relationships were seen as being highly differentiated— husbands were expected to work for a living, whereas wives were to stay at home and take care of the children. Indeed, the most honorable position for a man, in many ways, was that of the diligent but firm father, who showed his love not through outward affection but rather careful stewardship of his children. Both men and women were exhorted to work hard for hard work was seen to be morally redeeming, but men's work was out in the world while women's was largely domestic. Obedience to one's parents and superiors was also emphasized.

At the same time, people who embraced this dominant variety of modern morality demonstrated their virtuousness through "proper" conduct that entailed a avoiding a series of behaviors. These included a rejection of overt sexuality, gambling, gluttony, alcohol and drugs, and self-indulgence in general. This attitude was sometimes taken to extremes—many people who endorsed these values believed that the entire female body had to be covered so as not to tempt men, and even body parts like the "leg" could not be mentioned in polite society.

Such values were widely discussed and constantly reinforced in culture and the press. Morality was a key theme of novels, speeches, newspaper articles, and daily discussions in the nineteenth-century societies in which it took hold. Moreover, its proponents saw the spreading of their morality as an important evangelical act akin to evangelical Protestant missionism. Educating the poor, and foreigners, about proper behavior was seen as being a virtuous act of its own.

Where was Enlightenment notion of "progress" in all of these restrictions? Where was Enlightenment "liberty" in the aversion to gambling or exposing an ankle to view? Philosophers such as Locke and Rousseau suggested ways in which morality and behavior could be tied to liberty and humanism. Essentially, their argument was that only proper "breeding" and behavior made it possible for people to exist together in a civil, enlightened society. A man and citizen earned his political rights by acting like a rational, moral, honorable adult. Women and children could not enjoy the same rights because they did not possess the same measure of honor and rationality. Nevertheless, women were often seen as the key moral guardians of the era, for they were the guardians of hearth and family and the educators of children. Thus their behavior was perhaps the most rigidly controlled.

The picture painted in the paragraphs above is of a strict and obedient society. Yet this picture is not entirely true, because even in evangelical Protestant societies, there were multiple modernities beneath the dominant model. In fact, nineteenth-century industrialized societies were full of dissent and misbehavior even by their own standards. Gambling and drinking were in reality rife, and opium-based drugs widely available. Illicit sexuality was also present, if often hidden behind curtains and closed doors, and many moralists either looked the other way or partook themselves. Moreover, the Enlightenment values of liberty and freedom helped to make dissent not only possible, but even a national value in some cases. Even in Britain—perhaps the society most obsessed with proper behavior of the time—the legal record is full of individuals swimming naked in order to protest decency laws, and of novels whose antiheroes flout convention in bursts of individual righteousness. Laws of free expression and a culture of liberty made such actions possible, although their practitioners were often seen as "eccentric."

Nevertheless, the new morality was extremely powerful in global affairs. One of the areas in which it was most on display was in the quest to abolish the Atlantic slave trade. It is ironic, of course, that formal, organized abolitionism emerged earliest and most strongly in two countries that had benefited greatly from the Atlantic slave trade—Britain and the United States. Yet abolitionism was so closely tied to Enlightenment and evangelical values that in some ways it is no surprise. From an Enlightenment position, slavery was a moral ill. Rousseau, for example, wrote that "the right of slavery is null, not simply because it is illegitimate, but because it is absurd and meaningless. These words, *slavery* and *right*, are contradictory. They are mutually exclusive."[3] Moreover, enslavement went against the capitalist precepts of free work, free will, and free labor. From a religious perspective, slavery was a moral sin that needed correction. In both the United States and Great Britain, it was women, the key religious moralists of the era, who were at the forefront of the movement to end this sin that shamed the nation.

Of course, the forces fighting to defend the institution of slavery also mobilized Enlightenment and Evangelical arguments to support their position. They argued that Africans were not rational, and hence did not have rights. They also suggested that slavery actually protected the enslaved from their own bad judgment, with the planter acting as a sort of fatherly figure. Pro-slavery arguments also invoked sections of the Bible that referred to slavery, or suggested that Africans were the descendants of individuals cursed by God. Plantation owners even claimed that the work of slaves redeemed them morally, since hard work was seen as a means of purification in evangelical moral codes. Slave-owners made these arguments to such great effect in the United States, at least, that many Protestant congregations were torn in half by the abolitionist struggle. In the end, however, the moral arguments of the abolitionists won over much of society, leading to the abolition of the Atlantic slave trade for these two countries in 1807–1808. Britain outlawed slavery across its empire in 1834–1835.

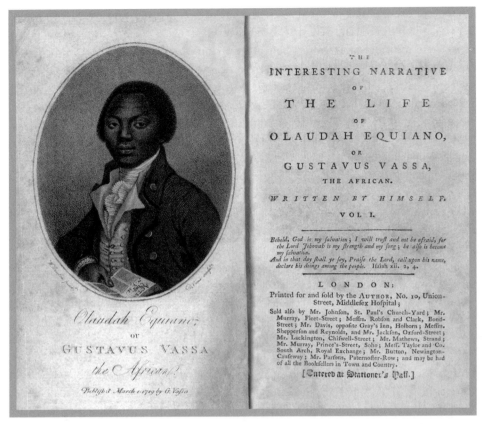

Figure 2.7 Autobiography of Olaudah Equiano. Certainly one of the most important documents of the abolition movement was this autobiography of Olaudah Equiano, a self-emancipated slave whose descriptions of his own enslavement and experiences were important in winning popular support for the abolition of the slave trade. Equiano was assisted by a network of evangelical abolitionists, many of whom were women. Note that the volume begins with a prayer.

Other European states gradually followed, although slavery remained legal in much of the Americas, including in the United States, until well into the mid-nineteenth century.

Sex, gender, and morality

The new morality also reshaped matters of sex and gender, especially in rapidly modernizing societies. Modern-era rules of behavior influenced by the Enlightenment and evangelical Protestantism carefully regulated the conduct of both men and women. Both were expected to control their behavior in schools and at home. Men were instructed as to how to act with honor in the public sphere—business and politics—and women were taught to provide the stability at home to enable them to do so. The particular role of the homemaker was venerated for women, who were told that being a mother and homemaker was of great value to society, even while they were restricted from the public sphere. Many people connected women's behavior to the strength of the nation, arguing for example: "[H]ow intimate is the connection which exists between the women of England and the moral character maintained by their country in the scale of nations."[4]

Publications sprang up in this era to assist young men and women to learn to act correctly, stressing that polite behavior was the wellspring of civilized domestic and public life. Consider this advice for women:

> It is a want of true politeness that introduces the discord and confusion which too often make our homes unhappy. A little consideration for the feelings of those whom we are bound to love and cherish, and a little sacrifice of our own wills, would, in multitudes of instances, make all the difference between alienation and growing affection. The principle of genuine politeness would accomplish this; and what a pity it is that those whose only spring of rational enjoyment is to be found at *home*, should miss that enjoyment by a disregard of little things, which, after all, make up the sum of human existence![5]

In cities like London, Philadelphia, and Buenos Aires "benevolent" societies—many of them tied to evangelical organizations—arose in the late eighteenth and early nineteenth century to help impose or teach such rules of proper behavior. Some of these focused on alleviating bad habits—drunkenness, gambling, and sexual transgressions. Indeed, sex was obsessively discussed even in polite nineteenth-century bourgeois society, although usually along strict gender lines. Meetings to discuss sexuality might involve women or men, but rarely both. Sexuality was, in fact, deemed something of a problem, and benevolent societies actively sought to reform or eliminate prostitution, premarital sex, inter-racial sex, and other acts that transgressed the rules of behavior.

For women especially, the message was that sex was something to be endured rather than embraced. Some writers advised that sex be limited even in marriage. An 1894 pamphlet from New York gave advice for brides for their wedding nights:

> One cardinal rule of marriage should never be forgotten: GIVE LITTLE, GIVE SELDOM, AND ABOVE ALL, GIVE GRUDGINGLY. Otherwise what could have been a proper marriage could become an orgy of sexual lust. On the other hand, the bride's terror need not be extreme. While Sex is at best revolting and at worst rather painful, it has to be endured, and has been by women since the beginning of time, and is compensated by the monogamous home and by the children produced through it.[6]

The orthodox idea of men as promiscuous and women as sexually reticent dominated industrialized societies in this era. It was part of the broader language of sexual morality that was so central to the dominant strand of modern behavior. Even science was mobilized in an attempt prove that sex was unhealthy, that masturbation caused insanity, and that sexual "excitability" left women ill. Connections between promiscuity and venereal diseases were used as evidence in campaigns to outlaw prostitution in the 1870s and 1880s as well. Yet, again, these ideas were not always honored. We know that in fact even in the capitals of countries like Germany and the United States, prostitution remained extremely active, that this was a time of sexual experimentation including the invention of the vibrator, and that pornography proliferated.

Something similar is true in terms of same-sex relationships as well. Technically, "irregular" sexual activities were frowned upon or outlawed beginning around the 1880s in Britain and the United States and soon after in many other countries. Famous gay men such as Oscar Wilde, the British playwright, were prosecuted and imprisoned. This was also the period in which doctors and scientists began to argue that homosexuality was a result of some disease or inherited disability, even while religious leaders depicted it as a sin or moral failing. Nevertheless, homosexuality remained very visible in society, if technically clandestine. Both male and female couples were active in high society, including the partnership of French painter Rosa Bonheur and American actress Charlotte Cushman. Defenses of "homogenic love" were written and published. For example Edward Carpenter's 1894 text argued using science and logic that homosexuality was not a disease, but rather that persecution was damaging to gay youth.

> It is difficult of course for outsiders not personally experienced in the matter to realize the great strain and tensions of nerves under which those persons grow up from boyhood to manhood—or from girl to womanhood—who find their deepest and strongest instincts under the ban of society around them; who before they clearly understand the drift of their own natures discover that they are somehow cut off from the sympathy and understanding of those nearest to them; and who know that they can never give expression to their tenderest yearnings of affection without exposing themselves to the possible charge of actions stigmatized as odious crimes.[7]

Carpenter, like many other activists and writers who defended homosexuality as natural and normal, drew on the global encounters of the era. They pointed to the fact that many societies in other parts of the world tolerated or even embraced same-sex relationships. Carpenter even argued that it was tough and masculine nations (he cited Polynesian Islanders, Celts, and Albanian mountaineers) whose societies included open male same-sex relations.

At the same time northwest Europeans strove to limit these practices and behaviors in their colonies. Suppression of same-sex relationships was the key goal in the agenda of Protestant missionaries in Uganda in the nineteenth century, for example. Missionaries and colonial officials also tried to extend their moral code in other areas of life. In Polynesia, for example, they sought to ban nudity and especially to convince women to cover their breasts and to stop public breastfeeding of children. In India, they discouraged traditions of cross-dressing.

Paternalism and the Indian Uprising

Thus we can see that missionaries and other Europeans campaigned to modify the societies in which they were active and to encourage them to emulate Europeans' own stated morals and values. At the same time, however, they often believed their duty was to protect indigenous people against what they saw as the excesses of imperialism. In southern Africa and North America, Protestant missionaries in a few cases even helped arm local inhabitants to so that they can protect themselves from settlers who wanted their land. They thus sometimes found themselves at odds with settlers, colonial administrators, and others from their own society. These conflicts help show that colonialism was not a single, unified view but rather a set of overlapping but distinct projects. Missionaries wanted to create a Christian utopia. Representatives of corporations wanted to make a profit from the labor and resources of the colonial subjects. Officials wanted to manage the colony without great expense or disruption.

Nevertheless, colonialism contained a philosophical shared message that brought together evangelical and Enlightenment ideals and that was broadly shared by missionaries, officials, and settlers alike. At the heart of this message was the superiority of European forms of thought, knowledge, and behavior. We have already introduced this as the idea of the civilizing mission (Chapter 1), and we can see it played a role in religious missionism as well. An important component of this message was the concept of **paternalism**. Derived from the Latin word for "father," paternalism was a way to explain why liberal, Enlightenment societies like Britain and France could exclude the inhabitants of their colonies from political rights. It began with the argument that only rational adults could be political participants. It then defined colonial subjects as not being rational adults because they acted in "childlike" ways. Finally, it justified ruling these colonial subjects without their participation by arguing that Europeans (or European Americans) would act like fathers toward them. This sense of fatherhood that was used was that of the enlightened father: a stern punisher, but also an effective guide.

The concept of paternalism was deeply embedded in colonialism, and as part of the civilizing mission it was a core, shared intellectual ideal of the colonizers. This was nowhere more so than in India, which over the course of the period 1750–1914 functionally became one large British colony. The British East India Company's (BEIC) administration had become entrenched in the rich Bengal area following key victories in the Seven Years War, and spread rapidly. By the 1820s, the colony was secured by a vast military mostly manned by local troops—the so-called Sepoy

Regiments—with European officers. The colony's limits in the north were Muslim Afghanistan and the Sikh kingdom of Punjab, both of which resisted fiercely.

Although the BEIC at first managed its new empire much in the style of the Mughals who had previously ruled the region, Enlightenment and evangelical ideals quickly infiltrated their administration. Evangelical missionaries arrived in the late eighteenth century, seeking to "save the souls" of Muslims, Jains, Sikhs, and Hindus. They were often met with anger and resistance by local religious leaders, and the Company's officers sought for a long time to ban them in order to maintain the peace and placate the local population. Nevertheless, European values and ideas infiltrated Indian society, both purposefully brought as part of the colonial civilizing mission and adapted by members of the local population. These ideas sparked a series of debates known as the Hindu Renaissance, especially in Bengal Province. Led by Ram Mohun Roy, whom we have already met in this chapter, Bengali thinkers sought to reinterpret ancient Hindu texts like the *Upanishads*. They used this knowledge to respond to evangelical missionaries in languages of faith and belief, published in poetry and journals that sprang up in the region.

Meanwhile, Enlightenment ideals also began to affect the way that the Company ruled its Indian colony. In the 1830s, for example, the administration outlawed a number of religious practices, arguing that they were doing so "for the good of mankind." Whether or not some of these decisions were done on humanitarian ground, they were all taken with little consultation with the local population. Moreover, they were applied unevenly. Where the needs of European investors and administrators conflicted with humanitarian concerns, they usually decided in favor of profit and power. For example, rather than eradicating the hierarchical Hindu caste or class system, the British solidified it into its current form, using these socioeconomic divisions to split the population and hence strengthen their own power.

The tensions of colonial rule finally provoked a unified response in the Indian Rebellion of 1857, surely one of the most important events of the period. This uprising began among the Sepoy Regiments on which the British relied to administer the colony. Some of its causes were political, the result of frustration at colonial land-grabs. Some of them were based on economics, as real wages for sepoys declined in this period. Race also played a large role, as British officers increasingly maltreated local soldiers whom they felt were racial inferiors. However, religious and intellectual conflict provided significant fuel to the fire. Evangelical activity had increased heavily in the 1840s and 1850s, and many Hindus and Muslims believed that the Company was trying to convert the entire population. At the same time, the British had begun to disregard important Hindu, Sikh, and Muslim religious rules. For example, some Hindu sepoys had a religious objection to crossing bodies of water. The last straw came when the soldiers were ordered to use cartridges greased in pig and cow fat, forbidden by religion to Muslims and Hindus, respectively.

PUNCH, OR THE LONDON CHARIVARI.—September 11, 1858.

THE ACCESSION OF THE QUEEN OF INDIA.

Figure 2.8 An 1858 cartoon, from *Punch*, depicting an Indian woman—perhaps the rebel leader Rani of Jhansi—kneeling to Queen Victoria of Great Britain. The cartoon demonstrates both the government's assumption of formal colonial rule in India and British satisfaction that rebels had been reduced, once more, to children kneeling at their feet.

The resulting sepoy mutiny soon gained support from the civilian population and seized much of northern India back from the Company. Rural peasants, many of whom had been coerced to produce raw materials for British factories and companies, rapidly joined the rebels. The arrival of British reinforcements and loyal sepoys eventually reversed the uprising, but the rebellion nevertheless caused massive changes in the way India was managed. Following the uprising, the British government formally took over the administration of the colony from the Company. Moreover, in a frenzy of revenge and anger, the government abandoned any projects designed to inculcate Enlightenment ideals of liberalism in the Indian population, and also reined in Evangelical missionaries. They still did so in the language of paternalism, deciding that their Indian subjects needed a "stern" father rather than a "loving" one. The result was a more racialized and formalized form of rule. In this way, their response ushered in the form of colonialism that would be replicated around the world in the twentieth century.

Rejoinders and reactions

So far, much of this chapter has focused on Protestant evangelism and the Enlightenment. It might seem strange for a world history text to spend so much time on ideas coming out of a single region of the world. Yet for better or for worse, these two forces had an enormous impact on the development of modernity around the world. This does not mean, however, that either the European and North American lower classes or people in other regions simply accepted these religious and intellectual ideas and morals. Instead, they responded with a variety of strategies, some of which sought to assimilate and modify them, and others of which rejected them.

Resistance strategies

The spread of Enlightenment ideas and Protestant missionism threatened enormous disruption to societies around the world, including within Europe. One of the institutions that felt this threat most was the Catholic Church, whose political power within Europe was deeply threatened by nationalism and liberalism as well as by the arrival of Protestant missionaries in many Catholic regions. Within Italy, especially, the Catholic Church felt threatened by Italian nationalists' attempts to build a secular nation-state, a project that threatened Rome itself.

In response, Pope Pius IX called together the First Vatican Council. He planned a months-long conference to confirm the power of the popes and to commit Catholics to a conservative policy of rejecting accommodation with liberal Enlightenment ideals. In the end, the council affirmed that the Pope was infallible and had full power over the church. However, many other parts of his planned conservative agenda could not be adopted because war broke out while the conference was in session. In September 1870, the forces of the Kingdom of Italy captured Rome and made it the capital of the new Italian state.

Pius IX pursued a conservative response to what he saw as a major threat to the Catholic Church. Some societies responded even more dramatically through **millenarian** responses, movements that believed that they were seeing world-ending or all-transforming events and that responded with society-wide rituals and efforts. In many cases, these rituals were both attempts to recall or return to older rituals and spiritual authorities but at the same time they made use of ideas entering from outside the society, especially from evangelical Protestantism.

One significant millenarian movement was the Taiping movement in China, from 1850 to 1864. This rebellion was largely a peasant response to economic hardship whose causes included mismanagement, plundering by Europeans, and land shortages. China's humiliating defeat at the hands of the British during the Opium Wars of the 1840s and the diminishing authority of the Qing emperors helped to stimulate the uprising. Evangelical Protestantism also played a role in the rebellion in two ways. On the one hand, many Chinese were offended by the spread of Protestant missionaries into China. At the same time, however, Christianity was officially banned by the Qing, which meant that it was increasingly associated with rebellion and opposition to an unpopular government. While the doctrine of the missionaries themselves was not enormously attractive to most Chinese citizens, intellectuals and religious figures like Taiping leader Hong Xiuquan made use of them to develop ideologies that could appeal to the masses.

Hong believed that he had discovered he was Jesus Christ's brother through a series of dreams. These dreams included prophetic visions of a sort familiar to followers of Taoist Chinese sects like the White Lotus. Hong left out of doctrine many parts of Christianity that did not resonate with Chinese culture—like the notion of original sin. He focused instead on the Ten Commandments and other teachings that had some similarities to Confucian moral teaching. Yet Hong also rejected many Confucianist teachings. Having himself failed the Confucianist civil service exam, he was happy to use evangelical teachings such as the rejection of "false" gods and idols to justify destroying Confucian schools and, eventually, to attack the Qing Dynasty itself.

At the height of the rebellion he led, Hong claimed to be building a Heavenly Kingdom whose members were required to live by the mix of Christian gospel, Taoist, and Confucianist beliefs. Personal piety was rigorously enforced through daily rituals. In a reflection of evangelical Protestantism, the genders were segregated, and opium and other "depravities" were outlawed. Such values were taught through songs like the "Ode on the Origin of Virtue and the Saving of the World":

Of all wrong things licentiousness is the chief;
When man becomes demon, Heaven is most enraged.

Debauch others and debauch oneself, and both are monstrous....
Depraved customs change men; who can set them aright?
All that is needed is a reformation of faults; so urgently renew yourself.

Yet while some Taiping values were imported from evangelical Protestantism, European missionaries themselves were seen as outsiders to be shunned. In fact, the Heavenly Kingdom's leaders preached that there was a special holy role for China that Europeans could not achieve. In response, European Protestant missionaries ended up generally supporting imperial Qing efforts to eradicate the rebels.

Throughout the 1850s, disaffected Chinese peasants rallied to Hong's banners, hoping that he would be able to overthrow both an unpopular government and an economic system that they found oppressive. Taiping troops control of important cities, including Nanjiang and declared the Taiping Heavenly Kingdom to be an independent state. However, forced to constantly fight imperial troops aided by Europeans, the Taiping were eventually defeated and the Kingdom eradicated in 1864.

Hong Xiuquan had adapted evangelical teachings in his claim to be a messiah. In Sudan, a religious leader known as Muhammad Ahmad resisted colonialism through a Muslim language of resistance. Seeking to overturn British and Egyptian rule over the region, Ahmad claimed to be the Islamic Mahdi—or promised redeemer. He

Figure 2.9 Portraits and a landscape from the Taiping Rebellion, from the *Illustrated London News*, February 24, 1855.

created space for both a fundamentalist message and local Sufi practices of Islam to coexist, and he demonstrated his authority both by claiming to have experienced a number of signs and miracles and by reenacting many of the important events in the life of the Prophet Mohammad. He claimed that his personal authority was above that of the established religious books and figures other than the Quran itself. Many of the different Muslim communities of the region flocked to his side, although religious officials in cosmopolitan Cairo rejected his authority. When Egyptian and British authorities tried to arrest him, he declared a divinely inspired war against both. His army, with vast popular supported, defeated an Anglo-Egyptian force and captured Khartoum, the regional capital. However, after he died in 1885, his forces were eventually defeated by a British army equipped with modern weapons.

In North America, indigenous communities resisted European American visions of Christianity and faith through a variety of strategies. Often, resistance took the shape of religious revivals that incorporated Christianity into local religious practices. The Ghost Dance movement of the 1870s and 1890s was one of these. Led by the Paiute prophet Wovoka, the movement taught that the people should return to traditional rituals of dance. This practice would bring the dead to life and send the Europeans back from whence they had come. Dancers were expected to enter into a trance during which they would acquire symbols and ceremonies of power from ancestors. The movement quickly spread from across different groups and across a wide swath of the western United States. Some adopters, like members of the Lakota community, militarized the ceremonies to protect themselves in their conflict with U.S. soldiers. Their leaders preached that the ritual could protect the population from the modern guns and bullets of U.S. soldiers. Eventually, government agents moved to violently suppress the Ghost Dance movement. This repression culminated in a massacre of 300 men, women, and children of the Lakota and related groups at Wounded Knee.

Reform strategies

While the spread of Protestant missionism and the export of Enlightenment ideals threatened long-existing religious and political structures around the world, people in these regions often saw some advantages and opportunities in these new worldviews. They sought to adapt lessons from modernizing Protestantism to their own needs and religions. These efforts frequently resulted in **reformist** movements. The reformers drew on both imported ideas and long-standing internal resources and patterns of thought as they sought to change their governments and religious institutions from within.

Reformers often moved to reinvigorate or create rational, critical studies of their religious tradition that helped them to integrate the ideas of liberalism and the Enlightenment with their own worldviews. Muslim scholars such as Sayyid Ahmad

Khan and Muhammad Abduh, for example, argued that there were ways to use rational calculation to understand the will of Allah and the working of the world. Other reformers emphasized the formalization and uniformity of rituals and rites as much as they tried to introduce new ideas. This was especially the challenge for Hindu reformist leaders, who had to meld together many diverse religious practices from across South Asia in to a single "religion." They wanted to create a new and unified vision of Hinduism, one that could bring together the local traditions of millions of people in thousands of communities across South and Southeast Asia. They accomplished their goal partly through voluntary associations that funded temples, supported pilgrimages, and endowed religious charities. They also did so almost entirely without the support of the colonial authorities.

Still other reformers created new religious denominations suited to the realities being experienced in the nineteenth century. The Church of Jesus Christ of Latter Day Saints, founded in 1830 by Joseph Smith in the United States, was built around biblical teachings but had its own holy book. By incorporating the Americas into biblical narrative, this *Book of Mormon* helped to make Christianity more relevant for some inhabitants of the United States. In Persia, meanwhile, Shi'ite Muslim leaders Sayyid Ali Muhammad Shirazi and Mirza Husain Ali Nuri preached a cosmopolitan, adaptable philosophy that developed into the new Bahai religion. Their teachings were particularly useful to Persians adapting to a rapidly changing world, because they aligned with Enlightenment ideals like gender equality and called for the reconciliation of science and religion. In fact, in some ways the Bahai faith was much more successful in delivering on modern Enlightenment ideology than any other.

Judaism also faced the question of how to adapt to the new world order of the nineteenth century. Nationalism provided one route, as some Jews—persecuted in many parts of Europe and especially Russia—sought to establish a national homeland in Ottoman-ruled Palestine. Their movement, known as Zionism, gradually came to embrace the idea of a Jewish nation-state. Another route to modernization, especially for Jews in the United States, was that of reform. In 1885, proponents of Reformed Judaism in the United States met in Pittsburgh. They rejected traditional ideas that they saw as having no "rational" basis—for example, kosher dietary laws. At the same time, they embraced many core humanitarian ideals of the Enlightenment. Yet the Pittsburgh Platform, as their statement was named, still called upon Jews to embrace their own unique culture and spiritual life.

The movements described above focused on religion outside the sphere of politics. Reformed Jews, for example, defined Judaism as a religious community while recognizing that they were also citizens of the nation-state in which they lived. In some parts of the world, however, governments exerted control over religion and culture by restricting some sects and sponsoring others. In late nineteenth-century China, for example, political leaders tried to promote Confucianism as a national religion and a way to push back at missionary Christianity. In Japan, Shinto was promoted by the Meiji state at the expense of Buddhist sects.

Many government-sponsored reforms were explicitly political or economic, but necessitated religious and intellectual change as well. The Tanzimat, or "reorganization," of the Ottoman Empire was an important reform movement that began in 1839. To a large degree, this effort began within the government of the Ottoman sultan. The main promoters of this movement were military officers, some of whom had studied in northwest Europe. The reforms they promoted were partly prompted by their awareness of the dangers of growing nationalism among the ethnic and national groups of the empire—Armenians, Kurds, Arabs, and Slavs especially. In order to appease these movements somewhat, the reforms extended some civil liberties and property rights to all Ottoman subjects. They also modernized the military and updated the national financial system. At the same time, the reformers realized that political and financial changes weren't sufficient, and that intellectual and religious reforms were also necessary. A law passed in 1856 guaranteed the rights of non-Muslims to practice their religion, an important improvement for Jews as well as Armenian and Syrian Christians. In addition, they created a modern education system that included a number of universities and teacher training colleges and an Academy of Sciences.

Similar reforms were periodically attempted in China under the late nineteenth-century Qing emperors. The most important was the Hundred-Days Reform of 1898. The need to reform China's political and cultural system had been made clear by the Taiping Rebellion, the Qing military's defeat by Japan in an 1894–1895 war, and the erosion of Chinese sovereignty at the hands of European powers. The 1898 reforms, which were pushed by a small group within the royal court, aimed to improve economy, modernize the military, and industrialize production. More importantly, perhaps, the reformers pushed for a culture of "self-strengthening." They sought to remain true to Confucianist morals while still adapting some Enlightenment methodologies and ideas. Despite some initial progress, however, these reforms were quickly cut short. Following a struggle within the imperial court, the reformers pushed out of power by conservatives led by the Empress Dowager Cixi, who believed the new policies would ultimately threaten authority of the Qing Dynasty.

Subversive trends in European thought

Within European society, as well, individuals and groups often found the dominant moral and cultural norms to be restrictive or threatening. Their responses tended to reflect strategies for dissenting from the center, rather than the periphery. For example, some northwest Europeans and North Americans developed an ethos of primitivism that embraced the art and cultural expressions of societies otherwise deemed to be "barbaric" or "savage." Artists like Paul Gauguin "escaped" Europe

Figure 2.10 Paul Gauguin's paintings of Tahiti. Executed in the 1890s, the paintings show a wistfulness for the laid-back, simpler life that he sought. Gauguin fled to Tahiti in 1891, abandoning his wife and children and all of his responsibilities as well as the rules of middle-class post-Enlightenment European life.

and found—to his mind—a simpler way of life in the South Pacific. Pablo Picasso, similarly, sought inspiration and the inner soul of humanity in the art and cultural objects of African societies.

Primitivism was a critique of "modern" morality, the Enlightenment, and evangelism. Even while extolling African, Pacific, and Native American societies as virtuous, however, primitivists still tended to accept the view that they were simple and savage. Primitivists therefore ironically contributed to the dominant view of these societies as being unchanging, if not backward.

Agnosticism was another moral viewpoint that arose in this period. Broadly defined as a skepticism of the idea that some things were unknowable, agnosticism was in particular the lack of acceptance in an unknowable and all-powerful God. It was related to older types of skepticism from around the world, but was based in Enlightenment concepts of science and reason. Agnostics like the mid-nineteenth-century British philosopher Thomas Henry Huxley rejected mystical or religious ideals that they saw as having no basis in evidence.

Agnosticism was a set of loosely shared ideas. By contrast, **nihilism** emerged in the mid-nineteenth century within a concentrated faction who aimed at overthrowing all

authorities, conservative *or* liberal, religious *or* secular. Nihilism was born in Rus
where the Orthodox Church and the state closely monitored and quashed reformist
or even moderately liberal movements. In response, nihlists argued that all power
structures impede the individual and needed to be destroyed. They acted, often with
violence, to do so. Perhaps the most important nihilist intellectual was Friedrich
Nietzsche, who especially aimed his critique at Christianity. Adopting a stance
similar to the agnostics, Nietzsche argues that Christianity built a power structure
on the argument that the Bible contained all meaning, which he rejected in favor of
individual rights. In fact, Nietzsche rejected all forms of collective moralization. He
called on individuals to instead be free spirits, actively promoting their own values
and ways of life.

First-wave feminism

Among the most important critics of the ascendant morality of the time within
Europe and the Americas were women who organized responses that we now call
first-wave feminism. Feminism is the advocacy of equality across the genders as well
as women's social, political, and economic rights. First-wave feminists were the first
groups and individuals to advocate these rights and equality using the vocabulary
and ideas of modernity.

The first-wave feminists of the late eighteenth and nineteenth centuries were
influenced to various degrees by Enlightenment and/or evangelical ideals. Some,
like Olympe de Gouges in eighteenth-century France and female anarchists and
socialists in nineteenth-century Russia saw women's struggles for rights as part of a
wider fight for political participation and better conditions for all citizens. Others,
like the women who sat on the board of the American Anti-Slavery Society in the
1840s, were motivated by religious and liberal ideas of free labor, personal salvation,
and humanitarianism. In the United States and Britain, many early feminists were
involved in anti-alcohol movements. They were motivated both by distress over
the damage done to families by alcoholism and by the bourgeois morals of their
society.

While these early movements made use of the dominant moral and philosophical
ideals of the time, they were also implicitly rebellions against them. In particular,
many women who were leaders in these movements also questioned the ways in
which women had been excluded from political and economic equality. In 1848, a
number of U.S.-based women organized a conference in Seneca Falls, New York,
at which they issued a declaration stating thus: "Men and women were CREATED
EQUAL; they are both moral and accountable beings, and whatever is *right* for a
man is *right* for a woman."[8] Their calls for political equality were repeated in Britain,
Germany, and France in subsequent decades. Moreover, they were also echoes in
Latin American middle-class communities. In Brazil, a feminist periodical titled

O Journal das Senhoras was published in 1952. In Mexico, women—who could not vote—pushed the Liberal Party to extend educational and other rights to females. By the beginning of the twentieth century, women were beginning to gain the vote in Western-style parliamentary democracies and republics. Their victories were examples of the rebellions that would create a tension between a single, and multiple, visions of modernity in the twentieth-century world.

Key terms

acculturation [49]

agnosticism [64]

Enlightenment [36]

evangelism [34]

first-wave feminism [65]

fundamentalism [69]

inculturation [49]

millenarian [59]

missionaries [48]

nihilism [64]

paternalism [55]

primitivism [63]

reformism [61]

secularism [36]

social sciences [43]

syncretism [49]

travelogue [38]

Further readings

Several histories of Enlightenment thought exist, although most are focused solely on Europe. One of the most accessible is Margaret C.C. Jacob's *The Enlightenment: A Brief History with Documents* (Bedford St. Martin's, 2000).

One of the more remarkable books about the global and intercultural creation of evangelical Protestantism is John Sensbach's *Rebecca's Revival: Creating Black Christianity in the Atlantic World* (Cambridge: Harvard University Press, 2006). This narrative follows the story of Rebecca Protten, a freed African slave whose evangelical mission covered three continents.

The Taiping Rebellion has received a great deal of scholarly attention, but it's often difficult to find primary sources. This problem is rectified by Franz Michael and Chung-li Chang's *The Taiping Rebellion: history and documents* (Seattle: University of Washington Press, 1966).

One book that explores the connection between ideas of "civilization" and gender in modern moralism very well is Gail Bederman's *Manliness and Civilization* (Chicago: Chicago University Press, 1995).

Interlude 1: Fundamentalism

American modern society is the grandchild of both the Enlightenment and Protestant evangelism. As a result, it embodies both a strong evangelical tradition and a separate secular, political realm. The defenders of this "division of church and state" worry about those who do not agree with these two discrete categories. Indeed, there are many people in the world for whom it makes perfect sense for government and law to be driven by belief and religious practice. Americans tend to call these people **fundamentalists**, and what they say about fundamentalism tells us a lot about our vision of the past and the present.

The modern term "fundamentalist" was a title claimed by some evangelical Protestants of the late nineteenth-century United States. Its proponents were religious figures like R.A. Torrey who called for a return to the "fundamentals" of Christianity. Torrey and his colleagues called for a revival of basic faith, personal piety, and biblical morality as a safeguard against industrialization, secularism, and vices like alcohol and gambling. Fundamentalists split with their fellow Protestants who accepted the Enlightenment liberal emphasis on rationality and who sought to reconcile religion and Enlightenment ideals. Instead, they embraced a passionate, belief-driven defense of biblical truth.

Quite quickly, however, the label "fundamentalist" came to have a negative connotation for many. Urbane, cosmopolitan intellectuals depicted fundamentalists as throwbacks to earlier times who rejected all the new ideas and the exciting opportunities of modern life. Very few evangelical Protestants of the early twentieth century embraced the label, preferring to call themselves conservatives or evangelicals. In the modern United States, it is mostly secular liberals that uses the term, and usually as a pejorative. Over time, moreover, the meaning of the term has changed. While critics still use the word to imply that their opponents are backward, it also connotes that they are violent and dangerous, rather than passionate or strong in belief. Thus is a very useful label to use in domestic politics, because it brings up frightening specters of cults, witch hunts, and religious fanatics.

The term "fundamentalist" has also become widely applied to groups beyond the Christian world. Although the label was at first used to describe Protestants, in the twenty-first century we hear most about Islamic fundamentalism. This is a label that is applied both to the Sunni Osama bin Laden, descendant of the eighteenth-century founders of the Wahhabi movement in Arabia, and the Shiite leaders of Iran. As such, it is intended to be negative and is applied only by outsiders: whether orthodox or revolutionary, Muslim religious leaders do not use the term to describe themselves. What critics of these leaders and movements are trying to do by using this term, therefore, is to argue that they are opposed to the values that we hold dear such as progress, rationality, and separation of church and state and moreover that they are violent.

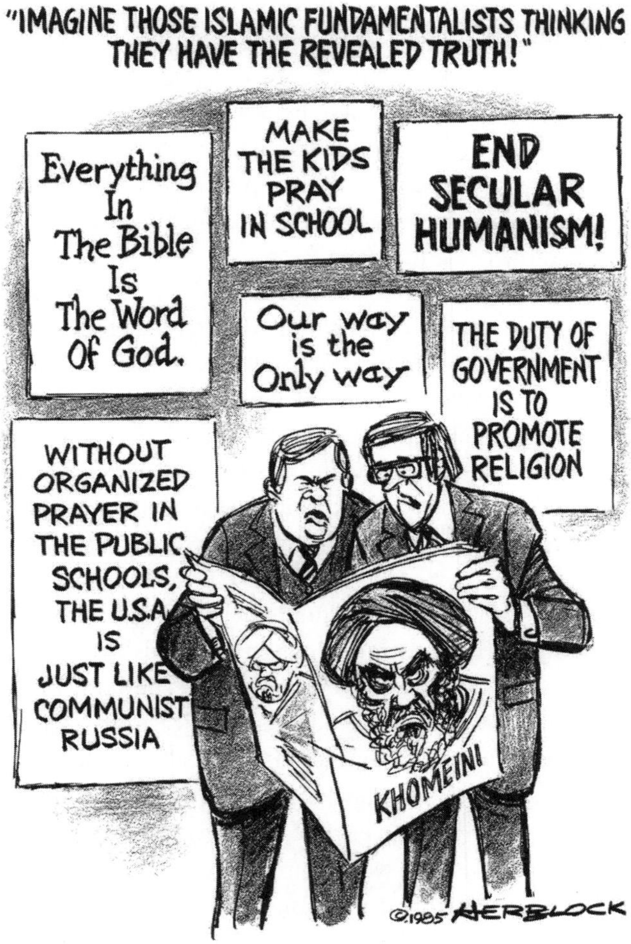

Figure 2.11 A 1985 cartoon, from the *Washington Post,* by artist Herbert Block, depicting Christian "fundamentalists" condemning Ayatollah Khomeini and of Iran. This was a commentary both on international affairs and domestic politics in the United States.

The contemporary use of the term fundamentalism reflects the notional division between evangelical religion and secularism that grew to be pronounced in the period described in Chapter 2. Thus it is a useful term to explore following reading that chapter. At the same time, however, it's important to question whether the use of the term as a negative reflects reality or just starkly divides things that are actually more complex. Historically, for example, Protestant "fundamentalists" in the United States have not only been conservatives but also modernizing reformers. They were key abolitionists, fighters for a national education system, and sought to limit the influence of drugs and gambling. As is often the case, reality is more complex than what a simple label seems to make of it.

3

Nationalism and the Nation-State

Chapter introduction

In this third chapter of the book, we will look at a fundamental transformation in the political structures through which human societies were organized in the long nineteenth century, and the cultural shift beneath it. This transformation was the emergence of the nation-state, the political institution through which the modern world came to be organized. There have been many flavors of the nation-state in the past century, from secular centralized democracies to somewhat decentralized federations to states like modern Iran where religion and governance go hand-in-hand, a diversity that gives credence to the idea of multiple modernities. Nevertheless, all of these models draw on the animating ideals and structures of the nation-state that emerged in the course of the long nineteenth century.

That popular ideal which gave birth to and animated the nation-state was nationalism, and while, again, there are many flavors of nationalism, the identification of the people as a nation in search of a state is fundamental to all modern societies around the world.

Figure 3.1 Eugene Delacroix, *Liberty Leading the People*, 1830. The French Revolution was a decisive moment in the development of the modern nation-state, and such symbols as the female "Liberty," often known as Marianne, were used to mobilize nationalist sentiment in the years that followed.

These two features of modernity—nationalism and the nation-state—are the intertwined themes of this chapter. In particular, we will look at how they came about in the first years of this period, and how they spread around the world and were adapted to new settings throughout the nineteenth century.

Among the key concepts we will explore in this chapter are **nation, nationalism, classical liberalism,** the **Social Contract,** and the **nation-state.** We especially look at specific forms of nationalism including **creole nationalism** and **ethnic nationalism** Together, these terms and narratives will help you to understand the core of modernity from the point of view of political culture and institutions.

By the end of this chapter, you should be able to:

- Explain the origins of modern forms of political liberalism in this period.
- Discuss the process by which nation-states became a leading form of state organization over the course of this period.
- Describe how nationalism developed during this period, and how it shaped the culture and experience of people in many regions.
- Interpret the development of the culture of nationalism through writing, art, and other forms of expression.
- Compare and contrast the nation-state form of government described in this chapter with the empire form described in Chapter 1, by identifying overlaps that explain how they could at times exist within a single society.

The emergence of modern nationalism

We live today in a world of **nation-states,** one particular kind of political unit. The kind of state that is most recognizable to us has relatively uniform laws, strictly delineated borders, and an extensive bureaucracy and apparatus of government. Moreover, it is built on the idea—whether true in practice or not—that all of its citizens are members of a **nation,** a group with a shared cultural identity and history.

Even as late as the nineteenth century, however, a number of different kinds of political entities had coexisted, many of which were not nation-states. Many parts of the world were characterized by types of chieftaincies led by elected or hereditary rulers who governed without the help of a professional bureaucracy. Confederations, states in which power was balanced among several powerful families or regional governments, could be found in many regions of Asia, the Americas, and Africa. To be sure, just about every part of the world included some centralized states and even large empires, but even in most of these, the idea of the nation as a popular identity with a political will had not yet emerged.

However, in the centuries leading up to the events described in this chapter, the groundwork for a world of nation-states had begun to be laid. As we discussed in

Chapter 1, by the fifteenth and sixteenth centuries highly centralized states in Eurasia and North Africa had begun to make use of a combination of increasingly sophisticated bureaucracies and gunpowder firearms to assert the power of the state—the central government and its agencies—over large populations. Many of these states expanded rapidly into the Asian interior (Mughal Empire, Ottoman Empire, Ming and Qing Dynasty China, Safavid Persia, and Romanov Russia) and across oceans into the Pacific and the Americas (Portugal, Spain, England, the Netherlands, and France). The states of the Atlantic seaboard of Europe states were especially poised to take part in long-distance trade.

By the mid-eighteenth century, three northwestern European states—England (now Britain), France, and the Netherlands—had become especially involved in long-distance trade and in all of the cultural and economic innovations this commerce helped to stimulate. It was in three states in this region, and more importantly in their American colonies, that the particular set of political ideals linked to the modern nation-state first began to emerge. These ideals are discussed in this chapter as liberalism and nationalism. Although these were not the only political innovations in this period, for political innovation is a feature of societies everywhere, they proved to be the ones with the greatest impact.

The birth of political liberalism

The foundation for modern nationalism was the late eighteenth- and early nineteenth-century ideology of liberalism, and in particular its earliest modern form: **classical liberalism**. Liberalism first evolved in northwestern Europe and the European colonies in North America. It stemmed from a distinct intellectual and cultural trajectory that focused on the importance of personal liberty and freedom, hence the root of the term liberalism in the Latin origin word *liber*, meaning free (man). Liberalism was to some degree a product of the sixteenth- and seventeenth-century religious movement known as the Reformation, which had challenged the power of the state and church. In the process, its proponents promoted individual liberties like freedom of worship. Such fracturing of the long-established power of religious and secular institutions was further exacerbated by the movement of Europeans overseas to the American colonies. Far away from the centers of political authority, these groups had greater freedom to experiment with styles of governance and organization. The expansion of trade within Europe and the colonies and the emergence of new groups involved in commerce and finance also helped to stimulate this process, as these individuals, finding themselves excluded from a government of the landowning aristocracy, sought to parlay their economic wealth into political clout.

Perhaps the most important cultural context for the rise of liberalism, however, was the Enlightenment, the series of intellectual trends discussed at length in the previous chapter. As we've seen, the intellectual and cultural debates produced by

Enlightenment thinkers were shaped partly by trends within North America and Europe. They were also informed by the increasing stream of information about governance and politics from other parts of the world brought back by merchants, traders, and emissaries. Their observations and studies of the world around them allowed European intellectuals to develop an emphasis on reason, a rejection of tradition, and a belief in progress. One idea that emerged from this period was the argument that a contract should exist among citizens at all levels of society, known as the **Social Contract**. This theory led to such work as Thomas Hobbes' emphasis on the relationship between citizens and government and John Locke's advocacy for the rights of life, liberty, and property.

By the 1750s, these ideas had coalesced into the embryonic ideology of liberalism. Liberals tended to believe in governing through the rule of law rather than through the rights of aristocrats and monarchs, and they even went so far as to demand that laws be applied equally to everyone, or at least to a large number of educated men. They worked toward what they saw as a rational government and political system. Most importantly, however, liberals had a commitment to a particular set of liberties, especially the freedom of individuals to choose their religion, to speak, to assemble, to a free press, and ultimately, to the right to aspire to a life of freedom with hopes to advance in society. They also supported free trade, individual property rights, and open markets, concepts that will be discussed in Chapter 4.

Importantly, these ideas developed in a region where the governments were rapidly becoming both larger and more highly organized. Where once northwest Europe had been a patchwork of relatively weak kings dependent on powerful landowning aristocrats, by the early nineteenth century, Britain, France, and the Netherlands were governed by kings who had at their command armies of lawyers, bureaucrats, accountants and tax collectors, and—increasingly—soldiers. The governments of these states were much more deeply involved than ever before in building infrastructure, enforcing laws, and managing their economies. In degree of organization, they were finally catching up with China, which had had a large and well-organized professional class of public officials for several centuries.

The modern idea of the nation

Together, liberalism and the centralized state were conditions that made possible the modern nation-state. Understanding this connection requires us to follow a cascade of ideas, the first of which is the nation. The term **nation** was originally a French and Spanish word used to refer to communities of aristocrats or intellectuals who were in correspondence with each other and who debated important topics. In the sixteenth and seventeenth centuries, these "nations" tended to be rather small and exclusive groups of men (and occasionally a few women). Perhaps the most important innovation of eighteenth-century liberals was that they came to understand the "nation" as including a much broader group of *the people*, and not just a small body of intellectuals.

It is important to state here that this early nationalism was not necessarily democratic: the concept of the nation did not at this time necessarily imply that all people should participate in government. In fact, early nationalism restricted political participation to relatively small groups of formally educated, relatively wealthy adult men. They believed these men could be trusted to express the interests of the people. Of course, this meant that the early notion of the "nation" was restricted to people who to a large degree really did share a sense of history, culture, ethnicity, and belonging.

Over the years that followed, the meaning of the nation would be expanded as political debates emerged as to whether or not to include the poor, women, ethnic minorities, and others within the political realm of a single state, region, or language group. These groups did not necessarily initially have a strong common identity or sense of belonging. As a result, the nation would need to be *imagined* by those who were trying to give large groups of people a common sense of identity. The leaders of the nation would try to stir a sense of belonging by creating symbols like flags, preaching brotherhood, by writing national histories and shared school curricula, and by creating holidays and buildings. All of these projects combined to create a nationalist ideology.

The emergence of nationalism

Nationalism is the ideology by which the leaders and proponents of the nation argue that the nation should govern its own state. This idea was reflected best, perhaps, in the 1795 French Declaration of Rights. In the words of this great liberal document, "Each people is independent and sovereign, whatever the number of individuals who compose it and extent of the territory it occupies. This sovereignty is inalienable."

The aspirations of nationalists to attain sovereign control of a state might involve taking over from a king or aristocratic elite. Indeed, in its earliest period, nationalism was largely a challenge to the monopoly that aristocrats possessed on political power in northwest Europe. However, nationalism could also be used to argue for a nation's separation from a larger state or empire, or merely the creation of a nation-state where there wasn't one before. Both of those uses would become common later in the long nineteenth century.

Why did nationalism emerge so powerfully in this period, and not before? There are several theories, many of which are described briefly in a previous section of this chapter as contributors to the development of political liberalism: religious Reformation, Enlightenment ideas, the semiautonomy of settlers in far-flung colonies, the political aspirations of merchants and financiers, and the generally increasingly rapid spread of ideas around the world.

An additional key factor was probably the expansion of the state. In the nineteenth century, northwest European states employed many more government workers and administrators than in the earlier era. These administrators were trained together in universities that brought together students from around the country—especially in Britain, France, the Netherlands, and the German principalities. They were educated to believe in a shared civic culture and in loyalty to the state. These administrators were among the important early nationalists who worked to help spread ideas into the broader population.

Another transformation in this era was the breakdown in historically strict class boundaries. As it became increasingly possible for workers and peasants to become entrepreneurs and artisans, they began to build relationships across the usual boundaries of class position. At the same time, rising trade helped to get people to move across their countries, sharing ideas and building relationships that overcame provincial isolation and differences. All of this social and geographic movement helped to build a sense of a broad national community.

Technological innovations were also important, especially newspapers and the growth of literacy. By the late eighteenth century, relatively large groups of Europeans—as well as European settlers in the Americas—could read. This expanded literate community resulted in the publication of several national and imperial newspapers and pamphlets that spread ideas rapidly and effectively throughout a country or colony.

Lastly, the military transition to firearms also had its own implications, since states had come to rely on large groups of peasants who increasingly owned their own firearms or could be quickly trained to use government-provided weapons. While effective for a state that wanted to direct its soldiers against rebellious aristocrats, putting weapons and power in the hands of the commoners also created a danger to the state itself.

It is important not to overstate the importance of any of these changes or the influence of nationalism in this early period, however. These were for the most part quite gradual changes (firearms being an exception). Moreover, these new national identities were built on a bedrock of group identities that already existed to some degree. For example there had already existed, by the late eighteenth century, a sense of "Englishness" based on the profession of a Protestant faith, the shared English language, and a pride in entrepreneurship and commercial success. This identity was quite ready to coalesce under the right conditions in the nineteenth century into an English nationalism.

Nevertheless, political nationalism was in many ways something new. In 1750s' northwest Europe, as in most of the rest of the world, most people still lived in small villages, spoke regional languages, and were generally isolated from broader trends. Only gradually did national forms of identity seep into the consciousness and the homes of large numbers of regular people, beginning in this region and spreading widely before 1914.

The invention of nationalism, c.1750–1820

Nationalism became a decisive political force on both sides of the Atlantic during the period 1750–1820. In Europe, nationalism emerged most dramatically in the French Revolution and its aftermath. In the Americas, liberal nationalism was the core ideology of revolutions in both British and Spanish colonies, and it also contributed to the Haitian Revolution in the French island colony of Saint Domingue.

Creole nationalism and the American War of Independence

It was in the American colonies, rather than in the European metropoles, that liberal nationalism first emerged as a really powerful political force for change. We tend to apply the term **creole nationalism** to the ideology as it was expressed in these colonies. As we saw in Chapter 1, the term *creole* was used in the Spanish colonies to denote individuals of European heritage who had been born in the Americas. As an analytical term, however, it is equally useful when talking about British and French settlers.

In all of the European colonies in the Americas, creole classes occupied a relatively high social position and enjoyed some economic success, but despite some functional autonomy, they generally lacked both political authority to govern their own societies and representation in the governments of the metropoles that ruled them. Governors of the colonies were normally officials imposed from Europe, rather than selected from among the settler population. Similarly, laws arriving from European capitals were usually written without consultation with the settlers and were often imposed without appeal. The inability of the creole classes to rule themselves or to shape the laws that governed them caused a great deal of individual frustration, and colonists shared that frustration through each other through newspapers and other means of communication. Much of their writing was inspired by the classical liberalism of Enlightenment thinkers, whose work was increasingly available in the colonies in French, Spanish, and English languages. By the late eighteenth century, therefore, networks of creole intellectuals, merchants, planters, and artisans were debating the ways in which the ideas of liberty and equality related to them.

Increasingly, creoles found themselves in an ambiguous position. On the one hand, they still were very deeply connected to their homelands and identified as European. On the other hand, they resented the imposition of political authority in which they had no say. This was true for example in British North America, where until the 1750s, at least, most settlers identified closely with Britain. Indeed, loyalties were

Figure 3.2 Paul Revere, *The Bloody Massacre,* 1770. The Boston Massacre, which the British called the Boston Riot, occurred on March 5, 1770, when British soldiers fired into a crowd of American colonists. The confrontation was touched off by a private dispute over a debt between a British soldier and a colonist, but resentment at British policies turned it into a mass protest that ended in bloodshed. Anti-British colonists were quick to use the event as nationalist propaganda in paintings, poems, and pamphlets.

especially strong during the Seven Years War (1756–1763) in which British troops assisted English-speaking American colonists against French rivals. So long as the British government allowed the settlers to run their day-to-day affairs without too much meddling and backed them up with troops when needed, they were content to be British subjects.

However, the Seven Years War itself threatened this complacency. First, the British government imposed a series of taxes on the colonists to help pay for the Seven Years War against France, as well as to help support the British East India Company, which was suffering due to competition with independent merchants in North America and elsewhere. British King George II also imposed a new and more interventionist set of policies that took what limited power elected groups of colonists—the burgesses, congresses, and parliaments of the colonies—had to rule themselves. These actions drove both long-term settlers like Thomas Jefferson and new immigrants like Thomas Paine to take the ideas of personal liberty that were floating around and form them into a unified call for revolution against British rule. Most significantly, they filtered their calls for independence through the idea of nationalism. They increasingly claimed that the settlers constituted a new nation, separate from British society, and deserved a state of their own. This idea soon got its own heroes and shared emotional episodes in the dumping of British East India Company tea and through the national martyrdom of protesters in the "Boston Massacre."

Within a few years, a new and embryonic national identity had begun to form in British North America. In 1776, a congress of representative settlers declared themselves independent from Britain. Many of the colonists might still have felt some attachment to Britain, but this attachment was ended by the violence and ill-will created by the War of Independence fought between 1776 and 1781. In the end, aided by Britain's European rivals, the colonists managed to win independence and to establish themselves as the United States of America, a brand new nation-state.

The French Revolutionary years

The French King Louis XVI had been particularly generous in providing aid and support for the rebels in British North America, thinking to unsettle his British rivals. Instead, the French war effort helped to topple their own king and, indeed, the entire French system of government. Over the decade that followed 1781, the ripples from the American War of Independence promoted nationalist sentiment in France, where much of the population similarly felt alienated from a government in which they were not represented and which was not responsive to their needs.

Political authority in late eighteenth-century France was monopolized by the king and his close advisors. So long as the population had largely consisted of an illiterate rural peasantry, this system could endure. However by the 1780s a large public sphere had developed. Within this loosely-knit group, members of the lower aristocracy mingled with merchants, artisans, and a small but important group of intellectuals. This cosmopolitan community was largely literate and entrepreneurial. They had a financial as well as a cultural stake in the laws by which they were governed. In the years following the massive expenditures on wars in the Americas, they began to question their government more stridently. However, most of them, especially members of the growing middle classes, had no access to the government. They were frustrated by this exclusion, not least because the monarchy of Louis XVI failed to implement laws that would have made business activities easier. In their anger they even found common cause with the peasants and the rural poor who suffered from an inefficient government response to a series of bad harvests in the 1780s. Even aristocrats struggled to get policies implemented to help them through financial crises resulting from changing land values.

Each of these frustrations affected different classes of France's population. However, the means to bind them together in common cause was emerging. Education was expanding in France and the ideas of political liberalism had attracted those who could read the new national and regional newspapers and the books of Enlightenment philosophers. Returning French soldiers and volunteers from the American War of Independence helped to stoke these ideas by sharing the writing and sentiments of American nationalists. The result was a growing, shared sense that the French state should belong to or at least be responsive to all of the classes of the "nation," no matter what their particular needs.

In 1789, an assembly of French representatives called together by the king to help raise funds for the government instead turned on him. Quickly, the representatives formed a National Assembly that demanded power from the king, whom they forced out of power. At first, aristocrats and the middle class dominated the new government. However a 1792 invasion of France by conservative European forces backing the restoration of the monarchy led to the mobilization of an army of peasants and workers, and this force in turn helped to create a truly "national" government for the first time.

In 1799, following remarkable successes in the battlefield leading French armies in Europe and Egypt, a young general named Napoleon Bonaparte seized control of the government. Bonaparte's initial popularity with the masses was based largely on these successes, and his continued effectiveness against France's enemies. Between 1793 and 1815, Bonaparte led French armies against several coalitions of European opponents, including Prussia, Austria, Russia, and Great Britain. Although he suppressed many of the liberties established by the French Revolution in France, Bonaparte's armies did help spread the revolutionary ideas of social and political freedoms and of nationalism across Europe. With French support, sympathizers established liberal national governments in the Netherlands, Central Europe, and elsewhere. Ironically, Napoleon's opponents in Austria, Egypt, Spain, and elsewhere responded by calling on their own populations to defend their countries in the same language: the name of national sovereignty. Even after France was defeated in 1815, many of these nationalist movements remained important throughout Europe, as we will see.

Revolution and rebellion in Latin America

The French Revolution and the American War of Independence played a large role in catalyzing nationalist sentiment in the Spanish colonies of Latin America, as well. Here, creoles in many capital cities such as Buenos Aires and Cartagena were linked via networks of newspapers, travel, and political and family ties. In a pattern that we have already seen, they were largely barred from political office and instead ruled by administrators, governors, and bishops sent out from Spain, many of whom acted and believed that they were culturally superior to creoles. Responding to their exclusion from power, the creoles began to create a sense of their own national identity, making considerable use of religion as a binding force. They embraced religious stories that asserted the importance of Latin America in Catholicism, especially the memorialization of the purported appearance of the Virgin Mary in Tepeyac, Mexico in 1531. They began to write of themselves as the rightful inheritors of the mantle of power once wielded by the Inca and Mexican (Aztec) ruling classes. In the 1780s, for example, a leading Peruvian creole who rebelled against Spanish governors did so under the name of Tupac Amaru II, claiming to be the heir to the last Inca emperor. At the same time, the creole classes increasingly read, absorbed, and contributed to the work of the Enlightenment, offering insights on scientific ideas as well as the new philosophy of liberty.

Napoleon Bonaparte's successful invasion of Spain in 1808 and the placement of his brother Joseph on the Spanish throne ignited these existing ideas and discontent into a revolution. In spring of that year, groups of creole nationalists in Spanish America removed royal officials, especially those who seemed to be willingly cooperating with the new Bonapartist regime in Spain. They quickly organized committees to rule themselves, and then set out to appeal to the broader population. Over the next 10 years, inspired by events in Europe but acting in their own national interests, these colonies would win their independence and become the modern nation-states that make up Latin America.

The Haitian revolution

Creole nationalism in Latin America successfully transferred power from imperial officials to local representatives over several decades. However, it always veered between an inclusive and exclusive notion of the nation. Some of the leaders of

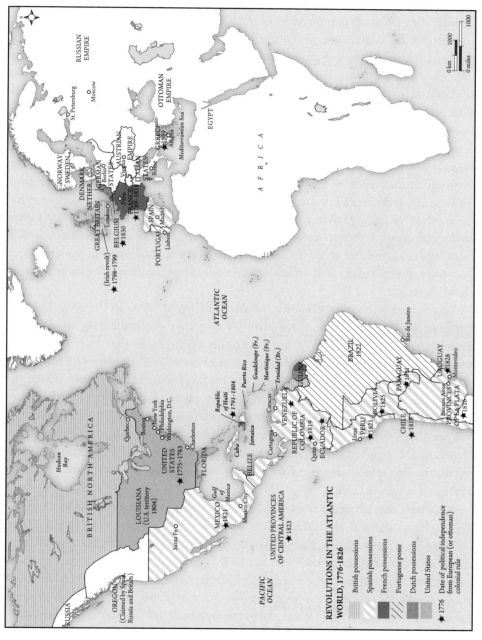

Figure 3.3 Revolutions in the Atlantic World, 1776–1826.

these rebellions against foreign rule saw themselves largely as representatives of a class of people of European descent only, while others sought to include people of mixed heritage and the indigenous population as full members of the nation. This more inclusive definition of the nation was both pragmatic—for the revolutionaries needed the arms and participation of these large populations—and in many cases inspired by the ideals of classical liberalism.

However, there was one group that was seldom included in the creole definition of the nation: the large population of people of African descent. The importation of enslaved Africans by Europeans into their American colonies dates back to the fifteenth century, and by 1800 more than eight and a half million humans had been forcibly embarked on such voyages. For many years Africans outnumbered Europeans in both Caribbean and mainland American colonies, their numbers steadily increasing over the years. For example, more than two and a half million Africans disembarked in Brazil alone by the beginning of the nineteenth century. They and their descendants often labored under horrific conditions, but they were not complacent or willing laborers. In that Portuguese colony alone, Africans led three major rebellions in the nineteenth century as well as many smaller uprisings. Similar uprisings occurred frequently in British, French, Dutch, and Spanish mainland and island colonies. Acts of small-scale rebellion, noncooperation, and sabotage were too many to record.

Undoubtedly the most effective rebellion led by Africans in the Americas was the Haitian Revolution that took from France its most profitable colony. Saint Domingue was the source of huge amounts of sugar, indigo, and cotton that together were the mainstay of the French economy. In 1789, a rebellion erupted among white and mixed-race artisans and traders on the island that mirrored the revolution in France. The conflict was meant to sideline the largest population of the island—enslaved and free people of African descent. In 1791, however, this very population took matters into their own hands through a mass insurrection that brought together hundreds of thousands of enslaved Africans and their free brethren. The rebels organized themselves into regiments based partly on their region of origin in Africa.

Although they shared a hatred of the imperial French administration, however, these groups did not align themselves with the middle-class white rebels' liberal nationalism. Instead they called for a new order that, in particular, outlawed slavery. Many of the revolutionaries in fact hoped a system led by a king bound by social obligations akin to that of the Kingdom of Kongo in west-central Africa from which they came. Ultimately, their revolution was victorious and despite French attempts to reoccupy the island, the former slaves managed to establish an independent state, the modern country of Haiti, with its own sense of identity based partly on its titanic struggle against colonialism and slavery.

A world of nations, 1820–1914

Beginning around the 1820s, nationalism spread rapidly outward from the north Atlantic to new regions. Groups around the world found it a useful tool for their political ambitions and hopes. But they also found that they had to adapt nationalism and the nation-state to fit existing cultural institutions and local ideals. As a result of these new environments, as well as changing times and technologies, new flavors of nationalism came into being and nationalist sentiment was expressed in an expanding variety of ways in the mid-nineteenth century.

Ethnic nationalism and new nation-states

In the nineteenth century, as "race" was becoming accepted as an important category for defining large groups of people, especially in the context of empire, the related notion of ethnicity came to dominate political nationalism. One reason for the merging of ethnicity and nationalism was the infiltration of classical liberal ideas into two great empires composed of many different peoples—the Habsburg and Ottoman Empires. In both of these empires, the state kept power over many diverse religious and language communities partly by setting them against each other and partly by sponsoring and protecting their interests. In the mid-nineteenth century, however, the spread of liberal ideas promoted nationalist sentiments among these minority communities and channeled anger among those that felt excluded from opportunity and power. These communities began to conceive of themselves as new nations based on a shared **ethnicity**—that is to say, a mixture of common descent, language, and culture.

For both the Habsburgs and the Ottomans, **ethnic nationalism** quickly became a destabilizing force. The Habsburgs, based in Austria and the Balkan Peninsula, faced these kinds of nationalist sentiments among Hungarians, Slovenes, Czechs, Croats, and even the privileged German-speaking population. The Ottoman administration encountered nationalist movements in Egypt following the French invasion there in 1798, and soon after among the Greek, Armenian, and other religious communities within their far-flung provinces. In the 1820s, Ottoman officer Muhammed Ali managed to win partial independence for Egypt by promoting a new sense of Egyptian nationhood among soldiers and other local elites. This sentiment spread among Egyptians as Egypt, along with other parts of the Ottoman Empire, came under the economic control of English and to some degree French bankers. By the early 1870s, Egyptian army officers and intellectuals together demanded the expulsion of British and French debt administrators and the creation of a constitutional representative government. Representing themselves as the guardians of an Egyptian nation, this group slowly won widespread support from a broad cross-section of the Egyptian public.

Greek nationalists presented their own challenge to the rulers of the Ottoman Empire as early as the 1820s. A lack of opportunity in Greece led many young men to travel to western Europe in search of employment. When they returned, they brought back with them newfound nationalist sentiments that had spread throughout Europe with Napoleon's armies in the previous decades. They applied this nationalism to the argument that their own lack of jobs, and Greece's problems more broadly, were a result of Ottoman mismanagement. As an alternative to Ottoman rule, these young men promoted an idealized sense of what it meant to be Greek, an identity that excluded many people living in parts of Greece who weren't considered culturally or physically "pure" enough, including Macedonians living on its northern fringe. The young nationalists adopted Greek Orthodox Christianity as a central feature of

February, 1898.

Saved !

(Scene from Grand International Nautical Melodrama, first performed in 1833, and now revived with all the Original Scenery and Effects.)

Figure 3.4 A British cartoon from the 1830s, by Sir John Tenniel, depicting the Ottoman Empire as a lascivious man holding Greece (as a young woman) captive. The woman is about to be saved by European sailors. Many British, French, and German newspapers of the day used cartoons to support Greek nationalism. The use of gender in images like this one helped to promote the idea of western Europeans as virile, male nation-states.

their national identity, and soon began to attack Muslim mosques as well as Ottoman political institutions. When the Ottoman government responded by arresting church and community leaders, the result was an uprising in which idealistic British, French, and Russian liberals, including the renowned poet Lord Byron, volunteered to assist the rebels. Thus Greece won its independence in 1830 with the help of committed nationalists from all over Europe, and partly through an ethnic expulsion of Muslims and others deemed to be non-Greeks.

In Central Europe, nationalist sentiment erupted among liberals in the form of a series of uprisings in 1848. These uprisings were partly the result of a series of crop failures that in turn led to commercial and then financial collapse across Europe. They were also inspired, contradictorily, by both the aspirations and a desire for change among the emerging European upper middle class and resentment at the rapid pace of change by members of outmoded lower middle-class artisans. But all of them took on flavors of nationalism. Many, although not all, were aimed against the Habsburg state. Some of the fiercest rebels emerged among the Italian-speakers and German-speakers within the Habsburg Empire and in neighboring principalities. While the uprisings ultimately failed to achieve their goal of winning independence for these groups, but they did create networks of largely liberal German and Italian thinkers who thought the solution to their problems was to form unified "ethnic" Italian and German nations, neither of which had existed in the modern era. Over the next few decades, nationalist newspapers emerged in both languages, and their readership grew rapidly. In 1867, for example, there were 1217 newspapers in Germany, many of them openly espousing nationalist rhetoric and ideas. Nationalist mass movements in both states soon coalesced around certain princes who openly spoke of unifying the nation into a single state. In Germany, this was the Prussian Prince Wilhelm I. In Italy, it was King Victor Emmanuel II. Although many liberals were wary of cooperating with these conservative rulers, they generally suppressed their suspicions in pursuit of the immediate goal of creating a unified nation independent of the Habsburgs. Despite a series of internal conflicts and external wars that hampered progress toward statehood, both Italy and Germany emerged as nation-states in 1871.

Nationalism and imperialism

The new imperialism of the late nineteenth century also stimulated the spread of nationalism, most notably in the rival imperial metropoles. Germany and Italy joined such "great powers" as France, Britain, Russia, and later the United States and Germany in vying for domination over large parts of the world. In order to rally public opinion in favor of imperialism, they promised their populations cheaper goods and better lives, all to be delivered by new colonies. Demagogues and authoritarians seeking power painted neighboring nations as natural enemies and themselves as patriots as they sought to use imperial nationalism to distract the population from domestic problems and to redirect dissatisfaction outward. The master of this strategy was the conservative German Chancellor Count Otto von Bismarck, who held out the fruits of new colonies to diverse groups of German voters. He used imperial nationalism to convince Germans to support his campaigns first to defeat his rivals, especially working-class political parties and liberals who questioned his disdain for democracy. To secure popular support against these movements, he argued that the German people's problems would be solved not by social change or greater democracy, but rather by the acquisition of new colonies.

The political link between nationalism and imperialism is perhaps even more starkly illustrated in the case of Japan, where the Meiji Restoration of 1867 combined central elements of both philosophies. This transformation was led by members of the samurai warrior class, who resented the ruling Shogun and saw a restoration of the emperor as a way to get some access to government. The spark for their revolt was the unexpected arrival of American warships, which gave clear evidence of foreigners' military superiority. Because the literacy rate was enormously high in Japan for the time—estimated at 43 percent for men and 15 percent for women—a wide body of the Japanese public was able to read about these events. Consequently, when the insurrectionaries promised to make Japan a great industrial and military power, a great proportion of the population was inspired to offer their support. Popular backing contributed to the victory of the rebels, who took on an aura of nationalism by claiming to represent the whole body of Japanese people.

The new government put in place by the Meiji Restoration carefully constructed an emerging Japanese nationalist identity around the person of the emperor, whom they restored to power following the expulsion of the Shogun, ending almost 700 years of military rule. He became a symbol of the nation as a whole. To further build support for their rule and advertise Japan's status as a modern nation-state to the world, the ruling coalition decided that they needed to invade Korea. This decision was partly based on a need to access Korea's natural resources, but even more by a desire to demonstrate that their nation-state could be as imperial as the United States and Britain. A final motivation was the desire to build domestic national pride and support for the new government. Hence national pride again slid easily into imperialist expansion.

Hybrid models of nationalism in West Africa

At the same time as nationalism and imperialism were growing in tandem, however, liberal forms of political nationalism that contradicted imperialism were spreading around the world. Unlike imperialism, nationalism could spread by voluntary subscription and adoption. In West Africa, for example, black English-speakers born in both Africa and the Caribbean began in the late nineteenth century to write about their desire to create African nation-states based on local ethnic and cultural identifications.

The Sierra Leonean doctor James Africanus Horton was a leader in this respect. He helped several groups including the Fante-speaking and Ga-speaking populations of the Gold Coast (today Ghana) to write constitutions and to build structures similar to that of European nation-states. Horton wrote, "If Europe… has been raised to her present pitch of civilization by progressive advancement, Africa too, with a guarantee of the civilization of the north, will rise into equal importance." Horton was joined by men like Joseph Casely Hayford and John Mensah Sarbah who tried to define the characteristics of the Fante nation and its right to be independent. Casely Hayford, for example, argued that the Fante nation, unlike European nations, had no rich or poor, but rather a unique type of equality. Sarbah argued that the people of the Gold Coast needed to be independent because under European rule they had no opportunities or political representation.

Although they were opposed to European colonial rule, many West African nationalists of the late nineteenth and early twentieth centuries believed that Britain's stable political model or Germany's struggle for unity might show the way to their fledgling nation-state. Others, like Edward Wilmot Blyden, promoted the idea of an intrinsic connection among all Africans that could help create a unified pan-African nationalism. However, these nationalist leaders had to struggle with two major challenges. The first was that Europeans often opposed the creation of African nation-states because sovereign states so close to their colonies threatened their own influence and authority in the region. The second major challenge was that the forms of nationalism promoted by these men were imported ideas, and still alien in this period to most West Africans.

The Fante Confederation of 1868–1872 is one example of a West African nation-state that almost was. It was based on a long-standing alliance among many small, coastal West African states in the Gold Coast, a region that traded heavily with Europeans. This region faced threats both from a large rival state—Asante—and from European colonialism. A group of Western-educated but locally born men such as James Hutton Brew and Robert Ghartey believed that they could create a constitutional state that would give reformers like themselves power through a form of parliament. They hoped by stirring up nationalist sentiment, and especially by identifying the outside threats the Fante faced, they could gain popular support. To that end, they promoted the idea of a Fante "nation" that featured a shared sense of cultural values including commercial entrepreneurship and Christianity, a shared set of symbols in the traditional chiefs and kings whom they encouraged to join them, and a shared history of opposition to Asante as well as frustration with European interference.

In the end, the Fante Confederation did not last long. Historians have long argued that this was because their nationalism was too much of a threat to the British, and it's true that by 1874 the British had de facto annexed this territory. However, another interpretation is that the common people of the region largely weren't attracted to the new government, which didn't appeal to their cultural sense of themselves. The highly centralized state, Christianity, and the whole idea of a Fante nation held less appeal than their own local communities and systems of governance. The absence of local national newspapers and associations in favor of a Fante state also hamstrung their efforts. Thus, following victory over of an Asante army in 1868 and the end to that threat, the people of this region saw little need to unify under the banner of a Fante national-state. By the time the British put the finishing touches to this project by imprisoning its leaders, there was little real support for it. This does not mean that the Fante wanted to be colonized—they assuredly did not—but rather that they did not see a modernizing form of Fante nationalism as an attractive alternative either.

Nationalism against empire

The opportunities and limitations associated with liberal nationalism in this era were also on display in China, where the 1897–1901 Boxer Rebellion drew on the concepts of the nation but filtered it through local language and ideological frames until it became an anticolonial tool. The rebellion's protagonists were brotherhoods called the Societies of Harmonious and Righteous Fists (hence "Boxers"), which drew on Chinese Taoist tradition and practice. Their main concern was to put a halt to European's undermining of Chinese state, religion, and culture. They were particularly frustrated by the special rights and economic control won by Europeans in the Opium Wars of the 1840s and afterwards, inequalities that had a very real material as well as cultural impact on the lives of many Chinese. The Boxers also took aim at Christian missionaries who were working arduously to convert Chinese from worldviews such as Confucianism, Buddhism, and Taoism to evangelical Christianity, a topic discussed in the previous chapter.

In 1897, Boxer organizations led the first protests against German missionaries who were preaching in Shandong province. When German troops intervened, fighting spread. Soon receiving widespread popular support, the rebels were able to surround the foreign diplomatic and trade zone in the capital of Beijing. The imperial powers—Britain, France, Japan, United States, Austria, Russia, Italy, and Germany—responded by sending an international force to reassert control. In the process of combating this international force, the rebels took on an anti-outsider attitude that celebrated the Chinese "nation," and in particular the Han culture that described most (but not all) of China's population. Chinese citizens who were not Han, including Muslims from the west of China, fell under suspicion alongside Europeans. Also deemed suspicious were the Qing royal family, whose ancestors were Manchu originating from outside of China.

Ultimately, the rebellion failed. Rather than seeing the Boxers as potential allies in asserting their sovereignty against Europeans and Japanese, the Qing were wary of the rebels, who they felt had the potential to bring down their government. Thus they refused to support them in their battles with the international forces. By 1901, the Qing Empress Dowager, Cixi, chose to support European, Japanese, and American troops that broke the siege of the international quarter of Beijing. The Boxer Rebellion had failed, and the Qing Dynasty ended up even more deeply indebted and beholden to outsiders than it had been before the uprising. Underneath the surface, however, the rebellion had helped to create a sort of nationalist sentiment. Chinese citizens increasingly spoke of the Manchu Qing rulers as "foreigners" in the years that followed, and intellectuals circulated documents like Zou Rong's "The Revolutionary Army" that called upon the citizenry to "annihilate the five million and more of the furry and horned Manchu race." Such propaganda would eventually help to bring about the end of the Qing Dynasty following the death of Empress Cixi in 1911.

In the Ottoman Empire, meanwhile, nationalist movements continued to spread in this era among merchants and intellectuals and sometimes gained widespread support among many of the empire's ethnic communities. An Ottoman military defeat at the hands of Russia in 1877–1878 stirred up nationalist sentiment among Slavic peoples of the empire: those ethnically related to Russians, including Bulgarians, Serbians, and Romanians. It was in this period, for example, that Serbia fought to win its independence from the Empire. The desire for an ethnic nation-state also stirred up movements among the Kurds of eastern Anatolia and the population of Armenia, both of which ground on deep into the twentieth century. One Ottoman response to this rising tide of ethnic nationalism was a series of reforms and protections for various groups within the empire in order to quell discontent. These reforms, known as the Tanzimat Reforms, were discussed in the previous chapter.

Ironically, even the ruling Turkish-speaking community of the Ottoman Empire was coming to embrace a sense of ethnic nationhood by the early twentieth century. The increasing availability of Turkish-language newspapers alongside increasing interaction with Greek and western European nationalists brought in ideas of liberal nationalism that were interpreted into a local cultural context. What resulted was a uniquely Turkish form of nationalism, based on the translation of Islamic manuscripts into Turkish and a newfound sense of a particular Islamic mission for Turks. By the late 1880s, this new type of Turkish nationalism was transformed into a cultural movement sponsored by a group called the Young Turks. This cultural movement gradually became political as well. In 1908, this group of intellectuals, military men, and political leaders seized power in the Ottoman Empire. They called for the implementation of a new, culturally Turkish society within the empire. Their ideas did help the Turkish-speaking population of the empire to develop a unique sense of nationhood. Yet they also further alienated the other communities of the empire such as Armenians, Arabs, and Kurds.

The powerful appeal of national identity also manifested itself at the very heart of the largest nineteenth century global empire, as British rulers faced a reenergized Irish nationalism. The Irish people, long partially subjugated by English rulers, had formally become subjects of the United Kingdom in 1801. However powerful Irish cultural leaders loudly denounced British rule in the last decades of the nineteenth century, strongly proclaiming a pride in Irish culture and pushing for land reform to help impoverished Irish farmers and to win political semiautonomy, or "Home Rule." Some of the members of this movement also called for the expulsion of British rule altogether, and the formation of an independent Irish state.

In the last years of the long nineteenth century, many of these nationalist movements would erupt: in the 1911 creation of the Chinese republic, the Arab uprising against their Ottoman rulers during the First World War, the Armenian genocide of 1915, and the Irish rebellion of 1916. Nationalism had come to stay, and it would shape the world of the twentieth century as well.

Experiencing and imagining nationalism

Nationalism, like all political ideologies, was produced in different settings by groups of people who discussed, wrote, imagined, performed, and fought to achieve the aspiration of having a state for their nation. In this section we ask who the groups were that developed and expanded the idea of nationalism, and how they sold it to their societies. We also look at how nationalism was experienced by the men and women of those communities. We discuss the ways in which nationalism brought people together to share an identity, but also inevitably excluded some from membership in the group. Finally, we discuss two broad cultural frameworks around which nationalism was discussed, written, and performed in this period: romanticism and rationalism.

Producing the nation

The different examples of political nationalism discussed in this chapter were all popular political movements that captured the imagination and support of large communities of people. However, they were usually initiated by relatively small groups of politically active intellectuals, artists, and businesspeople who met to discuss the new ideas flowing around them. Their meeting places included taverns in 1770s Boston, the salons of important women in 1780s Paris, union meetings in 1830s England, and coffeehouses in 1840s Frankfurt and 1880s Istanbul. These locations shared the characteristics of being public or semipublic spaces where people could talk and congregate without necessarily attracting too much attention, being somewhat removed from governmental interference, and usually being pleasant places to sit, drink, and eat while considering how best to improve their country. In these settings, men and women could open their minds to new ideas through untold numbers of casual conversations as well as formal presentations. In this way, relatively small numbers of committed nationalists could together construct a brand new way of seeing the relationship among themselves and with their communities and governments.

These places were also sites where nationalists could strategize about how to share the political ideas with large numbers of their fellow citizens. Nationalism only gradually entered the everyday lives of most people. But once nationalists took power, they turned the institutions of government to the task of promoting nationalism and educating people about the benefits the nationalist leaders believed the nation-state brought. State-run education systems, many of which became compulsory in the nineteenth century, were one place to inculcate attachment to the nation. Their curricula often included explicit "civic instruction." In postrevolutionary France, for example, a program was created in 1794 to educate students around the country in a standardized French language, "morality," and the history of revolutionary heroes and French glory. Similarly, the new government of Japan in 1891 promoted a national school reform aimed at creating a Japanese nationalist sentiment among the country's youth.

These education systems often held the explicit goal of creating a unified nation. The French curriculum, for example, was uniform across the country. One of its goals was to teach minorities like Breton-speakers in the west and Provencal-speakers in the south to speak and act like Parisians. The Japanese curriculum was designed in part to stop the spread of Christian ideals, which were deemed nonnational, and instead promote "traditional" Japanese values. Through this process of enforcing a nation-wide conformity, political leaders incorporated the majority of citizens into a nation that was more efficient and more easily controlled.

Public rituals and nation-wide celebrations were also an important component of the saturation of the people in nationalist ideals. In revolutionary British North America, for example, British holidays like Guy Fawkes Day were quickly replaced by nationalist American rituals such as the Fourth of July, which celebrated national independence. At these events, effigies of King George and the traitor Benedict Arnold were burned. In France immediately following the revolution, religious holidays were replaced by the celebration of the July 14 storming of the Bastille Prison. In 1790, at the first such celebration, revolutionary leaders shared a secular "mass," after which military cadets swore an oath to the "fatherland." At the next year's celebration, the Enlightenment philosopher Voltaire was laid to rest before a vast crowd in a national funeral.

Figure 3.5 Nationalist symbols and ideas of the French Revolution made their way even onto playing cards, replacing Kings, Queens, and Dukes (or Jacks). Here: "The genius of business," "long live liberty," "freedom of religion," and "equality."

Nationalists also moved to quickly replace the monuments that kings and emperors had erected in their own honor. In post-1870s Germany, for example, statues of the princes of the now-extinct small states that had made up the region were exchanged for nationalist German cultural figures like the philosophers Goethe and Schiller, as well as the new monarch of all Germany, Wilhelm I. In early nineteenth-century Latin America, monuments were erected to liberation heroes like Simon Bolivar and others who had led the break from European rule.

Newspaper nationalism

Alongside holidays, schools, and monuments, newspapers were important vehicles for diffusing nationalist ideas to a broader, increasingly literate, population. Before the nineteenth century, the most effective form of political literature was the pamphlet— single-topic booklets or leaflets that were produced in relatively small numbers and distributed as best as possible. Newspapers, by contrast, were multitopic, produced by a team, and appeared at regular intervals. With the development of new machines such as the keyboard-operated linotype, they could be produced relatively easily and sold cheaply.

Newspapers took the nineteenth-century world by storm. In Canada, 30 million newspapers were sent by mail in 1880. This in a country of only 4.3 million people. The United States, following the development of the linotype, produced 15 million newspapers a day in 1900. Nor was this revolution restricted to North America and Europe. The first newspaper in India was produced in 1780. The first mass-printed Chinese newspaper was introduced in 1842. African newspapers such as *The African Times* began to circulate in the 1860s, although most of these newspapers were printed in English at first, and only a relatively small readership who read English, French, or Arabic could enjoy them. This wasn't the case everywhere, however. The first Chinese newspaper, *Jingbao*, which appeared in limited form in the 1730s, was printed in Chinese and maintained a large readership throughout the nineteenth century. A weekly newspaper appeared in Arabic during the Ottoman Empire in 1861.

The political power of newspapers was so dramatic that liberal states made freedom of the press a key policy. In Great Britain, publications critical of the government had been relatively safe from censorship since 1695, and in the United States, the First Amendment to the Constitution came to protect the press soon after the revolution. Other European states followed, and even Tsarist Russia gave certain guarantees in 1865. Egypt also introduced laws protecting freedom of the press in the 1860s. By contrast, some conservative and monarchical states sought to limit the scope of these freedoms. In Germany, for example, newspapers were still liable to censorship into the 1890s. The same was true in the imperial periphery. Even liberal states like Britain and France often censored or limited newspapers in their African, Asian, and Caribbean colonies.

The development of newspapers influenced the daily experience of those who could read them. News was suddenly available rapidly, often accompanied by political opinion. Some of the events covered occurred far away, while others were local. Newspapers could call people together to exercise their political rights or to enjoy a play. Advertising meant that consumers could learn about new products and purchase them more easily. Public opinion, stoked by editorials, coalesced quickly in the era of the newspaper, and thus became more influential in the politics of the day. In particular, jingoistic publications fuelled the fires of nationalism and helped to sway the population in support of wars like the Spanish-American War, which was heavily promoted by publishers William Randolph Hearst and Joseph Pulitzer in the United States. Hearst's 1898 wholly unsubstantiated allegations that the Spanish had blown up the U.S. Battleship *Maine*, an attempt to turn national sentiment in favor of conflict, was a key factor in the declaration of war that year.

Nationalism as experience

Nationalism shaped people's consumption of goods as well as of news. For example, it was nationalism that led many English-speaking North Americans to switch from drinking tea to consuming coffee! Most of the European settlers in America drank tea before the 1770s, but following a parliamentary act that allowed the British East India Company to undercut American merchants in 1773, they began to forgo and even burn their tea (or dump it in Boston harbor). Rather rapidly, drinking tea came to be seen as a declaration of loyalty to Britain rather than merely an act of consumption, while drinking coffee became an open act of defiance. The result was a rapid rise in coffee drinking that has never been reversed in the United States.

Nationalism also manifested itself deeply in changes in everyday manners and even notions of morality. In highly hierarchical societies like those of the prenationalist European monarchies, the manners of the working classes and peasants weren't important to the political elites because they were not regarded as equals in any way. There was no need to discipline with the unruly behavior of the masses except to demand respect for the powerful and rich. Nationalism, however, cut across classes to make the nation, and therefore the upper classes became invested in proving how great the nation was by promoting what they considered to be proper morals and good manners. Since the people now represented the nation, if one nation was to be superior to another, so the behavior of its members must be proper. Moreover, the growing middle class of industrialists, shopkeepers, and professionals tended to support such reforms both because they too were nationalists and because they believed that emulating social elites would help them buy their own way into respectable society.

An example of just such a transition took place in the city of Philadelphia. Prior to the spread of liberal nationalism, city leaders paid relatively little attention to the morals and manners of the urban poor and minorities. As a result, marriage was it had been for most of history, often quite informal: children born out of wedl were considered legitimate, and a great range of liaisons between men and women were largely overlooked. By the early nineteenth century, however, liberal reformers began to argue that this state of affairs was bad for the image of the American nation. They argued that having sex outside of marriage was immoral and urged the working classes to practice restraint for the health of society. They also persecuted women who had children outside of marriage and prosecuted prostitutes. This imposition of marital, sexual, and social behavior from above, alongside the eradication of casual long-standing attitudes toward marriage, was quite a big change for the city.

One of the biggest changes that liberal nationalism brought was the extension of political rights to a wider section of society. One of these rights, at least briefly, was the possibility of participating in the writing of a constitution—a set of laws that formed a contract among members of the nation and between citizens and rulers. In general, however, constitutions were written by small groups of elites— predominantly men. A somewhat more widespread right was the casting of votes for public officials. In the decades before 1914, the right to vote spread in some areas to large portions of the male population and in a few cases even to women. Being a voter meant more than just living the experience of casting a vote on a particular day; it also often involved participation in mass political parties. The earliest of these parties emerged in late eighteenth-century Britain, where widespread political campaigns presented voters (and, coincidentally, nonvoters) with printed political advertisements, sponsored events like fairs and picnics, and public speeches. Participation in these organizations altered the mindset and broadened the political consciousness of many middle-class people. Nevertheless, most citizens' consumption of such events remained limited because they were too poor to participate, too busy working, constrained by the fact that they were women, or otherwise excluded from voting.

Inclusion and exclusion in nationalism

Liberal nationalism became such a powerful political force in the eighteenth century because it cut across class boundaries that had defined societies around the world for centuries, if not millennia. In eighteenth-century France, the power of this new force brought peasants, artisans, workers, and even aristocrats together in revolution. In the Americas, creole versions of liberal nationalism attracted planters and landowners, merchants, artisans, and at times even the laboring classes on plantations and mines. By the late nineteenth century, ethnic nationalism created an even more powerful sense of a unified people or, as German nationalists put it, a "folk." In societies enduring the considerable stresses of increasing long-distance migration and rapid urbanization, such a sense of inclusion across classes helped to build a sense of stability and to support internal trading networks. It also fostered cultural celebration and led to gradual create political change.

Yet nationalism, by creating a more rigid if broader sense of who was "inside" the nation, inevitably defined groups that were "outside" and hence excluded from participation in national politics and culture. Women, depicted even by Enlightenment thinkers as nonpolitical or nonrational, were both inside and outside the nation. They generally belonged to the national culture, but were excluded from politics. Thus for example, French Revolutionary leaders, while creating a much wider political body, largely excluded women from playing a political role in the revolution. Early feminists pointedly noted the hypocrisy or short-sightedness of this. The famous *Declaration of the Rights of Man and of Citizen*, adopted by the National Constituent Assembly in 1789 as the guiding statement of the revolution, said nothing about women or their rights. Feminist activists led by the revolutionary feminist Marie Gouze (Olympe de Gouges) protested this and urged the adoption of a *Declaration of the Rights of woman and the Female Citizen* that called for equality of women in all political and social rights, including in voting and office holding. Yet this statement was not adopted by the assembly. Overall, eighteenth-century liberal nationalism was a very masculine ideology. The nation was generally symbolized as a father, and the role of the state was seen as attending to and protecting women, lesser men, and children.

In fact, women's rights were slow in coming and faced one obstacle after another in nationalist societies. The rise of ethnic nationalism reinforced the depoliticization of women by emphasizing their role of serving the nation as mothers, rather than political contributors. In a desire to ensure the birth of many children who could serve the nation as patriots, workers, and soldiers, nationalist thinkers frequently called for women to produce many children and spend their time raising them. In Europe, especially, doctors and politicians enjoined women to stay home, not work, and to breastfeed for longer periods, all in the name of supporting their nation against others.

Other members of the community were also defined as outside of the political nation. Usually, leading nationalists were men with property, who conveniently defined those without property as unfit to participate. This meant that the poor and downtrodden were often excluded despite the intellectual and emotional promise of nationalist inclusivity. In revolutionary Latin America, for example, Mestizos, Indios, and people of African descent generally did not enjoy the political rights won by independence movements by 1820. Nor did the rise of nationalist governments really transform the economic conditions of the poorest Native Americans and inhabitants of African descent, most of who continued to labor in conditions little changed from serfdom. Their continued servitude was justified by the argument that they were not yet deserving of national citizenship. Some nationalists even claimed that including these groups might even drag the nation backward.

The nineteenth-century shift to ethnic nationalism exacerbated this exclusionary urge within nationalism and defined classes who lived within the borders of the state but were entirely excluded from the nation—or even defined as its enemies. Because ethnic nationalists tended to define the national community based on issues of blood, race, and culture, inhabitants of the nation-state who were seen as being ethnically different could face persecution, exclusion from power, or even exile. Particular groups especially faced exclusionary practices. In countries in Europe where Jews had lived for centuries, nationalists frequently pointed them out as different and undeserving of national status. In Europe, Jews were increasingly excluded from full citizenship of the nation in which they lived after 1870. Leading nationalists in Germany and the Habsburg Empire increasingly blamed their country's problems partly on Jewish populations. In Russia, anti-Semitism reached a fever pitch in the late nineteenth century. The ruling Romanov family confined the Jewish population to a small, impoverished region called the Pale of Settlement, and encouraged organized riots and massacres that killed thousands of Jews and triggered a Jewish emigration from the region. The Romanovs had discovered that blaming Jews was one way that they could claim the leadership of an Orthodox Christian, Russian nation.

Similarly, in England, large populations of Irish workers in the growing industrial centers were excluded from the nation by virtue of being Irish and Catholic. Turkish-speakers suffered greatly in late nineteenth-century Greece, just as Armenians and Greeks faced discrimination and dislike in an increasingly nationalist Turkey. Thus one of the central ironies of nationalism was that while it claimed to bring the national community together for the benefit of all, many minority inhabitants of nationalist states found themselves worse off than in previous eras. Thus nationalism operated to the benefit of some and the detriment of others.

Inclusion and exclusion in nationalism was partly driven by a central contradiction in nineteenth-century nationalist thought. Nationalists considered that the world was made up of a patchwork of different national communities, separate and unique, each of which deserved their own state. But they also imagined that their own nation was special and unique among the nations of the world. It was through this framework, for example, that French thinkers in this period began to promote the idea of the French as uniquely "civilized" based on their history, literature, food and culture, and indeed their lifestyle. Greek nationalists, too, held shared a belief that their nation was special, for they believed it was the root of European culture and the roots of European civilization. At the same time, many of these nationalist assumed that they had to emulate northwest European states in order to create their own nation-state. Such ambivalence toward northwest Europe was common in leaders and intellectuals in many parts of the world in the late nineteenth century.

Cultural expressions of nationalism

Nationalists talked about their nations in a variety of ways, but especially through the new languages of romanticism and rationalism. **Romanticism was a literary and artistic genre of the time that focused on heroic deeds, great epics, and emotional experiences of love and conflict**. The desire to advertise the nation fit well into this, especially in the form of stories about heroes who helped to formulate the nation or create the nation-state. Epic romanticist heroes included important national leaders like George Washington in the United States or Simon Bolivar in Latin America. They also included cultural heroes like William Shakespeare and the German philosopher Friedrich Schiller. Some national icons were mythical or resurrected from stories with deep roots in the past. French nationalists, for example, rediscovered the epic *Song of Roland* about eleventh-century Christian knights turning back an Islamic invasion. In Germany, Richard Wagner began to work on the *Ring Cycle* following the events of 1848. This series of operas followed mythic Germanic gods and heroes and stirred up a sense of national, pan-German pride. Other nationalist artists reached into Judeo-Christian myth. In Italy, for example, Giuseppe Verdi wrote the "Chorus of the Hebrew Slaves," implying that Italian suffering under the Habsburgs was akin to that of the Hebrews in Egypt. The song became immensely popular during the struggle for Italian independence and unity.

Among these stories, poems, and pieces of music, perhaps the most important were those that created a sense of a moment in which the national spirit was summoned into being. One of these founding stories was Ralph Waldo Emerson's "Concord Hymn," about the Battle of Concord, Massachusetts, in which American rebels defeated British troops for the first time. They hymn begins with the lines:

> By the rude bridge that arched the flood,
> Their flag to April's breeze unfurled,
> Here once the embattled farmers stood,
> And fired the shot heard round the world.

These famous words evoke the sense of a major moment in which mere "farmers" stood against royal troops and fired "the shot heard round the world." Other nationalist founding stories, however, took the form of long, heroic struggles. One example was "Prince Igor," a centuries-old story of a failed Russian raid against rivals in the Don River region, and the heroes' long struggle to return home. In 1890, it was adapted by the Russian musician and director Alexander Borodin into an opera in which the journey of the hero is a metaphor of the journey of the Russian people to statehood. Such songs and stories were learned, repeated, and chanted by those who found a sense of identity in their nation.

Romanticist stories of the birth of the nation were supported by Enlightenment arguments for the nation-state that stressed rational thought processes. From the days of the late eighteenth century, nationalists had promoted logical arguments for the existence of the nation. In prerevolutionary France, for example, the Abbé Sieyès, set out to logically explain what a nation is and why having one required the extension of equal rights, using the language of the Enlightenment to suggest that the exclusion of the population from the right to rule "deviates from the common order, the common law." Following the revolution, the connection between Enlightenment rationalism and French nationalism became clear in a misguided attempt to place time-keeping in scientific terms. Soon after the revolution, in 1789, the National Assembly passed a law that divided the day into 10 rather than 24 parts, with watches ticking every 100,000th of a day. They also tried to decimalize the week into 10 days. In order to make these weeks fit into a year, an extra five-day vacation was added to summer in honor of the workers. This calendar did not last long.

Of course, the cultural idea of the nation changed over time in every state. For example, we can look at the changing nature of the word "nation"—*kokutai*—in nineteenth-century Japan. Prior to the nationalist movements of the 1860s, the term *kokutai* was used to express the myth that the imperial family had ruled Japan continuously since its beginning. By the 1870s, however, nationalists had begun to use this same word to express the idea of a special link between the people and the imperial court. By 1875, when a court official named Sasaki Takayuki wrote that it was a word in seeming constant use, it referred instead to the land, people, and language of Japan. Fifteen years later, however, it was mostly used to refer to "the unique principle of each nation," or Japan's national uniqueness. Soon after, it was used in conjunction with adjectives meaning "glory" that clearly separated Japanese identity from that of others. Thus in half a century, the word had passed from a term applied only the imperial court to one that described the special qualities of the

Figure 3.6 Toyohara Chikanobu, *The Great Training Maneuvers by Various Army Corps*, late nineteenth century. Chikanobu was a noted nationalist Japanese artist and frequently depicted the emperor and Japanese military in his paintings.

Japanese nation. In similar ways in other societies, preexisting concepts were adapted to help define and describe nationalism at the popular and intellectual levels.

The internationalists

Not every nineteenth-century inhabitant was a nationalist, of course! Some people just didn't learn about or embrace nationalism, while others actively rejected it. Within liberal thought at this time, for example, there was a strand that was internationalist. Internationalists campaigned for the unity and welfare of all mankind, rather than that of the nation. The thinkers who espoused these ideas believed that liberty and equality could be best expressed by brotherhood (and sometimes sisterhood) across all societies on earth. The first modern internationalist thinker was perhaps the French philosopher Voltaire (François-Marie Arouet) who wrote that "it is sad that in order to be a good patriot one must be the enemy of the rest of mankind" and that "[h]e who should wish his fatherland might never be greater, smaller, richer, poorer, would be the citizen of the world."[1] A few decades later, the British-born American revolutionary pamphleteer Thomas Paine wrote that "the world is my country, all mankind are my brethren, and to do good is my religion." These two men, who were among the greatest influences on the French Revolution and American War of Independence, were also internationalists.

Other opponents of nationalism included leading socialists (see Chapter 4). Influenced by one of the most dominant thinkers of the modern period, Karl Marx, socialists generally viewed the world through a lens of struggle between classes, rather than nations. Thus they believed that nationalism divided the working classes of different countries from each other and instead exhorted workers to help each other across national lines. Yet while socialists and other internationalists provided an important alternative to nationalism over the course of the long nineteenth century, their message appealed to only a minority of people. Nationalism—liberating and anti-imperial or oppressive and discriminatory—was sweeping the world.

Key terms

classical liberalism [76]
creole nationalism [80]
ethnic nationalism [87]
ethnicity [87]
nation [77]
nationalism [78]
nation-state [75]
romanticism [102]
Social Contract [77]

Further readings

Steve Grosby's *Nationalism: A Very Short Introduction* (New York: Oxford University Press, 2005) is a good introduction to some of the key debates about nationalism, its history, and the way it functions today.

Ida Bloom and Karen Hagemann deftly illustrate the connections between nationalism and gender in *Gendered Nations: Nationalisms and Gender Order in the Long Nineteenth Century* (Oxford: Berg Publishers, 2000).

Undoubtedly one of the most important volumes on the ways in which nationalism is constructed focuses on nationalism in the nineteenth-century Americas and in twentieth-century Southeast Asia. This is Benedict Anderson, *Imagined Communities: Reflections on the Origins and Rise of Nationalism*, Revised Edition (New York: Verso, 2006).

One contrary voice in this debate is Israeli historian Azar Gat, who argues that nationalism was not primarily invented in the modern era but also has deep historic roots. Azar Gat with Alexander Yakobson, *Nations: The Long History and Deep Roots of Political Ethnicity and Nationalism* (Cambridge: Cambridge University Press, 2013).

Interlude 2: The French Law of February 23, 2005

On the recognition of the Nation and the national contribution of French returnees

Historians have often argued over what constitutes a "significant" or "important" event or trend in global history. One definition is that events of world historical importance have an impact that is deep, sustained, and extensive. That is to say: they affect many people in profound ways over long periods of time.

Nineteenth-century nationalism and imperialism are both significant trends have left enormous legacies in the world in which we live today, although in different ways. Most—one could even argue all—countries today embrace the nation-state as their system of governance and their populations celebrate national holidays and embrace a sense of a national character. By contrast, very few governments or peoples outwardly embrace imperialism. Nevertheless, empire has left its mark on both former metropoles and former colonies. Moreover, in many cases, the heritage of the nation and the heritage of the empire are inextricably woven together, as the French Law of February 23, 2005 demonstrates.

Beginning in November, 2004, a series of protests and mass disturbances broke out in the suburbs of Paris, the capital of the Republic of France. Since 1789 (and even before), Paris has been a scene of frequent mass actions and strikes, often embodying the liberal themes of liberty and equality. The protesters this time were largely young men of African and Arab descent, mostly Muslim, whose families had immigrated to France from the former colonies of the French Empire. Few white French citizens joined them in the streets, and indeed few seemed to even understand what the protests were actually about.

This lack of understanding by France's white majority underscored the protesters' main complaint. While frustrated at high levels unemployment and poverty, the protesters were even more expressing their anger at what they perceived as ethnic discrimination against immigrants from former colonies. By and large, these immigrants and children of immigrants had found themselves culturally excluded from mainstream French life, treated poorly at school and in the job market, and

Figure 3.7 Muslim Parisians protesting in Paris, while a car burns behind them.

harassed by the police. In other words, they found themselves defined as being "outside" the French nation because of their culture, ethnicity, and heritage.

The question being asked by the protesters was whether and how a largely secular, European national political culture could embrace of large numbers of immigrants, many of them Muslim, whose culture and symbols were different from those of most native French citizens. This contest over the nation in the early twentieth century was not a purely French experience. A similar process could be said to be occurring in almost all nations that had engaged in imperial activities in the nineteenth and twentieth centuries, and which therefore had large populations of immigrants from the former colonies mixed in with those who considered themselves "natural" citizens on the basis of ethnicity and history. In each of these societies, the potent histories of empire and nation combined to fuel protests, debate, and sometimes violence in the early twenty-first century.

Nor was this contest carried out solely in the streets. In many cases, the halls of government were also a venue for challenging or defending traditional interpretations of the nation. In France, soon after the disturbances, of 2004, the government added fuel to the fire by passing a law, number 158 of 2005. This law called for the recognition of the positive character and contributions of the French overseas presence (in other words, the French Empire) and the "sacrifices" of the French army in the former colonies, especially North Africa. The law especially called for teachers to instruct students on the positive contributions that France had brought to local populations across its empire. As might be expected, this clause merely added salt to the wounds of those who already felt French imperialism had done great harm to their ancestors and themselves.

The Law of February 23, 2005 was an attempt to define the legacy of empire in the language of the nation. The law specifically addresses the relationship between France and its closest former colony Algeria, which is also the source of the largest immigrant population in France. The French occupation of Algeria, which began in 1830 and ended only in as 1962, was a living piece of history for those Muslims of Algerian origin living in France in 2004. But end of French rule in 1962 had in fact brought two groups to France. One were large numbers of Europeans who had settled in Algeria under colonial rule, and who enjoyed French citizenship, but who returned to France upon independence. The other were Algerians who had little choice but to move to France to find jobs and other opportunities. They were joined by other North African and former colonial subjects of the French Empire, some of whom spoke French but nevertheless possessed linguistic, cultural, and behavioral differences that ensured a difficult—some would say unsolvable—transition to life in France.

Once in France, each of these groups sought to find a place and status for themselves as part of the French nation. The white former settlers did this partly by trying to elevate the legacy of the empire and therefore of themselves as former agents of imperialism. They tried to make themselves and their experiences part of the narrative of the French nation as a way to overcome their own difficulties of reintegrating into French society. The law of February 23, 2005 was one element in this process. Through it, they hoped to convince or force schoolteachers and scholars to teach the next generation that the empire had carried the liberal ideals of the French nation—liberty, equality, and brotherhood—to the colonies, where, they implied, it had been sorely lacking.

Algerian and other immigrants who were former colonial subjects found it even more difficult to find a place for themselves in French society after 1962. Admittedly, French law was based on liberal Enlightenment ideals that supposedly made it possible for individuals of any religion or ethnic group to become citizens. On the other hand, centuries of French nationalism had had created a standardized idea of French cultural practices that mixed the secular state and of Catholicism, the French language, and French national history. It also assumed "Frenchness" to be normatively white and European. The new immigrants thus found themselves discriminated against on the basis of their religion, their language, their cultural choices, and even their skin color. Their story was also left out of the history curriculum they studied. Yet when they protested this discrimination, some native French citizens responded that they were purposely choosing not to assimilate, and therefore not to be part of the nation. Influenced by this line of thinking, French policymakers who supported the new law hoped it would force immigrants to assimilate partly by forcing them to recognizing the "value" that French culture and imperialism had brought to their societies. Thus although the new law purported to be about the past, it was also very much about contemporary issues of the French nation and society.

Outside of France, the law of February 23, 2005 provoked a furious response around the former French Empire. Protests broke out in the Caribbean island territories of Martinique and Guadeloupe, while journalists in former colonies like Cameroons and Senegal wrote scathing editorials. The government of Algeria broke off talks for a new treaty with France. Within France itself, history teachers were divided on the issue, with many calling for a recall of the law. Meanwhile, a new wave of protests broke out on the streets, and posters appeared on the streets of Paris calling for a law to teach the positive impact of immigration as a counterbalance to the February 23 law. Yet at the same time, the law received a great deal of support from among white French citizens, especially in the south of the country where immigration from Africa and the Middle East was highest.

Episodes like this one tell us a great deal about the ongoing impact of nineteenth-century ideas of nationalism and imperialism, as well as the limits of the ideals of the Enlightenment. Over the past two and a half centuries, the "nation" has become one of the most important categories of personal and collective identity on the planet. Yet the question of who belongs within the nation is often tied to a history of imperialism (and hence racism) through the vast empires that ruled much of the world during this period. This is nowhere more true than in France, one of the birthplaces of modern nationalism but also one of the largest modern empires, where different groups are still trying to define who is "inside" the nation and what that means.

4

Industrialization

Industrialization was one of the defining features of modernity, and like nationalism and evangelical Protestantism, it was a child of the long nineteenth century. As with the Enlightenment, it emerged first in Europe—specifically in Britain—but in fact had global roots. Its impact, too, was almost immediately felt around the world, both because of Britain's unique imperial connections and because industrial technology spread rapidly to other societies. By 1914, industrialized life had become a feature of many societies, empires, and nation-states.

Of course, this is not to say that there was a single, uniform industrial citizen of the world at the end of the long nineteenth century. People's lived experiences of industrialization varied greatly over the course of the long nineteenth century and across the globe. Not all societies became part of the global industrial economy on their own terms, or to the same degree. In some places, the advent of industrialization meant that within a few centuries much of the population came to work in factories whose lives were closely intertwined with industry. In other regions, change was not so rapid and dramatic. Nevertheless, most populations around the world gradually found their lives transformed, both negatively and positively, as their work and economies transformed to meet the needs of supplying raw materials for an increasingly globalized industrial economy.

Figure 4.1 Adolph Von Menzel, *Iron Rolling Mill*, 1875. Von Menzel's depiction of the interior of a German iron works conveys both the sophistication and the hard conditions of working in a factory in the period of industrialization. Von Menzel was a member of the realist school, who not only focused on industry as subject matter but also adopted its emphasis on precision and accuracy in their techniques.

In this chapter, we look at the Industrial Revolution first as a transformation in technology with results for the ways people worked, traveled, and lived their lives.

We explore this transformation through the processes and innovations that were central to industrialization, including **factories**, the **assembly line**, **enclosure**, the **segregation of tasks**, the **shift** system, and the use and production of **synthetic** materials. Many of the other terms introduced in this chapter have to do with the relationships between industrialized states and the societies that produced raw materials and consumed finished products they manufactured. These terms include **gunboat diplomacy** and **secondary imperialism**, **deindustrialization**, **commodity replacement**, and **dependency**. We also explore **defensive modernization** as a response to these processes, and **realism** as one way in which industrialization was observed and described in art and literature.

By the end of this chapter you should be able to:

- Assess the role of global and local factors in shaping the first Industrial Revolution in Great Britain.
- Discuss three different processes by which industrialization spread: through informal empire, the diffusion of technologies to new areas, and the development of dependent relationships.
- Construct an argument connecting the Industrial Revolution to the themes of nationalism and imperialism discussed in Chapters 1 and 3.
- Compare and contrast the responses of different societies to the opportunities and pitfalls of industrialization that includes identification of ways in which some societies were hampered in their ability to fully participate.
- Examine the historical significance of the relative timing and sequence of industrialization around the world.
- Consider how art and literature of this period from both Europe and Japan reflect ambivalence toward industrialization and a recognition of its costs as well as its advantages.

The first Industrial Revolution

Beginning around 1750, the rhythms of daily life and economic activity were radically altered by a technological and social transformation that we call the Industrial Revolution. I do not use the term "revolution" loosely here. Industrialization was probably a more dramatic change for real human experience than almost any other transition since the adoption of agriculture thousands of years before. Unlike cultivation, however, industrialization took place in world in which human societies were increasingly being drawn together. The rapidity of trade, the speed at which ideas could be shared, and the ability of some states to exert power across long distances meant that industrialization was both a very competitive process and one that was experienced quite differently around the world.

One way to understand the Industrial Revolution is as a series of massive changes in three, interlinked areas of human organization and technology. Perhaps the most fundamental area of transformation was the replacement of human and animal labor with that of machines that could speed up or improve productivity. A second related area of change was the reorganization of complex jobs into many, smaller, sequential tasks done repetitively by workers. Transformations in these two areas were facilitated by a third major innovation: the introduction of new sources of energy to fuel people and machines—fossil fuels for machines being the most important but coffee, tea, and sugar for people not too far behind.

Together, these changes helped to create economies that could mass-produce goods and deliver them to buyers more cheaply, more rapidly, and often with consistently better quality. These advances had wide implications in sphere of economics, of course, but also far beyond. The Industrial Revolution transformed the way people worked, their home lives, and the way they thought about their world and related to each other. Global in its implications, industrialization first emerged as a transformative experience in the island nation of Great Britain. There, the physical environment, political and legal framework, overseas empire, and social organization first combined to create the right context for industrialization.

Birthing the Industrial Revolution

The advent of the Industrial Revolution is often dated to the 1763–1775 development of the Watt steam engine, the first engine that could efficiently burn fuel to do such work as driving a shaft or turning a wheel. The Watt engine consumed coal to transform water into steam, and then used the steam to do the work that animals and humans had done for centuries. Its design was based on machines that used running rivers or the wind to do work, as well as earlier but less efficient models of a steam engine, but its introduction meant that machine production could be carried out away from rivers, even when the winds weren't blowing, and without large numbers of workers or wasted fuel.

Within just a few years, the Watt engine was being connected to such machines as Samuel Crompton's spinning "mule" (1779) and Edward Cartwright's power loom (1785). The resulting combinations created a massive increase in the speed and decrease in the cost at which textiles could be produced. Soon, many of these machines were being grouped together in giant buildings called **factories**. Aside from linking together multiple engines and machines, these factories were distinguished by the fact that they employed groups of workers in **shifts**, meaning that people worked in teams through specified recurring periods every day.

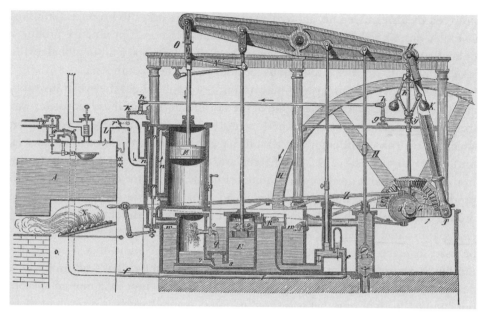

Figure 4.2 A schematic of James Watt's double-acting steam engine, 1769.

In some ways, the Watt engine was not so much a new invention as a refinement of earlier machines. Invention is often an incremental, collaborative process with many stages rather than a single moment of innovation. Specifically, Watt's engine was essentially a much more efficient version of the Newcomen steam engine of 1712, itself based on experiments carried out in seventeenth-century Italy. These Italian experiments were in turn arguably adapted from Islamic descriptions of even earlier Greek and Chinese technology. Similarly, the mechanized factories of eighteenth-century Britain were not the first time specialists had been organized into shifts to work multiple, linked machines. The assignment of individuals to shifts and specialist jobs had been a feature of slave labor in the sugar mills of the Caribbean for several decades. Likewise, Newport Evans's Delaware flour mill and eighteenth-century textile mills in China had linked many machines, as had colonial silver refineries in the Spanish Americas.

Nevertheless, the new factories with their steam-driven engines were so much more productive than both their predecessors and hand-worked textile production techniques that within only a few decades the global center of textile production for the world had shifted to a small area in northern Britain. For centuries, most of the world's cloth had been produced in South Asia. By 1800, however, Britain had become the world's first industrial textile-producing powerhouse. The small, incremental improvements in the efficiency of production introduced to British textile mills together added up to a huge advantage. By 1800, Crompton's yarn-spinning mule, powered by a steam engine, allowed a single English worker to produce 100 times as much yarn as a skilled Indian artisan, previously the most productive producer of textiles in the world. This advantage enabled a fundamental shift in global textile production, with massive implications for both Britain and South Asia.

The productivity advantages of industrialization soon caught the eye of investors and workers in other industries. One of the most important of these industries was iron production. Across the eighteenth-century world, iron was largely produced in small-scale furnaces although vast blast furnaces had existed in China as far back as the Song Dynasty (960–1279 CE). Charcoal was the main fuel used in manufacturing iron, but the metal it produced was quite brittle. Searching for new technologies to produce better iron, metallurgists in Britain adapted an innovation from the brewing industry. Beer-makers had already discovered in the eighteenth century that a refined charcoal product called coke—charcoal which had had the sulfur removed—could be used to make a better-tasting beer. Iron-makers soon found that it could also produce a superior form of iron. In 1784, Henry Cort combined coke-burning with a new process of stirring the molten metal with long rods to provide a more malleable but stronger form of iron that was soon in high demand. Largely as a result of these and other process innovations, iron production in Britain jumped from 25,000 tons (1720) to more than 250,000 tons (1804). Together, textiles and iron gave Britain's economy a decisive advantage.

The British origins of the first Industrial Revolution

Historians have long debated why Britain was the first society to industrialize. Was it because of some cultural superiority? Was it due to better environmental conditions? Was the Industrial Revolution's timing a result of political stability? Or was the reason not Britain itself but rather its large overseas empire?

At least part of the answer has to do with conditions within Great Britain itself. Fully unified in 1707, Great Britain was the amalgamation of Wales, England, and Scotland. It could also access resources from Ireland, which was ruled as a colonial possession. The environment of this unified state turned out to be uniquely suited to industrialization. In the first place, as an island Britain enjoyed special defensive advantages, sparing its government the cost of a large standing army. Britain also possessed massive deposits of coal, many of them close to the surface. By 1800, the country's coal mines would produce about 10 million tons of coal, and by 1850 around 60 million tons. Moreover, unlike in other resource-rich regions such as western China, the coal was very close to rivers upon which it could easily be transported to cities and factories. Fortuitously, Britain also had few mountains to get in the way of these rivers and the canals that were built to help transport fuel and materials. Coal, especially, could therefore be easily mined and cheaply moved to factory sites. In comparison, the island nation of Japan had no large coal deposits and was covered in mountains that impeded easy transportation.

Britain also possessed economic conditions that facilitated the Industrial Revolution. For example, wages for rural workers were much higher than in continental Europe, a situation that drove the search for machines to replace human labor. The political power of middle-class investors and business-owners, a special feature of the British parliamentary system, meant that the government was willing to invest in the infrastructure that supported industrialization. Throughout the long nineteenth century, the British government repeatedly proved willing to direct tax income to the building roads, canals, and later railroads. The government also supported the process of **enclosure**, by which small farms and communally owned land were turned over to wealthy sheep farmers. This process both helped to produce wool for the emerging textile factories and forced rural farmers and peasants off their land to become factory workers.

Culture, also, probably played a role. The scientific advances made by the Royal Society and other intellectuals in the seventeenth century, as well as Britain's economic emphasis on artisanal "tinkering," helped to create a culture of innovation that was both creative and practical. In Britain, inventions could give a person prestige, and also make them rich. Admittedly, culture has limitations as an explanation for Britain's industrialization. Many other societies also rewarded innovation. In China, for example, advances in agricultural production were both seen as highly desirable and often rewarded by the government since it solved China's principal problem— the need to feed a huge population on limited arable land. It just so happens that in Britain a culture of innovation combined with certain environmental, economic, and political situation so that industrialization became a possible pathway for British society.

The global underpinnings of the first Industrial Revolution

Yet, despite the suitability of Britain's own obvious environmental and societal traits, it isn't clear that industrialization would have happened there first if not for the existence of the British overseas empire. One of the big contributions of Britain's empire in 1750 was in the production of foodstuff. Calories flooded into the island from around the empire, so much so that many of Britain's workers may have consumed an average of 5000 calories a day. Approximately 20 percent of this food-energy came from Caribbean sugar grown and processed by enslaved Africans. Another important foodstuff to feed the emerging British factory workers was Atlantic cod, which was largely fished off the coast of the North American colonies. These provisions were supplemented by new high-calorie crops transplanted from the Americas to Britain and Ireland. The potato, which could grow in formerly unproductive, marginal, sandy soil, was particularly important. Together, Atlantic cod and newly adopted potatoes made fish-and-chips the great British food of the modern era. More importantly, the flood of calories from the sea and from the empire allowed the British to turn land over to the sheep farms and coal mines that were the key ingredients in textile industrialization.

Much of the financing that made the Industrial Revolution possible was similarly a product of empire and overseas trade. The Atlantic slave trade, in particular, generated vast profits for men who used them to build the banks that underwrote new businesses like factories. Plantation owners and slave traders also endowed universities like Oxford and Cambridge that were centers of experimentation and technological development at this time. Finally, the global corporations and trading institutions that had developed to service the slave trade and the empire had introduced organizational and management innovations that could be quickly applied to factories and industry.

In a similar way, the wars of empire also helped to drive industrialization. Britain's ongoing conflict with France and its allies—the Seven Years War, the American Revolution, and the Napoleonic Wars—were largely won through the development of better technology and a stronger economy. British strategies included the willingness of government to fund iron and coal production, the development of industrialized munitions factories, and finally the kinds of taxation and infrastructure spending that would help the effort to retain and build the overseas empire and, at the same time, markets for mass-produced goods.

Steam

The first Industrial Revolution was an age of steam, and by the early nineteenth century, engines that made steam and machines that used it were a common factor in Briton's lives. People experienced steam at work, where it was used to power spinning and sorting machines in the textile industry and to blast hot air into air furnaces and to turn giant rollers and stamps that turned out metal. Even in the cold of winter, many workers sweltered in hot, wet working conditions. In summer, factories could be deadly.

Steam also powered new vessels that transported people to work or moved them across oceans. The first steam ships were actually built in the United States, powered by a British-made Watt engine, but soon Europe's waterways were also full of them. These giant vessels burned either wood or coal. Early steamships fed this fuel to steam engines that drove giant pistons that in turn turned giant wooden paddlewheels. These propelled steamships up and down rivers or across bays, making them the superior ferries of their day. By the early 1800s, such ships were being built of iron.

Massive steamships could survive the buffeting of waves and currents, and thus could carry large amounts of people and cargo across the Atlantic and Pacific. By the 1870s, propellers had been widely adapted on ocean-going steamships, replacing the waterwheel. Liberated from the need to rely upon winds, steamships made possible the great migrations of the nineteenth century and also connected people to each other across the oceans.

The railroad was perhaps an even more significant innovation than the steamship. Steam-powered locomotives were developed as early as 1804, although it took the mass production of iron rails in the 1820s to really popularize them. The first commercial railroad line opened in British in 1825, and within the decade Britain was experiencing a railroad mania. Lines of track soon connected all of the big cities and many middle-sized towns as well as mines and factories, carrying both passengers and cargo. Coal, meant both for the locomotives and for factories down the line, was the leading cargo, but railroads soon carried just about anything. By 1840, Britain had 1490 miles of railroad track, and trains and rails were spreading in the United States, Latin America, and Europe.

Steam was also quickly adapted to military use. Ironclad steam-gunboats were used as early as the Anglo-Chinese Opium War of 1839–1842. Steam-driven machine guns were rapidly developed as well, as were cannon based on steam propulsion. Neither of these innovations really panned out, however, and advances in weaponry would spring more from later innovations in the area of chemistry. Nevertheless, the experiments in steam-guns are representative of the industrial ethos of the early industrial era—the idea that steam could drive any number of new innovations.

The Industrial Revolution and the British world-empire

By mid-century, British factories were producing the vast majority of industrial goods in the world. A large region of the country had basically become a giant machine that consumed local resources of coal, iron, and sheep and turned them into finished products, especially textiles, for British consumers. As the number and size of the factories continued to grow, however, they created a demand for raw materials from overseas and increasingly produced goods for an international market.

Ironically, this growing internationalization of British industrial networks occurred in a period in which the British government was seemingly uninterested in building formal overseas empires. The expensive war of the American Revolution in the 1770s soured Parliament on costly overseas empire-building projects for almost a century. But the ever-growing British industry and the investors who backed it needed the muscle of the military to explore new markets overseas. Somewhat reluctantly, therefore, the government was forced to lend its navy and its diplomatic corps to help open new parts of the world as potential markets for British goods. At the same time, almost without government sanction, British settlers and merchant companies began to claim new territory overseas where they could profit by producing goods for the industrial economy. Thus, as we saw in Chapter 1, the era of "informal" empire was born, and it was underwritten and shaped by industrialization.

Feeding the factories, feeding the workers

Britain's industries demanded two types of materials from overseas. The first was food to feed a working, urban population. More than in any previous society, industrial Britain's population did not grow its own food. Thus it built up a massive demand for such goods as Argentinian beef and grain from Canada. Entire regions of the world—especially in the Americas—soon began to specialize in producing large quantities of foodstuffs specifically for the British, and later the European, market.

Britain's second great need was raw materials for its factories. Textiles, for example, required not only wool or cotton but also dyes and gum for making patterned prints. Most of these materials were not found in Britain or even Europe. Gum was largely sourced from trees that grew at the edge of the Sahara Desert in Africa. Dyes came from Mexico, among other areas. Even cotton and wool were increasingly imported from the Egypt, the Americas, and Oceania. Other imported raw materials included rubber from Southeast Asia, copra (coconut) from the Pacific, and metals and nitrates from South America and Canada.

However raw materials were not the only imported industrial goods. Industrialization drove an increasing demand for lubricants, lighting, and soaps as well. These three needs were met by a global growing trade in oils. At first, many industrial lubricants, lamp oils, and soaps were manufactured from whale oils, much of which was imported from North America. Over time, however, the productivity of whaling declined due to overharvesting. The emphasis shifted to palm oil, which was largely produced in West Africa, by the late nineteenth century. Not only was palm oil itself useful for lubricant, soap, and lighting, but the kernels in which it was found could be used to make margarine, with the residual pulp being turned into cattle feed.

A number of competing networks formed in Africa to provide palm oil to Europe. Most of these were centered around trading conglomerates that developed along the rivers that connected palm oil growers in the interior of West Africa with the markets on the coast.

The main transportation technology of these networks was large canoes, and many of the competing African firms that emerged were organized through families of blood-related and adopted kin. This was especially true along the Niger River, perhaps the main highway for palm oil and palm kernels. By the 1880s, however,

British merchants had brought shallow-draught steamships to the river, allowing them to cut out Nigerian middlemen. The upshot was a series of conflicts between British and local merchants. Ultimately, these battles were resolved in favor of the British United African Company, partly because of its superior military technology. This outcome meant that a greater share of the profits from this trade found their way to Britain rather than remaining in West Africa.

Industry and the settler colonies

As British industry came to depend more and more on foreign raw materials for their all-important textile mills, British settlers began to carve out a new empire in order to produce the wool and cotton to feed them, almost without government support. To be sure, much of the raw materials that came to British factories continued to be imported from other countries. Independent Egypt was a major source of cotton, especially after the U.S. Civil War of the 1860s cut off supply from the southern states. Latin America, too, was important to British factories for not only sheep wool but also that of alpacas and llamas.

Aside from these international sources, British settler colonies began in this era to provide a great deal of the raw materials for British textiles, especially in the form of wool. New Zealand and Australia were probably the most important providers of wool for British factories. Australia had been settled by Europeans through several waves of migration. The first of these settlers were actually debtors and convicts exiled from Britain between 1788 and 1856. Many of them were rebels or even innocent bystanders swept up by British attempts to control Ireland. A much larger number of free colonizers came in the mid-nineteenth century, often assisted by the British government, in order to work in the wool and mineral industries starting in the territory. The Australian settlers found a sparsely populated land, a condition that they exacerbated by persecuting and hunting the indigenous population. Meanwhile, large numbers of British citizens began to settle in New Zealand in the 1840s. Here they encountered a much denser population—the indigenous Maori—whom they could only gradually and partially subjugate. In both cases the settlers rapidly turned to sheep farming as an occupation. Vast ranches spread out across the interior of Australia, especially. As early as 1838, Australia was annually exporting two million kilograms of wool to Britain. Although New Zealand lagged behind, it was also a major wool producer by the 1860s.

Another wool producing colony was founded in 1820 in the Eastern Cape region of South Africa. Originally intended by the British government to serve as a buffer between the Dutch-speaking population of the Western Cape and the indigenous Xhosa people, this colony was made up of 5000 English and Scottish settlers who were given funds and support to establish small-scale farms. Instead, most moved into local towns, turning their land over to a small number of ranchers who reared vast herds of sheep.

All of these settlers, and others in the Canadian provinces of British North America, demanded military and infrastructure support. For much of the nineteenth century, the British government was loathe to spend the money to support them or to build what was essentially a new empire. Gradually, however, Parliament complied with political pressure from settlers and their backers, especially financers hoping to get rich from investing in mining and farming in the colonies. British government services—from postal services to the army—slowly followed settlers into new regions. In turn, the settlers both provided raw materials for British industry and created new markets for the goods that rolled out of factories in England, Wales, and Scotland.

Gunboat diplomacy

While settler colonies made a ready market for British industrial finished products, other states tried to slow the flood of imports from Britain. Industrialization dramatically lowered the cost of producing goods in Britain, allowing them to outcompete locally made products in many regions. Some countries added taxes to imported British goods in an attempt to stop them from swamping local markets and driving out local producers. Others put a moratorium on some imports. Desperate to pry these markets open, Britain increasingly turned to the use of diplomacy and then military force. They especially used their new, advanced steam-driven gunboats to good effect. During trade disputes, the British would bring these gunboats into foreign port cities as an implicit threat to back up their ambassadors and merchants. For obvious reasons, this style of aggressive negotiation is often called **gunboat diplomacy**.

One of the most frequent sites where gunboat diplomacy was applied was in Latin America, which by the 1830s was divided into many independent states. British industrialists and investors saw these states as large potential markets for British goods. As early as the 1820s, 13 percent of British exports were bound for Latin America. This number tripled by 1860, while raw materials flowing the other way also increased rapidly. Meanwhile British firms invested heavily in industry in Argentina, Mexico, and Brazil. British iron and railroad firms made millions of pounds by providing the rail and locomotives that soon crisscrossed the region, serving the mines in the interior parts of Mexico and South America that provided the metals demanded by British industry. Most of the income from these activities ended up in the hands of British investors, while a much smaller percentage went to their local partners and governments.

Obviously, Latin American governments were not happy with this situation, and they frequently tried to change the conditions of trade to divert more profits to themselves and their merchant class. These attempts at renegotiation were met with furious resistance from British investors, who called upon their government to support their interests. As a result between 1830 and 1860, the British navy intervened with military force in the affairs of most Latin American countries, especially Uruguay, Argentina, and Brazil. Even more frequently, the threat of military force and demonstrations by gunships were sufficient to force local governments to come to terms favorable to British industry. This strategy continued to be effective until the mid-1860s. In those years following the U.S. Civil War, the United States began to challenge British preeminence in support of its own emerging industries and trading needs. This was not a favorable solution for most Latin American states, however, as it merely replaced one aggressive power with another.

The second wave of industrialization

The ability of the United States to nudge Britain out of its preeminent position in Latin America is one piece of evidence for the emergence of a second wave of industrialized societies that took place in the mid-nineteenth century. Even as Britain was building a worldwide network to feed its factories and buy its industrial goods, a number of rival states, and industrial and business communities, began to compete with British factories. This second wave of industrialization was especially focused in the Americas, continental Europe, and Japan. However these countries did not merely copy British innovations. The second Industrial Revolution also introduced new revolutions beyond steam, textiles, and iron—especially in the areas of chemicals and electricity.

A "second" Industrial Revolution

If the first Industrial Revolution was based on steam power and iron, the second Industrial Revolution introduced two major new innovations in the world of power: chemicals and electricity. Some of these innovations involved scientists and companies based in Britain, but many of the leading contributors were based in Germany and the United States.

In chemistry, this was the age of **synthetic** chemicals: substances created by men to replace or augment natural compounds. Some of the impetus for experimentation in synthetic chemistry was a result of new needs. For example, industrialization was a very dirty process, and oil stains in particular affected machines, people, and products. It is no surprise, therefore, that two of the first chemicals created by industrial chemists were soda and bleach!

Other chemicals were synthesized to replace expensive or rare natural substances. Synthetic purple dyes were produced by German and U.S. companies to replace such rare natural materials as indigo. Other chemicals were designed to replace rubber and cotton. Still others were advances in medicine, like aspirin. Perhaps the most momentous field of chemical innovation, however, was agriculture. Fertilizers had been applied to fields for millennia in the form of unprocessed human or animal feces, and a massive global trade in bird guano and other natural fertilizers had emerged early in the nineteenth century. But these raw materials were becoming increasingly expensive by the 1840s, hence the need for artificial fertilizers. By the late nineteenth century, the majority of fertilizers being used in agriculture in most parts of the world had been processed in factories in Europe or the Americas.

Chemistry also played an important role in the development of the electrical industry. Eighteenth-century philosophers and artisans such as Benjamin Franklin in the United States had sought to describe and understand electricity as a natural phenomenon, but they were unable to produce or harness it. In 1800, however, Italian scientist Alessandro Volta built the first basic battery that could be used to store an electrical charge. His "voltaic pile" was built using zinc, copper, and sulfuric acid or salt water. The implications of this invention became clear only gradually, but soon found many uses. The first significant application was probably the electric telegraph, which was demonstrated in the 1840s and that provided intercontinental communications beginning in the 1860s.

Two decades later, electricity had become increasingly useful to everyday people. Alexander Graham Bell introduced the electric telephone in 1876. Thomas Edison in the United States and Joseph swan in England both developed electric lights in 1878–1879. Edison went on to build the first system of switches, wires, and generators to

Figure 4.3 The electrified city: San Francisco with power lines and cable cars, 1890.

light up parts of New York City. Electric streetcars first entered widespread use in the early twentieth century. In order to provide the electricity to run all of these new systems, governments began to build vast turbines to collect electricity. The hydroelectric plant at Niagara Falls, perhaps the largest of its era, was built in 1886 and soon provided power to large parts of the northeastern United States and Canada.

The industrialization of North America and continental Europe

Many of these innovations were first developed and applied outside of Britain. The United States was among the earliest of the second-wave industrial nation-states. Although geographically quite different from Great Britain, it had notable advantages, not least of which was that the two countries shared a language and therefore ideas and technologies flowed fast across the Atlantic Ocean. The United States also had a significant labor shortage, making mechanization desirable, and possessed large deposits of key raw materials including coal, iron, and petroleum. Another impetus for industrialization in the United States was the U.S. Civil War, which helped to facilitate the growth of factories in both munitions and transportation fields.

The rapid industrialization of the United States was jump-started around the middle of the nineteenth century by the construction of a network of canals and railroads that facilitated commerce, industry, and the movement of people across the vast area of the North American continent. Growth in railroads was especially astonishing. In 1840, the United States had only 2800 miles of railroad but by 1870 it had 53,000 miles including lines that crossed all the way from the Pacific to the Atlantic. These connections catalyzed the colonization and settlement of this vast territory by the mainly European population of the Atlantic coast. This ironically created a **secondary imperialism** effect, in which the former colony of the United States became in its turn an imperial power. The population of the rapidly industrializing urban coast soon dominated large regions of the country to the west, often expelling or enclosing the Native American population of these regions. Some of these regions were industrialized in turn, others came to serve as areas for providing raw materials, while still others became relative backwaters in terms of industry.

Several densely populated regions of Europe also industrialized rapidly in this period. Belgium, the Ruhr and Saxon regions of Germany, the French provinces around Paris, and northern Italy became important centers of mining and factory production in the mid-nineteenth century. The Hungarian and Austrian provinces of the Habsburg Empire became a regional center for industrial production in eastern Europe. European Russia experienced some industrialization as well, although most of the country did not.

This patchwork pattern of industrialization left large parts of Europe that were underserved by the new transportation and communication services. Some of these were rural regions that continued to produce foodstuffs to feed the growing cities of Europe. The Netherlands, for example, was not particularly industrialized, but its enormous success in agriculture allowed its population to benefit by becoming the breadbasket that fed Belgium and parts of northern Germany. Others regions lacked the resources, government support, or economic conditions to either industrialize or profit from providing raw materials. These included the Mediterranean coast, relatively far from the industrial north of Europe. Other regions that lagged behind were surprisingly close to urban centers but were not favored by their governments. These included British-occupied Ireland and the south of France.

Measured in terms of overall industrial output, Germany was the most successful rapidly rising industrial power in Europe. As a collection of disassociated states before 1870, its governments and businesses independently built 11,150 miles of railroad. Once the country unified, the new Prussian-led German monarchy quickly focused on deepening industrial production. Following German occupation of the mineral-rich regions of Alsace and Lorraine in the 1870–1871 Franco-Prussian war, the country quickly overtook Britain in steel production. It also supported a scientific community that specialized in producing synthetic chemicals, making Germany the global leader in this industry by the early twentieth century.

Literature and art in the European and North American industrialization

It's easy to view the Industrial Revolution as a purely economic transformation, far removed from the world of culture in art. In fact, however, the impact of industrialization on human experience rapidly became a subject of the work of artists who sought to both depict and escape from the gritty realities of industrial life. In Europe and North America, two particular schools of art influenced by industrialization were realism and romanticism.

Realism was an approach to art that was very much in line with the rationalization of the workplace and daily life. Realist artists aspired to represent the world as it "really was." They strived to be as precise as possible, trying to perfect techniques for accurately replicating the world they saw in their art. Some realists did not even sign their works, preferring to present them as products of the world working through them. Working with pencil and paints, many of them chose to depict the industry that they saw in the landscape and lives of people around them. Albert von Menzel's image, which opens this chapter, is a good example. Some realists, like Gustave Courbet, used these images as social commentary on the problems associated with industrialization, but many realist artists were not critical of industrial modernity, preferring instead to benefit from the opportunities and materials industry offered.

Realism also featured in the literature of the Industrial Revolution. The British author Charles Dickens was one master of the industrial novel, depicting the reality of changing times—urbanization, child labor, mechanization—with precise detail. A factory worker as a child himself, he bemoaned the loss of individual enjoyment and idyllic childhood to the factories and workhouses of industrial cities. In novels such as *Hard Times,* he likened workers to the hands and feet of the machines rather than free people themselves.

By contrast, artists of the romantic school were very critical of the Industrial Revolution. We have already seen that romanticism, with its focus on heroes, nature, and humanity, was deeply tied to nationalist movements in this period. Romanticists wanted to celebrate human achievement and emotion. Many of them saw industrialization and its obsession with rationality as impediments to emotion and humanism. They intended romantic art to be an escape from this gritty reality. Instead of factories and railroads, these artists focused on folklore and classic heroes who seemed to inhabit a more humane past. The figures they depicted were usually posed in ways meant to express the noble emotions of lives lived from the humdrum of everyday factory work.

Figure 4.4 Eugène Delacroix, *Dante and Virgil*, 1822. Note how these figures of antiquity are in the throes of passionate struggle and heroism.

Some artists of the romantic school also focused on depicting rural landscapes, unspoiled by industry. This was especially true in Britain and the United States, where romanticists portrayed idyllic scenes in rural Sussex or coastal Maine as a means of appealing to human emotion and a love of the natural world.

Romanticism played on similar themes in literature, where they embraced a nostalgia for the past and for nature. William Wordsworth's early nineteenth-century poems, bemoaning the willingness of industrial man to abandon nature, are an excellent example:

The world is too much with us; late and soon,
Getting and spending, we lay waste our powers;
Little we see in Nature that is ours;
We have given our hearts away, a sordid boon![1]

Transforming Japan

The expansion of industry and the endeavor to open markets across the North American continent in the nineteenth century almost seamlessly led the United States across the Pacific Ocean. Their journey climaxed in 1853 with the arrival of U.S. gunboats under Commodore Matthew Perry in Tokyo Bay, Japan. As we saw in Chapter 1, their appearance was one of the signals for the Meiji Restoration of 1867, which replaced the last Tokugawa Shogun with an oligarchy of samurai and business leaders. The new Japanese government was both pro-industry and pro-expansion, and created Japan's first modern civil service to support the rapid industrialization of its society.

Japan prior to Perry's arrival is often depicted as an utterly medieval state. In fact, Perry and his officers were visiting a country that already had a smattering telegraphs and railroads. The rulers of the provinces of Satsuma and Choshu, in defiance of Tokugawa authority, had been building this kind of infrastructure and adopting such complex industrial tools as modern iron furnaces on a small scale for more than a decade. However, Japan's national industrialization really took off in years following Perry's visit, when the Meiji government acted to stimulate construction and economic development. Among the first new factories the government set up were shipyards capable of building vessels like those in which Perry had arrived. A large reason for this emphasis on a defensive naval industry was the Meiji recognition of the need for **defensive modernization**. The Japanese had been shocked by both the obvious military superiority of Perry's ships and reports that nearby China was being slowly pulled apart by industrial powers like the United States, Britain, and Germany. Determined to avoid a similar fate, Meiji administrators agreed to engineer a rapid modernization, and they recognized that the first step was to build a large industrial base.

Yet Japan faced some unique challenges to industrialization. Its mountainous geography meant that railroad construction was a difficult undertaking, and thus

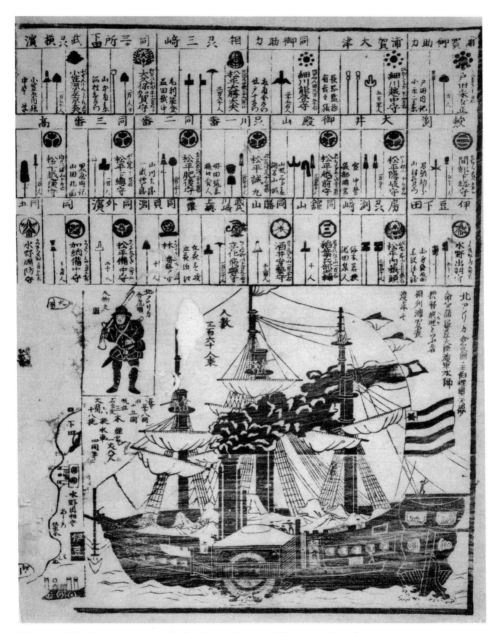

Figure 4.5 A Japanese artist's view of one of Commodore Perry's steamships, 1850s.

the country only built 100 miles of track in the years before 1880. It took concerted government investment and massive public works in the decades that followed to build a nation-wide rail network. Moreover, Japan lacked many of the basic resources that had enabled industrialization in North America and Europe. Simple materials, including coal, were not found in Japan and were often difficult to obtain. Finally, Japanese goods faced enormous import taxes in the United States and Europe, which were already trying to protect their own industries from competition. To address these problems, Japanese administrators and businesses turned to a policy of expansion into territories that could both provide raw materials for Japanese industry and open up markets for finished products. The largest of these was Korea, which first became a Japanese protectorate and then was formally and violently annexed in 1910.

Japan's lack of strategic resources also meant that its industrialization necessitated greater centralized planning than in many other states. Fortunately, the new Japanese government was well positioned to support industrial development. Its leaders included the heads of centuries-old businesses like the Matsui firm and of pro-industry provinces such as Satsuma and Chosu. Thus it is hardly surprising that Japanese industrialization was more dependent on government involvement than in Britain or the United States. Meiji administrators were particularly efficient at diverting tax money to industry, building infrastructure, and financially supporting large firms.

Together, these strategies constituted a national industrial campaign unlike any seen before. By bringing together local skills with imported expertise, this campaign managed to almost immediately vault Japan into a global leadership position in a number of industries. One of these was in textile production. Japan had historically been a major processor of silk. By adopting new machines and factory-style organization, and by excelling in quality, Japanese companies became the largest silk suppliers in the world by the beginning of the twentieth century. At the same time, Japanese producers studied cotton production and entered the market in cotton textiles as well, although here British corporations continued to lead until well into the twentieth century.

The literature and art of defensive modernization in Japan

As with Europeans, industrialization shaped the way that many artists in Japan described and commented on their world. In both societies, art became part of a debate over the costs and benefits of industrialization. Often, the cultural and even environmental costs of industrialization were recognized in works in both regions. At the same time, pro-industrialization lobbies sponsored art and literature that celebrated "modern" machines and other symbols. Yet despite these similarities between the two regions, Japanese art around industry and industrialization was of course quite unique.

In the early years of industrialization, the Meiji government promoted the adaptation of Western art and architecture forms that they saw as tied to the Industrial

Revolution. Western artists were invited to help to start schools like the Technical Fine Arts School (1883) and the Tokyo School of Fine Arts (1889). Many of the art produced by Japanese students at these schools was influenced by the European romanticist and realist schools.

Quite rapidly, however, some Japanese intellectuals and artists reacted to preserve local preindustrial artistic forms. In 1879, the Dragon Pond Society was formed to protect local art forms. In 1894, the artist Okakura Kakuzo formed a new art school, the Japanese Art Academy, which focused on traditional techniques. His students' artwork generally focused on preindustrial Japan, as if factories and railways had never sprouted across the land.

The existence of these two very different schools, however, does not mean that there were simply two opposed responses in Japan to industrialization: one a pro-Western, pro-industrial stance and the other a conservative, antimodernization stance. Instead, art and literature in Japan in this period often reflected the mixing of influences. For example, one popular form of Japanese novels of this period was the semiautobiographical "I novel," which figuratively represented the author's life. Because these lives were taking place in an era of great integration of Western and Japanese influences, they often blended motifs and symbols. A classic example was Natsume Sōseki's novel "I Am a Cat," which described the mixing of Western and Japanese culture through the eyes of a domestic cat, an approach that had been popular in pre-Meiji Japan but would have appeared strange to Europeans in the same period.

Unequal industrialization

Narratives of the Industrial Revolution in the nineteenth century often focuses on the pursuit of industrialization by Japan, the United States, and continental Europe. In reality, the story was a much broader one. The economic power of industrialization co-existed easily with the drive for resources and markets of the new imperialism. Together, industrial products and empire represented a dual threat that societies everywhere had to face. Governments and people around the world recognized that they needed to industrialize merely in order to defend their economies and sovereignty, but they faced many challenges. First, there was the difficulty of reconciling the changes industrialization brought with the existing needs and structures of their societies. Even more significantly, they faced resistance from states that had already industrialized and that sought to keep industry from shifting to these new regions. The racism, economic aggressiveness, and militarized foreign policies of these industrialized states restricted the opportunities of other societies. Gradually, this inequality created a global "dependency" cycle through which some areas became wealthier centers of industry while others were increasingly impoverished.

The struggle to industrialize: Egypt

Egypt's experience is a prime example of the difficulties faced by late industrializers. In 1810, Egypt was a semi-independent province of the Ottoman Empire led by Muhammad Ali, a general who had successfully repelled an invading French army with the help of the British navy. Recognizing the need to industrialize in order to stave off further invasions, Ali embarked on a three-step economic program. First, he raised money by exporting food and other agriculture products to Europe. He then invested this money in growing cotton, which he could sell as a cash crop to British textile mills. These two initial steps were successful, although only by forcing peasants to labor in government cotton fields and reducing the amount of food available to them.

By the 1830s, Ali was ready for the third step: creating factories in Egypt itself. The earliest of these were munitions factories and shipyards designed to help Egypt defend itself. Soon, however, Ali's government began to constructing textile factories so that the country could process its own cotton. However, the Egyptians faced a problem typical of newly industrializing economies in this period. European countries, which had already developed textile industries of their own, imposed vast taxes on Egyptian cloth in order to try to halt its importation. At the same time, Britain used gunboat diplomacy to force the Ottoman Empire and North African states to accept British textiles tax-free. Thus Egypt had no natural market advantage in its surrounding region. Together with a lack of coal to fuel their machinery, this situation caused Egypt's factories to collapse in the 1840s.

Another region whose population attempted significant defensive modernization in this period was coastal South Asia, although here the involvement of government was minimal. The main focus of industrialization in this region was transportation—in particular shipbuilding—led by companies hoping to participate in the growing trade between India and far-flung regions of the world. The main South Asian shipbuilding centers that emerged in the 1790s were in Gujarat on the western coast and Bengal on the eastern coast. One factor that helped this industry was a shortage in timber in Britain and continental Europe, itself partly a result of their industrialization.

South Asian shipbuilding centers benefitted from the introduction of new tools and from the demands of customers like the British Royal Navy. Shipbuilders in this region increasingly developed or adapted innovative metalworking and woodworking techniques. For two decades, these shipyards thrived. Around 1820, however, European customers began to move their orders back to European shipyards. This was partly because they wanted to take advantage of new chemical and metallurgical techniques developed in Europe and partly because European governments wanted to build their own ships for strategic and economic reasons. Yet it was also very much a result of the policies of imperial powers that were slowly gaining control of South

Asia. Britain, in particular, was purposefully dismantling South Asian industries because they competed with British companies. Instead, corporations like the British East India Company, which occupied Bengal, focused on transforming this region into a supplier of agricultural goods, in particular opium and cotton.

Deindustrialization in Asia

The dismantling of South Asian manufacturing was part of a process of **deindustrialization** that occurred in many regions during the nineteenth century, even as others were industrializing. Once the heart of global textile production, South Asia became instead a net importer of cloth by the First World War. Partly, this decline was a result of the competitive economic practices of the British East India Company, which sought to monopolize textile production in the parts of India it controlled by forcing local producers to sell their products only to the company even though it offered 15–40 percent less than other potential customers. As a result, many weavers left the industry. Also significant was the company's emphasis on agricultural production to the detriment of industry. This policy contributed to the most important factor in the region's deindustrialization: British factory owners wanted South Asians to be consumers of British textiles, rather than producing for themselves or for export.

Processes of relative deindustrialization also took place in other regions of Asia. In China, the weakening Qing Dynasty remained focused on feeding and effectively administering a vast, widespread population. A series of revolts and internal issues such as the Taiping Rebellion of and Boxer Rebellion made stability even more difficult for this vast kingdom. However, the intervention of outside industrial power and military might played perhaps the key role in the collapse of this complex state. Beginning in the 1810s, British companies had begun to profit significantly from the sale of opium to China. Millions of ounces of silver flowed out of China to pay for opium in the 1820s and early 1830s, enriching Britain and contributing to both the decrease in Chinese productivity and the dwindling amount of money available there for investment in new industries. When the Qing government tried to halt the sale of opium and to reverse these trends, Britain backed up its drug-dealing merchants with steam-powered gunships. Between 1840 and 1842, these industrial weapons allowed a British army to inflict a terrible defeat on China. In the ensuing Treaty of Nanjing, China agreed to pay millions of dollars in costs and reparations, and also turned over the island of Hong Kong to Britain. This was the beginning of the process by which other industrial powers would come to occupy large coastal swathes of China for their own economic benefit.

The process by which deindustrialization occurred was not always quite so violent. The Ottoman Empire, for example, experienced deindustrialization largely through subtle but significant **commodity replacement** trends. In the mid-nineteenth century, as European industrial production ramped up, the Ottoman Empire became on open market for their products. Because European goods were produced using industrial techniques, these were usually cheaper to produce and purchase than locally made products. As a result, Ottoman handicraft producers saw a rapidly diminishing market for their own goods. This doesn't mean that the Ottoman sultans and businesspeople did not pursue their own industrial policies. These included the construction of munitions factories as well as textile mills. In 1842, Ottoman officials even designated a large industrial zone near Istanbul for metal and textile works. Most of these factories were abandoned within 15 years, however, largely because of competition from established European companies that could dump their products on the Ottoman Empire due to the lack of import taxes, a policy forced on the sultans by the stronger European states.

Dependency and the "global south"

Nor was deindustrialization confined to Asia during the nineteenth century. Commodity replacement in Africa meant that local metalworks, pottery, and consumer goods were rapidly replaced by industrial goods from Europe. Something similar occurred in the Pacific, where both settler and indigenous societies began to consume large amounts of industrial goods from Europe, the United States, and Japan. This process was often hastened by ecological change. Throughout the nineteenth century, plants and animals from Eurasia and the Americas were imported to Polynesia, Australasia, and other parts of the Pacific. These new species either replaced or destroyed many of the local materials historically used for clothing and other goods.

A similar process, if more decentralized, also occurred in Latin America. As in the United States, industrialization in Latin America largely occurred in urban centers with populations largely of European descent, which in turn gradually opened up rural areas to settlement and economic exploitation. The populations of these areas rapidly became producers of raw materials for urban factories and consumers of their finished products. Nor did these rural regions produce raw materials only for the big cities of the coast. With both the United States and Britain actively angling for their mineral and agricultural bounty, Latin American states turned into mass exporters of raw materials. This began a centuries-long process of the overexploitation of local products for the benefit of distant populations. Sugar, tobacco, and coffee from Brazil became the stimulants that helped keep British, U.S., and European workers at their machines. Argentinian beef fed them when they returned home. Peruvian guano—bird feces—kept their fields productive. Meanwhile, industry in Latin America stagnated. By 1900, only Argentina had been able to develop much industry, largely in the area of meat processing and packing.

Why had Latin America remained relatively agricultural while the United States became an industrial powerhouse? One explanation is that Latin America's economies were captured while still in their youth by the earlier industrializing powers. Before the 1830s, Great Britain used gunboat diplomacy and other strategies to force Latin American countries to provide raw materials and to not levy taxes on imported British goods. In the late nineteenth century, the United States largely took over that role. Admittedly, however, they could not have succeeded in capturing Latin American economies without the assistance of some local elites, particularly mine owners and ranchers, who also profited from this unequal trade.

Thus by the end of the long nineteenth century, large areas of the world were economically tied to the global economy in a subordinate position. They generally produced only raw materials, for which they were paid little, and consumed finished products, for which they paid too much. Most of the profit in this exchange went to large, industrialized economies. We tend to call this subordinate position a condition of **dependency**. Such dependent societies were especially concentrated in the southern hemisphere of the world, while most of the industry was in the north. This global inequity has remained largely true to this day.

Living in a world of industry

Wherever industrialization took hold, it produced changes at the most basic levels of human existence. Home, travel, work, and daily activity were all affected by the advent of modern industry, sometimes in ways that were quite profound.

The industrial city

The transformations wrought by industrialization were most obvious in the cities and large towns of highly industrialized societies, beginning with eighteenth-century Britain and spreading to parts of North America and Europe as well as Japan and later cities in other parts of the world. These cities were every bit as much a product of the Industrial Revolution as the factory or the railroad, and in fact the three were complementary. Factories need large pools of labor, and thus tend to be located near cities. Railroads brought workers and goods to the city, and carried away finished products. The populations of cities need to earn money since they cannot easily produce their own food, and thus turned to factories for work and wages.

Globally, cities grew rapidly over the course of the nineteenth century, especially in Europe and North America. At the beginning of the century, seven of the 10 largest cities in the world were located in Asia, with only London, Paris, and Naples as the European exceptions. By 1900, London had overtaken Beijing as the largest city in the world, followed by New York, Paris, Berlin, and Chicago. Among Asian cities, only Tokyo remained in the top 10. The fastest urban growth rates represented either cities that had industrialized rapidly—such as Manchester, England and New York—or colonial cities able to exploit vast resources at the frontiers of European expansion—such as Philadelphia, Buenos Aires, and Sydney.

Within these cities, factories and urbanization had an impact on daily life and health that was in many ways quite negative. Large processing plants tended to produce a lot of pollution. Coal was one of the key culprits in the decline in the health of city-dwellers, since factories belched out soot and smog all day and night. In these cities, black dust coated everything, including people's lungs. Textile factories, paper mills, and metallurgical plants also used dangerous chemicals like arsenic and mercury, often concentrated and their remains dumped directly into urban drinking water. Together, pollutants made life in cities quite difficult. Smog was so bad in London that at times the municipality had to shut down. At its worst, in 1858, a combination of pollution, human waste, and heat made the city smell so bad that most people refused to go out of doors.

Even seemingly harmless products could be deadly when stored in large amounts in crowded urban areas. In 1919, a molasses tank exploded in Boston, killing 21. One Boston newspaper reported that:

> Fragments of the great tank were thrown into the air, buildings in the neighborhood began to crumple up as though the underpinnings had been pulled away from under them, and scores of people in the various buildings were buried in the ruins, some dead and others badly injured.[2]

As poor peasants moved in from the countryside and even poorer immigrants arrived from abroad, cities also became sites of squalor and suffering. New arrivals were densely packed into tenements. Often lacking the kinds of extended family support structures that had helped them in the countryside, these families tried to recreate the institutions of their villages. This often meant the public house or pub, a place to congregate after work, talk about the day, and eat and drink. These buildings also functioned as dance halls for evening gatherings. In late nineteenth-century industrial Belgium, some cities had as many as one tavern per 25 inhabitants! But they did not really recreate the support structure of the rural village.

It wasn't just poor workers who flocked to the cities. The growing number of factories and the emerging finance and transportation companies that served the cities also needed administrators, supervisors, and other professionals. These workers and their families constituted a class who could afford more than just a poor tenement and access to a public house. Increasingly concentrated in segregated, well-to-do neighborhoods, this emerging middle class demanded entertainment, and they could afford it. They also frequently had evenings and weekends off. Their demand for entertainment helped to create leisure activities that typified the city. Ticket-paying urban customers created professional leagues for sports like baseball in the United States, stimulated the growth of theater and opera, and lobbied for parks. Their ability to participate in "respectable" leisure activities helped distinguish the middle class from the factory workers. Yet evidence suggests that they also often went "slumming"—visiting the pubs and dance halls of the poor.

In fact, even for the poorer classes, the industrial city was may not have been a bad place to live compared to impoverished rural areas. Some large European and North American cities developed innovative running-water and sanitation systems in the nineteenth century that (finally) brought them up to the level of cleanliness enjoyed for centuries by Ottoman cities like Damascus. These systems advanced fastest in places where city governments were strong and representative. New York created a system of pipes and drinking water reservoirs in the 1840s. London developed its public water supply around the same time. Then they went even further than New York, and built the first great modern public sewer system. This innovation was prompted in part by "The Great Stink," a horrible stench that rose from the Thames River in 1855 due to the backup of raw sewage. By 1868, the City of London had laid 1300 miles of sewers to pipe waste away from the city. Modern sewer systems spread rapidly after this date, including to Calcutta in 1865 and Shanghai in 1883. Another great amenity of city life was development of first gas and then electric lights. Lighting allowing city-dwellers much more mobility and flexibility at night than that enjoyed by their rural countrypeople.

Other innovations attempted to give workers better lives. In response to the poverty and suffering they saw around them, some industrialists tried to create special, enlightened towns for their workers. One of these, Hopedale Community in Massachusetts, was an attempt to meld Christian ideals with industrial work. It offered workers a chance to vote and participate in industrial as well as community decisions. In Scotland, Robert Owen built New Lanark, a planned town that offered factory workers health care, an art program, and even a nursery school. Yet despite these few experiments, city living remained difficult for many throughout this era.

New vistas

By the mid-nineteenth century, the industrial middle class began for the first time to travel away from the city for vacations, emulating the wealthy aristocrats of earlier generations. They vacationed in the countryside, toured such great sites as the Imperial Exhibition at Crystal Palace, and even began to visit other countries. Tourism was largely a product of the growth of the middle class and the development of rail and steamship routes. Some regions that were well served by railroads, like the Hudson Valley and Switzerland, became favorite vacation places for city-dwellers. Hotels soon emerged along these routes, and guide books were written for visitors. Specialist companies like Thomas Cook (Britain) and the Stangen Brothers (Germany) began to organize group tours to the Alps, the cities of Italy, and beyond.

Steamship lines crossing the Atlantic brought Europeans to New York and European Americans back to visit their ancestral homes.

In the 1870s, Europeans increasingly also began to visit the Ottoman Empire, Egypt, and the Holy Sites of Islam. However, they were found themselves in the company of a much larger group of travelers. Steamships and train lines had also developed to facilitate the Islamic pilgrimage to Mecca—the Hajj. A combination of ships and trains connect Muslims from as far away as West Africa and South Asia to the Arabian Peninsula. The numbers of pilgrims rapidly increased over the course of the century, a trend that had important repercussions. Religious and philosophical approaches like Wahhabism were soon brought back from Arabia by pilgrims to their home countries, while the cosmopolitan experiences of the pilgrims helped to reinforce the idea of a shared Islamic world despite the political divisions under which Muslims lived.

Railroad lines in India and Africa may have facilitated travel to Mecca, but they failed to provide other new kinds of travel opportunities to most Africans and Asians within European empires. This was partly a result of the planning and design of these lines, which were largely built to help bring resources out of these regions to European

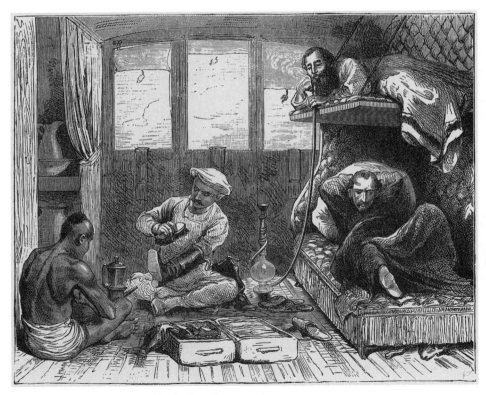

Figure 4.6 Railway travel in India, nineteenth century.

factories. Thus although India by 1910 had the fourth largest railroad system in the world, many of the lines were not widely used by South Asians themselves. Some had been built to move British troops to frontiers, while others almost exclusively moved freight. In 1882, India's rail system moved four billion ton-kilometers of freight. However, passenger travel still cost too much for most people, despite the fact that South Asian subjects of the British Empire supported the railroads through their taxes.

Factory and mine

For most inhabitants of industrialized societies, the Industrial Revolution was not so much about the opportunities of tourism and travel as the daily grind of labor. In factories, mines, and fields, work was increasingly regulated by the authority of the supervisor and the clock. Jobs were standardized through the **segregation of tasks**, which meant that workers specialized in a particular role and performed it over and over. Even the production of such basic materials as thread or wire required many different steps. The most efficient way to produce industrial finished products was to arrange workers to specialize in individual tasks, as they could learn through repetition to be very good at their tasks. Factory labor was made even more efficient through the introduction of the moving **assembly line** around 1900. In this system, complicated products moved along a conveyor belt from worker to worker, gradually reaching completion. This system was especially useful for difficult and complex products like the car.

Specialization and the segregation of tasks was highly efficient. It was not, however, a particularly healthy scheme for the workers. Repetitive tasks stressed muscles and joints, especially when combined with the long hours worked by many factory laborers. Moreover, dangers abounded in factories, from the moving parts of machines like the assembly line to open forges and dangerous chemicals. In rural areas, the gathering of raw materials was often equally dangerous. Mines in particular held numerous hazards from collapsing rock to toxic materials like coal dust and mercury.

The dangers of industrialization were not restricted to adult male workers. Children and women were frequently assigned the worst and most dangerous tasks in factories, principally because they could be paid less but also because of their smaller size. Traditional European notions of gender roles played a part in these assignments as well. Women were largely seen as "helpmeets" of men, and thus given roles that were perceived as less important and hence poorly paying. Another reason for the concentration of women in factory work was historical. Women had traditionally been the most important producers of textiles in Europe, and because early industrialization occurred in this field, it was women who moved into factory jobs first.

Figure 4.7 Women working at the Hanks, Wells and Co.'s factory in Birmingham, England, 1951. They are sharpening the nips of pens using grindstones driven by a steam-powered belt and shaft.

As the nineteenth century continued, women continued to work in factories, but often in segregated settings. Moralists of the period worried about the intermixing of women and men in the workplace, and sex-segregated factory floors were seen as more "respectable" and were therefore preferred by middle-class managers. However, when moral values interfered with profit, such restrictions often collapsed. Girls and women were regularly employed alongside men and boys in British coal mines, for example, and often under terrible conditions. In 1842, the British government probed working conditions in mills and factories and found that workers suffered from joint injuries, lung diseases, hunger, and lost limbs. Even more troubling to some investigators, however, was the mixing of girls and boys in conditions they deemed immoral:

> In two other pits in the Huddersfield Union I have seen the same sight. In one near New Mills, the chain, passing high up between the legs of two of these girls, had worn large holes in their trousers; and any sight more disgustingly indecent or revolting can scarcely be imagined than these girls at work. (N)o brothel can beat it.[3]

Industrial-style labor conditions came into existence in some parts of the nonindustrialized world as well. Palm oil plantations in West Africa, opium fields in Bengal, and diamond mines in southern Africa were increasingly organized along industrial lines over the course of the nineteenth century. In some of these places, like Egypt, women and children labored alongside men. In general, however, men dominated the wage labor market in raw material production, whereas women were assigned to domestic labor and growing food for the family. This was also true in Japan, where female participation in the industrial workplace was much lower than in the United States or Europe.

A world run by pocket watch

Railroads organized by schedule and factories run in shifts were symptomatic of the increasing importance of measured time in the industrial age. Workers and trains were expected to show up when they were due, and people planned around these expectations. But how did anyone know what time it was? Before 1800, there was no such thing as synchronized time. The needs of industry, however, made uniform time measurement a requirement. Over the course of the nineteenth century, therefore, most countries adopted a synchronized time signal, coordinated eventually by telegraph pulses sent out from a national center. In large countries, like Russia and the United States, multiple time zones emerged. Business quickly fell into line with national systems. In 1870, there were over 70 different railroad time synchronizations among the 400 or so companies in the United States. By 1900, they were synchronized to each other and to the national clock.

The final stage in this process was the synchronization of countries with each other through a series of international agreements. An 1884 conference divided the world into 24 zones, each roughly 15 degrees of longitude in length. However, the delegates had difficulty agreeing on a single standard for noon (the zero longitudinal meridian) largely because nationalism stoked disagreements as to whose capital would be the standard from which everyone would add and subtract hours for their own time zones. It took a few years for everyone to agree that Britain's Royal Observatory at Greenwich (outside of London) would be the globally recognized zero meridian. The French government resisted agreeing to this measure until as late as 1911.

At a much more personal level, people's homes—and even their pockets—were gradually also tied into this universal time system. By the 1870s, the cheap pocket watch and affordable, mass-produced desktop clock had become common in the hands of middle-class people everywhere in the world. As the clock and pocket watch became symbols of civilization and modernity, they were be awarded to those who aspired to be considered civilized or imposed on those who came under modernity's rule. In Japan, the Meiji emperor began to award pocket watches to successful students. In East Africa, colonial planters forced locals to show up for work when the plantation bell rang and to leave only when they were dismissed. Since only settlers owned watches, the laborers were captive to those who held authority in their pockets. The watch was just one manifestation, really, of the changes wrought by life in an industrialized world, but it was a potent symbol of the power of modernity to people everywhere.

Key terms

assembly line [139]
commodity replacement [133]
defensive modernization [128]
deindustrialization [133]
dependency [135]
enclosure [117]
factories [114]
gunboat diplomacy [122]
realism [126]
secondary imperialism [125]
segregation of tasks [139]
synthetic [123]

Further readings

Recent scholarship on the origins of the Industrial Revolution has focused in part on the interaction between the global and local dimensions in Britain. An excellent example is Robert C. Allen, *The British Industrial Revolution in Global Perspective* (Cambridge: Cambridge University Press, 2009).

An even more accessible history of the Industrial Revolution was written by prominent social historian Peter N. Stearns, *The Industrial Revolution in World History*, Fourth Edition (Boulder: Westview, 2013).

Andre Gunder Frank's original work on dependency and under-industrialization remains a classic in the field. Andre Gunder Frank, *Capitalism and Underdevelopment in Latin America: Historical Studies of Chile and Brazil* (New York: Monthly Review Press, 1967).

Prominent world historian Kenneth Pomeranz has edited a significant anthology covering industrialization in Japan and parts of Latin America and Southeast Asia. Many of the articles are authored by scholars based in these areas. Kenneth L. Pomeranz, editor, *The Pacific in the Age of Early Industrialization* (Farnham: Ashgate, 2009).

5

Capitalism and Socialism

The nineteenth-century world was a world in transition. Slowly in some places, rapidly in others, unevenly but emphatically, things were changing. A new world demanded a new economic system, and after many experiments and false starts, the system that emerged was modern capitalism. With its emphasis on free markets and individual profit, capitalism provided the funding for modernity, eviscerating other economic systems across the north Atlantic and then spreading rapidly around the world. Of course, modern capitalism did not emerge out of nowhere. The profit motive that was its primary feature had existed in many societies over long periods of time. But when harnessed to modern industry, it proved to be an incredibly powerful force for change, both on the macro-scale and for individual experience. Capitalism promoted a life that was generally more secular, more organized, and more regulated than the lives lived by people in precapitalist society. In other words, it was thoroughly modern.

Proponents of capitalism believed that through this economic system, individuals would become free to labor as they wanted, and as a result individual assets would increase. They saw capitalism as a meritocracy in which the hardest-working and most skilled would rise to the top. However, not everyone in the nineteenth century agreed that these changes were a good thing. Critics predicted that capitalism would bring about poverty for the mass of people while providing wealth only to a relative few. Gradually, they began to develop alternate economic doctrines. These culminated in the development of the socialist critique by the mid-century. This philosophy proposed economic equality as more important than the free market. By the First World War, the first major socialist revolution was underway in Mexico, foreshadowing the confrontation between socialism and capitalism that would reach its apex later in the twentieth century.

In this chapter, we look at capitalism as an economic system and as a set of real lived experiences for the inhabitants of the modern era. We especially explore industrial capitalism, the economic form that developed to support the Industrial Revolution and that connected capitalism to the nationalist and empire-building projects. But this history isn't just a dry account of prices and goods. The capitalist economic system that grew to dominate the world was alive and experienced, fought over and written about, loved and hated. Any history of capitalism in the long nineteenth century has to capture these realities.

This chapter also introduces a number of terms. Most of these relate directly to **capital**, **capitalism**, and the capitalist system. They include concrete ideas like the **market**, the **bank**, **stocks**, **bonds**, **bubbles**, the **profit motive** and **oligarchies**. In addition, we will look at intellectual and moral concepts like **free labor**, **free markets**, the **invisible hand**, and **regulation**. We will discuss the **industrious revolution** and particular models of capitalism like **laissez-faire** capitalism, **industrial capitalism**, **gentlemanly capitalism**, **utopian** ideals, and **utilitarianism.**

Other terms relate to global capitalist relationships. These include **core states** and **periphery**. We will look at the **proletariat** as a class and briefly discuss the **caste** system in South Asia as well as the expansion of the **nuclear family** form of kin organization. Finally, we will discuss ideas and movements critical of capitalism, including **luddites**, **trade and labor unions**, **socialism**, the **Marxist critique**, **communism**, and **anarchism.**

By the end of this chapter you should be able to:

- Describe how capitalism became the dominant global economic system, and how it changed over time during the long nineteenth century.
- Define capitalism and socialism, and compare and contrast them to each other as philosophies for economic organization.
- Account for the support of many members of the bourgeoisie in Europe and other parts of the world for capitalism.
- Evaluate the impact of capitalism on the lives of industrial and agricultural workers in several parts of the world.

The origins of a capitalist world system

Humans are innovative, and over the centuries human societies have developed many different kinds of economic systems. For much of human history, small-scale communities often had no real economy at all, each member of a group merely producing for their own individual requirements and the group's collective needs. But most larger-scale societies of the past developed ways of trading, sharing, and accumulating wealth in goods, land, and even currency. Sometimes gift-exchange dominated economic relations, or the powerful may even have periodically given away their wealth in order to gain social status. Often, different products were bartered between individuals or communities without money changing hands. Even taxes paid to governments frequently didn't come in the form currency. Most economic exchanges took place on a communal, regional, or state model, with long-distance trade being less significant and common.

By the beginning of the long nineteenth century, however, the population of the world was on an relentless pathway toward economic integration through a system that used currency, or **capital**, as its main means of exchange. Any history of the modern period from 1750 to 1914 must address this capitalist system and the principal ideologies of its supporters and its critics—capitalism and socialism. These are the subjects of this chapter.

What is capitalism?

Before we can explore the origins and functioning of **capitalism** in the modern world since 1750, we must first clearly define the term. To begin with, capitalism is a philosophy and an ideology that supports the creation of a capitalist system. This is a system of economic organization in which companies and productive assets are typically owned by private individuals or groups of individuals, rather than the government or the community as a whole. In a pure capitalist system, the goods provided by these companies, as well as the labor employed to produce them and the land on which they are produced, are all offered for sale on an open **market.** Perhaps most importantly, under a capitalist system people can lend or invest their money—or capital—to companies or economic ventures. Thus as well as markets, capitalist systems need **banks,** financial institutions that pool and invest money, often for profit the profit of their investors.

Of course, this is just a basic description of capitalism. As one of the most controversial features of the modern world, many people have offered definitions of capitalism, some of which are quite complex. Some see capitalism almost as a type of government, arguing that the market regulates human activity even more than the state. Critics of capitalism see it as a system of inevitable inequality, because the **profit motive**—the search for individual wealth—pushes some people to try to become rich while others stay poor. On the other hand, proponents of capitalism argue that its essential ingredient is freedom, because people can choose when and how to sell their labor by becoming employed and can buy or sell whatever they want, if they can afford it.

Figure 5.1 Thomas Rowlandson, *The Corn Exchange*, 1808. The painting depicts an important market in London where financiers, bankers, and merchants bought and sold shares and crops of grain.

Most economists and historians recognize that there has hardly ever been a case of pure capitalism. Even where there have been relatively free markets, historically, there is always some governmental intervention or cultural laws that imposes some **regulation** on these markets. Often, government regulations are meant to promote common welfare, like issues of defense or health care. Yet critics of government intervention usually see it as an impediment to the free flow of goods and wealth.

The global economic network in 1700

Capitalism emerged from roots in the early modern era before 1700, a period in which a global economic system existed, but was largely decentralized. In this era, we can speak of a world increasingly linked by commerce. Trade was becoming much more globalized than ever before, with galleons, dhows, and junks traveling back and forth across vast oceans carrying goods from one place to another. Labor, too, was also becoming increasingly globalized, with workers transported long distances such as from Africa to the Americas, and not always voluntarily. Money similarly flowed around the world. Vast areas of the world were connected by the shared currency of silver and gold, most of it coming from Spanish possessions in the Americas and ending up in India, China, or Japan. Increasing European maritime dominance also meant that many global trade routes were partly under their control, and some of the profits from this trade moved back to Europe. The Atlantic slave trade was also immensely profitable for some European societies. However, this was not a period of European economic dominance. Asia's productivity and demand for currency was immense, and most of the wealth brought in to Europe from mines and plantations in Latin America simply moved eastward, where it was used to purchase Asian goods.

Rather than a centralized global economy, we must regard the global economic situation in 1700 as a decentralized commercial network. Some areas produced more trade goods than and imported more material than others, although there were several important centers. East and South Asia possessed especially large economies. Trade routes stretched from these regions around the Indian Ocean to the East Coast of Africa, across Eurasia to Europe and hence the Americas, and east through Southeast Asia and the Philippines directly to Latin America. Along a single long trade route, there might be many investors and profit might be shared by many different people and organizations—merchants, governments, bankers, and others. This system had some features of capitalism, as we will see, but it was not yet integrated and did not yet have the sophisticated banking and finance institutions it would enjoy in the long nineteenth century. It also had relatively little impact on the lives of most people. In general, livelihoods, production, and household economies were purely localized and neither produced for nor consumed much in the way of long-distance trade goods.

The struggle for financial dominance

By 1750, the beginning of the long nineteenth century, East and South Asian economic dominance had begun to decline dramatically, as northwestern Europe and later the east coast of North America became major global economic centers. But the swing to Europe and the Atlantic was slow. Other regions continued to be important producers as well. Silk from China, cotton cloth from India, agricultural products from Southeast Asia, and minerals from West Africa and the Americas were particularly important global commodities.

 In fact, many Eurasian societies shared an expansion of both consumption and productivity in the late eighteenth century that is sometimes called the **industrious revolution**. As trade between these regions expanded, growing middle classes began to buy more and more goods, stimulating the production of foodstuffs and manufactured products. In Japan, the expanding samurai class needed fine weapons and clothing that were considered as status symbols. In China, merchant classes aspired to the silk clothing and porcelain that had previously been used only by state officials and wealthy landowners. Around the world, small communities of traders and rulers were increasingly demanding finished products from abroad. To feed this demand, merchants, landowners, and artisans had to increase their production of saleable commodities, whether by putting more family members to work, engaging paid laborers, or acquiring slaves.

In the northeastern European states of Britain, France, and the Netherlands, for example, new land was put to producing food and marketable goods like wool, women were increasingly absorbed into the workforce, while merchants expanded their investments in such businesses as slave-worked plantations in the Caribbean colonies and cod-fishing fleets. It was in this region that the industrious revolution became the Industrial Revolution through the process described in the previous chapter. However, it was not industrialization alone that made this region the economic center of the world in the long nineteenth century. Rather, it was the combination of industrialization and the development of a robust capitalist system that gradually gave the region's bankers a global financial dominance.

The late eighteenth-century accumulation of capital in northwest Europe was the result of a combination of cultural, political, and economic factors that are still being debated today. At least some of these factors had to do with the region's position in global trade and its growing numbers of colonies. For example, the development of a European-dominated opium trade from South Asia to China in this period began to bring silver, paid by Chinese buyers in exchange for opium, back to Europe for the first time. The Atlantic slave trade also paid very high returns to European investors. At the same time, the overseas colonies were producing more and more food for European consumers, allowing landowners back in Europe to turn their land into capital that they could invest rather than using it to grow crops. Together, the labor of conquered Americans and enslaved Africans, and colonized South Asians directed huge amounts of money to the bankers and investors of northwest Europe. The people who profited were the financiers who would build the capitalist system that came to characterize the modern era.

Northwest Europe's capitalists also rapidly found ways to secure the aid of their governments. National governments in this region needed to secure vast amounts of money for wars they waged partly for control of global resources, trade routes, and financial assets. The cycle of war and money led directly to many of the global conflicts that characterized the late eighteenth century. The Seven Years War (1757–1764), for example, was fought over control of the fur trade from North America, textiles from South Asia, sugar from the Caribbean, and even the slave trade from West Africa. Thus it's no surprise that battles in this conflict took place in points as disparate as Calcutta, Quebec, and Nicaragua.

In a similar way, many of the great rebellions of this era were at least partly motivated by concern over capital and finance. The American Revolution that created the United States, for example, was partly the product of a growing class of merchants and shopkeepers who resisted the drain of their finances back to Britain in the form of taxes. Thus, the American Revolution can be partially characterized as a middle-class, capitalist revolution. The French Revolution, too, was partly catalyzed to an explosion of petty capitalism. In the 1780s, France was characterized by small factories and workshops employing hundreds of thousands of workers and backed by banks and investors. Many of these investors were engaged in trade with the colonies. However, their success was constrained by a range of special privileges that gave the aristocracy a monopoly on some businesses and also the competitive advantage of a lower tax rate. Resentment at these privileges drove the capitalist middle classes to support the revolution and gave them a leading role in the French Republic that emerged from the tumult that followed.

Nowhere was the link between capitalism and governance closer, however, than in Britain. It was not without reason that Britain (and especially England) was labeled a "nation of shopkeepers" by its greatest enemy of the era, Napoleon Bonaparte. Large numbers of British citizens were invested in both local and international businesses, from the shop down the street to slave trading vessels to the vast English (later British) East India Company. This mass petty capitalism was partly a product of the British parliamentary system of government, by which wealthy commoners—many of them investors, bankers, or business-owners—could serve in leadership roles. It was also partly the result of Britain's immense commerce and colonial reach. Together, these developments facilitated the growth of massive insurance companies like Lloyd's of London and government-private partnerships like the Bank of England. Finally, the strength of Britain's capitalist classes was interwoven with the growth of its industry, each reinforcing the other. These factors helped propel Britain into global financial dominance around the beginning of the nineteenth century.

The flourishing of capitalist society

Capitalist financing made the expansion of European trade possible in the late eighteenth century. It also stimulated markets and encouraged profit-seeking behavior in other parts of the world. By 1850, it would have been difficult to find a part of the world where capitalist activity wasn't present. Yet in most regions, capitalist economic exchange was only a small part of the economy and often marginal to local politics. In some areas, like much of West Africa, capitalism came to coexist with exchange systems based on wealthy men and women redistributing their assets through gifts in exchange for noble titles. In the vast Ottoman Empire, banking and merchant classes flourished, but enjoyed little government patronage. The same was true in China. In Japan, most international trade was restricted to the port of Nagasaki, and merchants and bankers were largely seen as being either unimportant or crude.

While capitalism initially lay lightly upon some societies, in Northwestern Europe, especially Britain and the Netherlands, it rapidly became deeply integrated into society and politics as financial classes accrued both power and status. In rural parts of these countries, capitalism took the form of large landowners controlling

Figure 5.2 Plan of Nagasaki showing the Dutch trading island (crescent shape at left), by Yamoto-Ya. Japanese authorities very carefully controlled capitalist trade with the rest of the world between 1638 and 1854, but never halted it.

vast enclosed fields. Indeed, this enclosure of large fields was central to modern European economics, since it allowed landowners to use their land as collateral when borrowing money, which could then be invested in new businesses. Many of the factories that began to dot the landscape began as mills owned by individuals or small groups of investors for processing grain, coal, steel, cotton and wool, or dozens of other products that emerged from local lands. The mills were worked by crews of people who were paid wages. These workers, many of them former peasants expelled from the land when it was enclosed, did not own their own tools or mills. In fact, they owned nothing but their own labor, which mill-owners sought to regulate and command. Such workers came to be known as the **proletariat.** They included not only peasants, but also laid-off soldiers, landless vagabonds, and outcasts. As the use of technology increased, trained workers came to be increasingly valuable. Specialized mill- and factory-working classes emerged, but their labor, too, was tightly controlled and regulated in most cases.

Mill-owners came to play an important role in government in northwest Europe. Yet they were not the only emerging wealthy class. Aside from the old aristocracy, which still hung on if with reduced power, mill-owners were also joined by a whole class of people who supported the new capitalist economy. These included lawyers who protected their property, bankers and financiers who loaned them the money to start their mills and insured them against calamity, and a range of lower middle-class businesspeople including shop-owners and artisans. Together, these groups made up a powerful political class—the **bourgeoisie**—even in states where there was no permanent parliament to represent their interests. They used their economic power to increasingly protect their growing property and wealth with laws and, if necessary, with the use of force. For example, soldiers in Britain broke up workers' protests in 1779 and 1796, following which Parliament prohibited workers' associations meant to fight the mill-owners for better wages and working conditions.

The intellectual justifications for capitalism

As with other powerful classes in history, the bourgeoisie sponsored philosophies and intellectual developments that supported and justified the economic system that sustained them. Many Enlightenment philosophers were happy to build a framework for incorporating capitalism into their philosophy of liberties and freedoms. In some cases, their philosophical works broke ground for new capitalist enterprises, while in others, they merely recognized changes already happening in the society around them.

Probably the most important Enlightenment-era proponent of capitalism was Adam Smith, who wrote his famous book *An Inquiry into the Nature and Causes of the Wealth of Nations* in 1776, just as the American Revolution was getting into full swing. Smith was a Professor of Moral Philosophy at the University of Glasgow, in Scotland. There was no such thing as an "economist" at the time, and Smith's work began from a philosophical, rather than a scientific, position. He argued that capitalism made sense on the basis of human nature, reasoning that humans were special among the animals of the world because they had a "propensity to truck, barter, and exchange." The best economic system, he argued would be similarly based on trade, since it was such a natural thing for humans to do. More importantly, Smith argued, such a system would work best if nobody interfered with it, but rather if it were left to operate in an unrestricted manner. Smith called this system a **free market**, meaning that goods, labor, and capital would be bought or sold for whatever they could fetch. In such cases, Smith argued, the prices for goods and services would naturally find their balance through a process that he called the **invisible hand.** By this metaphor he meant that natural forces would guide the markets better than government intervention. In the process, he believed that individual profit motives would lead to wider societal benefits.

> Every individual is continually exerting himself to find out the most advantageous employment for whatever capital he can command. It is his own advantage, indeed, and not that of the society which he has in view. But the study of his own advantage naturally, or rather necessarily, leads him to prefer that employment which is most advantageous to society… He intends only his own gain, and he is in this, as in many other cases, led by an invisible hand to promote an end which was not part of his intention.[1]

Smith believed that all markets should be free to find the right price for a good or service. He even extended this to his own job as an educator, proposing that teachers should be paid by their popularity among students!

Smith believed that such free markets were tied to **free labor**. In other words, he maintained that all individuals should be paid as laborers according to what they could get for their work. This position was a significant challenge to existing economic systems, for it rejected both slavery and serfdom, both of which tied an individual to unpaid labor. Smith argued that these forms of labor were unproductive and should be abandoned. To some degree, these arguments formed the economic basis of the antislavery movement that emerged in Britain at the end of the eighteenth century. At the same time, Smith had no problem with some individuals acquiring enormous wealth while others were paid insignificant wages, so long as that is what the market ordained.

Nor was Smith alone in believing that it was okay to accrue large amounts of wealth while others remained poor. Around the same time, the Scottish philosopher David Hume was writing a number of widely read books that argued that trade was good, and so was greed. In the 1741 volume *Of the Independence of Parliament*, he stated that "greed must be made insatiable… ambition beyond measure, and all… vices profitable for the public good."[2] Like Smith, Hume believed that individual pursuit of profit was the root of progress.

Smith and Hume helped to transform British economic policy in the late eighteenth century from protectionist mercantilism to free-market capitalism. Of course, Britain had a major advantage in making this transformation. Because it was the most industrialized country in the world and had a production price advantage, Britain could afford to push for open markets, and British companies could sell their goods on those markets at relatively low prices. However, not all proponents of modern capitalist thought were British. Jean-Baptiste Say, a French merchant, ran a cotton mill and felt that his business suffered because of France's many restrictions and regulations concerning trade. In *Catechism of Political Economy*, he presented the idea that people added value to goods and in so doing created wealth, which he believed should be seen by governments as an important role individuals played in broader society. Thus, he argued, capitalism was an ethical good:

Q: How can the value that things already have be increased?
A: By increasing the degree of usefulness which existed in them when they were acquired… To produce is to give value to things by giving them a use
Q: To whom do the products created each day in a nation belong?
A: They belong to the industrious, the capitalists, and the landowners, who, either by themselves or by means of their tools, are the creators of these products, and are consequently what we call producers.[3]

These were merely the first philosophers who helped to create a growing field in the nineteenth century: economics. As modern capitalism extended around the world, new generations of thinkers began to elaborate on—and in some cases alter—Smith's work. One of the most important of these was John Stuart Mill, who was the father of the philosophy known as **utilitarianism**. This was the liberal philosophy that all decisions should be based on promoting the greatest happiness for the greatest number of people. In general, Mill believed that free-market economies met this test, and he supported Smith's idea of unregulated markets, which he termed **laissez-faire** capitalism from the French words for "leave alone." Mill, however, also believed that individuals should pay taxes and accept some limitation of their economic freedoms in favor of social good. He also came, over time, to believe that it was fair for workers to organize into collectives.

Hume, Smith, Say, and Mill are among the most important intellectuals of the eighteenth century, for they helped to spell out the justification and operation of modern capitalism. Even in their day, their work was called revolutionary by their supporters and held up as a blueprint for a better future. The great British liberal and supporter of the American Revolution Thomas Paine wrote in 1791 of his hopes: "The landholder, the farmer, the manufacturer, the merchant, the tradesman, and every occupation, prospers by aid which each receive from the other, and from the whole. Common interest regulates their concern, and forms their law."[4] Viewing the world around him, Paine truly hoped that such a capitalist utopia would come to pass: global, egalitarian, and enriching everyone.

Industrial capitalism

Late eighteenth-century philosophy, as much as economic development on both sides of the Atlantic, laid the groundwork for the global high capitalism of the nineteenth century. Yet the economic world that actually existed in the 1800s did not quite match Paine's hopes. Instead of ushering in a utopia, industrialized capitalism had chained as many people as it freed, and impoverished more than it enriched. In fact, capitalism in the nineteenth century tended to concentrate great wealth in the hands of just a few people in a few regions. On a global scale, this meant that some societies became capitalist **core states**. These states tended to have the greatest economies, the strongest centralized governments, and the most advanced technologies and infrastructures. Capitalist core states were often one and the same as the industrialized societies and imperial metropoles described in earlier chapters. By contrast, many parts of the world became part of the capitalist **periphery.** These societies tended to produce raw materials rather than possessing large industries, to have relatively weak or decentralized governments, and in some cases were formal or informal colonies of core states. Most of these states were found outside of Europe and North America in the nineteenth century. Cores and peripheries also functioned on a smaller scale. In many regions, like large parts of Latin America, big cities formed cores while rural areas served as their economic peripheries.

Industrial capitalism in Europe and the United States

Nineteenth-century capitalism was increasingly closely connected to industrialization. While land ownership and commerce remained important economic factors, development in this period was focused more than ever on the mill and the factory, the energy (mostly coal) needed to feed them, and the railroads and canals to transport the goods they made to market. In northwest and Central Europe, the United States, and later other regions, people who had wealth poured it into new factories and the infrastructure that fed them. These investments underwrote the Industrial Revolution, and hence we call this form of economy **industrial capitalism.**

Industrial capitalism radically altered the social structure of the societies it came to define. In the first place, factories and mills rapidly put many artisans out of work, so that the number of independent blacksmiths, potters, and weavers who had defined early modern economies rapidly declined. At the same time, the number of workers engaged in capitalist production rose rapidly. In Great Britain, for example, the number of workers in industry rose from 1.4 million in 1801 to 5.3 million in 1871. We have already seen what industrial life was like, but for economic purposes we must regard all of these workers as **wage earners**. Rather than producing food for themselves or making a profit out of their own handicrafts, they were paid money for the time they worked. As wage earners, they bought just about everything they needed from shops: their clothes, their food, the goods they needed for daily life. Thus in addition to being workers, they became **consumers** of finished products. Their demand for consumable goods in turn drove factories to produce even more. The availability of manufactured goods, and the need to pay for them, further drove the demand for more workers. Together, this cycle created a spiral of capitalism and industrialization.

Above the working classes, of course, sat the bourgeoisie. You will remember that these were individuals who had something to sell or some capital to invest other than their own labor. In nineteenth-century industrialized societies, what the bourgeoisie largely owned was not so much land but rather **stocks** in businesses, banks, mills, and factories. These were equal parts into which companies were divided so that many people could pool their funds in a single company or business. Increasingly, they also owned government and private **bonds**. These were loans made by individuals to the state or private organizations in return for a promised repayment with interest in the future.

Industrial capitalism had the potential to create some very rich people. Stocks, bonds, and other financial instruments were more efficient and legally enforceable than earlier agreements, and they helped to funnel money into innovation and economic development. This kind of innovation could be very rewarding. However, the misuse of financial instruments also caused great hardship. A number of economic **bubbles** occurred in the nineteenth century. In each of these, investors lost huge amounts of their money, mostly due to fraud. The result was economic ruin for many. At the same time, workers were often mistreated in order to increase the profits of stockholders. Sometimes, the whole system just broke down. The most dramatic example was the Long Depression of 1873–1879. Reflecting the new technology and communication speed of the industrial age as well as the global interconnectedness of markets, this depression started with a crisis of confidence in the Habsburg capital of Vienna on May 8, 1873 and rapidly spread. In the United States, several companies failed on September 18 and the New York Stock Exchange had to close temporarily soon after. In Chile, the price of wheat and silver dropped dramatically. In Britain, the economic growth rate was immediately halved. The Long Depression proved that global markets were now inextricably linked in a capitalist system.

Global commodities

In the international capitalist economic system of the nineteenth century, raw materials and finished products were sent back and forth across vast distances. In the previous era, long-distance trade had been more restricted and focused on expensive luxuries like silver, ivory, furs, and opium. Even everyday goods like cloth had been too expensive to ship long distances. In the nineteenth century, however, industrial technology and steam-powered transportation made possible the movement of more commonplace, everyday goods. Some of these, like palm oil, were the raw materials of the industrial system itself. Others were mainly the products of industry. Money and people flowed around the world following the demands of capital.

Undoubtedly the king of nineteenth-century long-distance trade goods was cotton. Textile industry based on cotton developed in France, the United States, Belgium, and even Russia in this era. The indisputable center of the cotton world, however, was Britain, and especially the city of Manchester. More than 30 factories were built in this city between 1820 and 1830 alone. Manchester was connected to the port of Liverpool, once a large slave-trading port but destined to grow into one of the world's greatest trading cities based on the cotton industry. British merchants, seeking supplies for this growing sector of their economy, promoted the cultivation of cotton around the world. A great deal was grown in the southern United States and in Latin America, but since it was subject to taxes imposed by the governments of those regions, British merchants instead sought in areas where they could control pricing and where there would be no additional taxes. Thus cotton fields sprang up across British-occupied South Asia and Egypt, which at first had its own processing industry but later came under British control.

Cotton production really spread far and wide in the 1860s, when the Civil War cut off supplies from the southern United States. Spanish Cuba rapidly switched from sugar to cotton. Egyptian production took off in this era, helping the government of Muhammad Ali to finance an expanding army and bureaucracy. The French Emperor Napoleon III unsuccessfully invaded Mexico partly in the hope of gaining control of a cotton-producing region. Russian merchants hatched a plan to grow cotton in areas of Central Asia, following a rapidly planned invasion of the region. The conclusion of the Civil War in 1865 then led to a surplus of cotton on the market, and reinstated the United States to its position as the dominant power in cotton production. The resulting crash in cotton prices contributed to massive financial crises in Egypt, India, and other states and may have contributed to the worldwide depression that was just a half-decade away.

If cotton was an obvious candidate for a great global commodity, guano was entirely obscure before 1830. Guano is nothing more than the feces of birds, but it makes excellent fertilizer for growing all sorts of crops because it is rich in nitrogen, phosphate, and potassium. In general, guano is only economical to collect in places where large numbers of birds nested closely together, and such concentrated nesting sites are rare. They exist, however, on small Pacific Islands, where thousands or even millions of large sea birds nested year after year. In fact, the richest guano sources in the nineteenth-century world were islands off the coast of Chile and Peru, where the Inca and their ancestors had been mining limited amounts of the fertilizer for thousands of years. In the 1830s, large companies became aware of this source of fertilizer and began to exploit these islands. The trade was so profitable that wars were fought for control of these islands, including the Chincha Islands War between Spain on the one side and Peru and Chile on the other and also the War of the Pacific which pitted Chile against Bolivia and Peru.

In general, the profits made from the guano didn't go to the local people or even to the workers, mostly from Polynesia and China, who were brought in to collect and process the guano. Rather, the companies that dominated the guano trade were largely from industrial societies—Britain and the United States especially. Even when Peru managed to reserve a large portion of the trade for Peruvian companies, it fell into a trap of borrowing money from European banks using guano as its collateral. When the guano ran out, Peru found itself suddenly bankrupt.

Not all of the commodities that flowed around the world had obvious productive value like guano or cotton. Gold, for example, had little value to industry at this time. However, its very rarity made it valuable, and governments as well as traders around the world agreed to recognize this value as an international currency. Increasingly in the nineteenth century, countries adopted the **gold standard.** This meant that their currency was considered to be worth a certain amount of gold. Other countries put themselves on a silver standard, backing their money with silver, although this became rarer over the course of the century.

The gold standard was made possible partly by the discovery of gold in new areas of the world that were increasingly being brought under European control over the course of the century. In North America, significant deposits of gold were discovered in California (1849) and in Alaska (1896). Gold strikes also occurred in British-occupied Australia (1851) and New Zealand (1861), and at the southern tip of South America (1884). Finally, the biggest strike of all occurred just outside of the British colony in South Africa in 1886. A decade later, the mines in this region were producing almost a quarter of the world's gold.

Laborers, miners, investors, bankers, and industrialists all flooded into the gold-bearing regions in massive gold rushes. Some miners would travel from one strike to another, following the opening of new mines from California to Australia and finally South Africa. Meanwhile, most of the gold flowed rapidly from periphery regions to financial cores—especially London and New York, but also Buenos Aires and Amsterdam.

Oligarchies in the United States, Latin America, and Japan

Over the course of the nineteenth century, industrial capitalism proved its adaptability to unique social and political situations in many parts of the world. Three places where specialized forms of capitalism developed in this period were in the United States, Spanish- and Portuguese-speaking Latin America, and Japan. In each case, economic and political power came to be concentrated in the hands of relatively small groups of very wealthy individuals—known collectively as **oligarchies**.

The economic system that developed in the newly emerging United States at the beginning of the nineteenth century was somewhat distinct from European capitalism. Land was more freely available to colonists, allowing for the creation of a large class of people who had capital tied up in land ownership. The country at first also wasn't highly integrated, meaning that there were many small markets rather than a few large ones. Moreover, the U.S. Constitution balanced federal rights to control commerce and industry with that of states and individuals. One result of this balance was the development of a variety of different economic systems in one country. In large northern states like New York, an exceptional diversification of products and industries developed. In others, especially parts of the South, older-style plantation economies specializing in single crops like rice or cotton predominated.

Over the course of the nineteenth century, this situation shifted radically. A massive burst of infrastructural construction tied together the different regions in the United States in the 1850s and 1860s and helped to spread massive privately owned firms that concentrated wealth in the hands of a relatively small group. The relative weakness of the Federal U.S. government and the lack of coordination between states meant that these firms were difficult to regulate in this vast country. By the late nineteenth century, an era of big business had emerged led by wealthy industrialists and financiers like John D. Rockefeller and Jay Gould who wielded massive economic and political power. Their political power helped them to manipulate a political system friendly to industrial capitalism, which as a result had few restrictions on individual accumulation of wealth. In this environment, big business leaders found that they could build vast, largely unregulated industries employing tens of thousands of relatively low-paid workers. Together with the availability of land in the western United States, their demand for labor helped to draw millions of immigrants to the country, but many arrived to find a system that favored business-owners over workers.

In the Spanish-speaking Americas, as well, small groups came to control much of the region's capital, or wealth, by the late nineteenth century. These oligarchs were not industrialists, but rather principally the owners of vast hacienda estates that grew raw materials and foodstuffs to feed workers and factories in Britain and the United States.

For a long time, historians argued that this continuous rural, agricultural focus on Latin American economies was a result of something intrinsic to the Spanish rule. However, the fact is that this region had a trajectory similar to that in the U.S. South and the English-speaking Caribbean until the nineteenth century. It failed to industrialize significantly in this period in part because of long legacies of inequality such as slavery and hacienda labor, which kept most of the local population from either buying goods or having money to invest. But this situation was exacerbated by the regional dominance of Britain and later the United States. The industries of these two countries demanded raw materials from Latin America. They found suppliers in the landowners of Latin America, who saw good money for themselves in providing sugar, guano, rubber, meat, tobacco, cotton, metal, and other resources. British, U.S., and even French banks were willing to fund this trade, loaning money to Latin American governments and landowners, usually at high interest rates. Together, the international financiers and local hacienda-owners used their money to control elections. Thus by the late nineteenth century, political and economic power were highly concentrated in the hands of just a few wealthy families. For the rest of the country, these arrangements led to a system of dependence, as described in the previous chapter, as the Latin American economics concentrated on selling raw materials and buying finished products, in the process leaving most of the profit to the industrial economies.

Japan, also, witnessed the development of economic oligarchies in the nineteenth century, in this case following the Meiji Restoration of 1868. As we have seen, the new government of Japan was deeply involved in industry, bringing shipyards, mines, and foundries under governmental control. Yet they did so in partnership with well-connected private individuals. A small oligarchy of very wealthy family corporations—such as the Mitsui, Mitsubishi, Sumitomo, and Yasuda—provided much of the funding and made much of the profit from these industries. They even organized themselves into a proto-governmental group known as the *zaibatsu*. Closely tied to the new Meiji rulers, this group had a huge influence on the creation of laws as well as foreign policy in the late nineteenth and early twentieth centuries.

Japan's commercial oligarchy and its government allies were particularly obsessed with controlling overseas areas rich in metals, foodstuffs, and other raw materials. Japan had a large population and hence plenty of workers, but few natural resources of its own. While the military and government saw overseas occupation as necessary for strategic and industrial development, commercial oligarchs saw Korea, China, and the Pacific Islands as places to put their capital to work through profitable investments, particularly because labor wages could be kept artificially low by Japanese imperial rule. It was this convergence of interests that led to such actions as the annexation of Korea in 1910.

Gentlemanly capitalism

Of course, Japan was not the only country whose empire-building was closely tied to financial and industrial concerns. Britain, France, the Netherlands, and the United States also built their empires in the late nineteenth century to not only provide resources and create demand for their growing industries but also to find places to invest for profit. It is not without reason that the great burst of empire-building known as the new imperialism occurred almost immediately following the long depression of 1873–1879. The new markets of the colonies held out the promise of a way out of economic stagnation.

One central debate in understanding this economic model of empire is how to separate the role of finance from that of industry. It's all very well to argue that empires were created to funnel raw materials into (and create markets for) European, Japanese, and U.S. industries, and another to suggest that support for empire was strong among bankers and financiers. Yet some scholars have noted that financiers and bankers played a bigger role than have factory owners, especially for Great Britain. This model of imperialism is called **gentlemanly capitalism**, and it suggests that the British Empire was largely the project of a commercial class of investors with plenty of money, most of whom lived in London. These individuals invested heavily in international trade and in government bonds that built roads, rail, and ports in the colonies, and they reaped huge profits from it. Because of these profits, they were the biggest supporters of imperialism. Of course, critics of this theory argue that factory owners, military officials, and settlers were also big supporters, but the role of bankers and investors can't be ignored. Financiers may have played a similar role in the Japanese, French, German, and U.S. empires.

Certainly, empire entailed the movement of vast sums of money and hence the potential for vast profit. Some of this potential had to do with the economic dependency of the colonies on the imperial metropole. Raw materials could be brought in from the colonies at rapid rates in many cases. France, for example, depended on foodstuffs from Algeria to feed factory workers and rubber from Indochina for automobile and other major industries. At the same time, finished products flowed back to the colonies. There was a great deal of profit in these trades.

However, a lot of the financial opportunity created by empire had to do with building infrastructure. Money to pay for roads, railways, ports, and stations was usually raised through government bonds or private stock offerings. Many investors saw significant profits from the interest paid on these local colonial bonds. The construction of huge, transnational infrastructure projects offered the potential for even greater rewards. European bankers flocked to invest in the Suez Canal that linked the Mediterranean to the Red Sea in Egypt, for example, and American investors poured money into the Panama Canal linking the Pacific and Atlantic Oceans. Of course, investors wanted to make sure their money was safely invested, and thus empire frequently followed capitalism. Britain occupied Egypt in 1882 largely to protect its control over the Suez Canal, and the United States intervened heavily in Panamanian politics at the beginning of the twentieth century to ensure the security and profitability of the canal.

Thus, through rapid empire-building that characterized the last decades of the nineteenth century, large parts of the world were drawn into the capitalist world economy. Railroads played an enormous role in this expansion of capitalism, just as they helped to spread empire. Russian rule over vast areas of central Asia was possible by a railroad that by the early twentieth century stretched all the way from the Moscow to the Pacific Coast. Along this railway, large groups of once self-supporting nomadic pastoralists became wage-workers on large cotton plantations, while previously self-sufficient Siberians increasingly became wage-laboring lumberjacks, cutting down timber to be shipped west to Europe. In the western parts of North America, as well, the construction of transcontinental railroads meant that the barter and exchange networks of the central plains and the west were replaced by money economies in which currency paid for local goods like hides and crops and went out again in exchange for industrial finished products.

Figure 5.3 Chinese gold miners in California, during the 1849 gold rush. The mania for gold brought immigrants and migrant workers from many parts of the world.

By the end of the nineteenth century, a connected, global capitalist economy truly dominated the world like never before. To be sure, small communities refused to be integrated or were so far from financial centers that they escaped integration. In the South Pacific, populations like those of the interior of Papua New Guinea continued to develop an economy in which social status depended on wealthy people giving gifts. In the Kalahari Desert of southern Africa, a nonmonetary, family-based exchange system continued to flourish. However, these areas were increasingly few and small.

This is not to say that capitalism was just always or entirely forced on new populations around the world against their will. In many cases, locals adopted capitalist economies willingly because they perceived some potential profit. Often, they came to desire industrial-produced goods both as good values and high-status items. At the same time, however, as local exchange systems dwindled and land was given to settlers, many people adapted to wage-working lifestyles and joined the global capitalist economy only because they had little choice.

Possession and dispossession

Capitalism helped to create enormous wealth and facilitate its movement around the world. But while intended to reward individual entrepreneurship and ability, the market in reality gave advantages and disadvantages to different groups based partly on class, race, nationality, and gender. Thus the new economy, rather than treating all equally, helped to create groups of haves and have-nots unevenly distributed across the world.

Bourgeois values and aspirations

Social class, or the ordering of society into groups by social and economic status, has existed in many places and times. For example, many rural agricultural societies before 1750 had longstanding distinctions between high class aristocrats and lower class peasants, often with smaller groups of artisans and merchants in between. However, the modern social class system is largely a product of industrial capitalism. Specifically, the introduction of capitalism saw the emergence of two distinct social classes: the middle-class bourgeoisie of shop and factory owners, professionals, and financiers, and beneath them the lower class proletariat of workers. Admittedly, this change generally took place slowly and exhibited unique features in each society and location. Nevertheless, we cannot talk about capitalism in the long nineteenth century without talking about this modern system of social class.

The bourgeoisie of the industrial capitalist system were the people who organized, owned, and managed the capitalist economic system. In much of Europe and Japan, the growing economic clout of this middle class diminished or even replaced the authority of the old elites—the landowning aristocrats. This middle class had different degrees of power and authority in different regions. In the United States, there was no large preexisting aristocratic elite. Hence the middle class managed to seize control of the economic system very easily. In some parts of the world, like Latin America, the Ottoman Empire, and Russia, the middle class was either integrated into or suppressed by the aristocratic elites. In a few areas, like Korea, a large bourgeoisie emerged but remained marginal to an economy that continued to be based on large-scale agricultural and artisanal production. In many colonies, the emergence of a local bourgeoisie was suppressed by the arrival of settlers and representatives of companies operating from the metropole.

Even within a single society, the real experiences of various members of the "middle class" could be quite different. At the top of middle-class society in London, for example, were some very wealthy commercial merchants and bankers and their families. These families owned large houses and employed numerous servants. They tended to be educated at the "best" schools, which were not necessarily academically oriented but rather taught the skills thought necessary for success in life—sports, classical history and languages, and sociability. They ate well, with cooks preparing meals with multiple courses at every sitting. On the lower end of the scale in the same society were the clerks, schoolmasters, journeyman artisans, and lesser clergy who had reasonable education and professional attributes but very little money. They often lived in small apartments, could not afford to employ servants, and ate very simply. Despite these broad differences, both of these groups saw themselves as middle class—neither as decadent as the aristocracy nor poor like the working classes.

One thing that drew all of these members of the British middle classes together was an aspiration to be recognized as being moral, political, and economic citizens. These aspiration often took the form of trying to be "gentlemen" and "ladies," in the language of nineteenth- century Britain. This meant that whatever their actual experiences, members of the British bourgeoisie tried to perform as models of the middle class. They attempted to dress and act to an idealized vision of a proper, Christian individual. Men espoused a code of honor, especially toward women and children. They rejected "vulgar" occupations like heavy labor. They joined clubs and took part in sports, including hunting. Women were expected to act with a sense of reserve and propriety. Middle-class families also purchased objects that would be easily seen as "middle class"—from fire insurance to three-piece suits. The ultimate middle-class possession was the piano, many of which were bought by families who could not really afford them. Having servants was also a mark of status. The middle class read novels and newspapers. They joined particular churches—especially Baptist and Methodist congregations—although Jews, Calvinists, and Catholics could to various degrees be accepted as class equals. Perhaps most of all, the middle class proved their virtue by "taking care" of the poor through evangelical societies, workhouses, and hospitals.

In general, of course, the members of the middle class were capitalists. Their place of business may have been a factory, mill, or field, but it was just as likely an office. Like the modern middle class, the modern office is a product of this time. Among the earliest purpose-built office buildings was the London headquarters of the East India Company, built in 1729. In this building, large numbers of clerks were employed in open areas, with individual offices reserved for managers. The clerk's workday was hard and boring, generally involving copying correspondence into letter books day in and day out. They also had to sign in every 15 minutes to prove that they weren't taking breaks. Managers had it somewhat easier, with long lunches and afternoons at the club. In some ways, little has changed.

Outside of Britain, of course, local conditions and ideas tended to influence the values of the middle class. However, some British and European values were globalized both because of colonialism and because of the economic strength of their corporations. West African commercial middlemen joined Christian denominations like the Baptists and took to dressing in three-piece suits. Chinese clerks working for the British banks took to reading English-language newspapers. Indian professionals ate toast with their tea. Yet this emulation left many of these individuals caught between local and European values. In economic terms, many of them came from societies that were less intensely capitalist, and often their extended families had the right or moral privilege to make demands on their income. Thus they had to both afford the trappings of the middle class and pay their own social and family obligations, a very difficult balancing act to perfect.

Workers' experiences

The middle class, however, was proportionally quite small. Most of the population of any nineteenth-century capitalist society were workers—individuals with no assets other than their labor, which they provided to farm, mine, or factory in exchange for a wage. In the capitalist system, these workers had to offer their labor on a free market. In principle, this meant that when there wasn't enough labor, they could charge high rates and get good wages. As the global population rose dramatically in this period, however, there were often labor surpluses, which meant that wages tended to remain low and large numbers of people were unemployed.

We have already explored working-class labor conditions in fields and factories in Chapter 4. However, the capitalist economic system shaped workers' lives outside of the workplace, as well. In urban areas like London, Paris, and New York, low wages were exacerbated by a lack of housing. Slum tenements were often thrown up to house large families who could pay little. They were owned by landlords who charged as much and put in as little maintenance work as they possibly could. Small rooms,

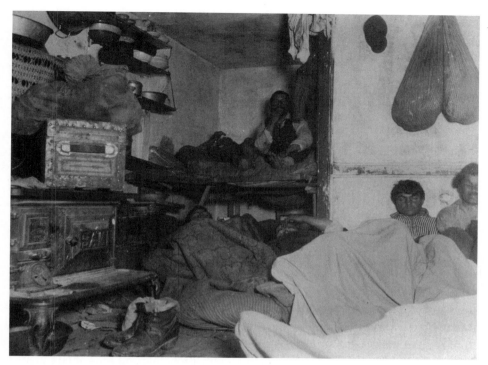

Figure 5.4 Jacob August Riis, untitled, 1890. These were typical living conditions for workers in New York tenements.

often without attached toilets, might be inhabited by dozens of people. In these tenements, people had to dump their waste into drains and sewers, often the same ones from which they got their drinking water. Homeless children wandered the streets. The middle class were not always sympathetic to this suffering. Their value code often implied that the poor deserved their poverty. The bourgeoisie tended to blame bad values for poverty, arguing that the poor wasted their money, gambled, and drank. In many cases, as this 1848 hymn suggests, they believed that poverty was God's will:

The rich man in his castle,
The poor man at his gate,
God made them, high and lowly,
And order[e]d their estate[5]

The capitalist financial system also contributed to periodic catastrophes that afflicted the poor. This was especially true in the case of famines. Most famines began with changes in the environment—diseases that struck crops or the lack of rainfall. However, industrial capitalism contributed to the suffering that followed. During the Irish potato blight of the 1840s, for example, free trade laws restricted the sale of food grown in Ireland to the starving. Ireland was under British rule at the time, and British landowners knew they could make more money selling their crops (other than potatoes) to English and foreign markets rather than distributing them to the starving Irish population. When some British leaders tried to pass laws that would have diverted the food to famine-stricken areas, they were defeated by "free trade" legislators.

Another famine in South Asia, in the 1890s, was made worse by the decline of the artisanal weaving occupation. Traditionally, weaving was the main occupation for those who could not farm, and in times of famine people turned to weaving to make money to buy food from abroad. But weaving jobs had moved to factories in Britain, and there was therefore no fallback occupation was available to farmers whose crops had failed. Meanwhile, British India continued to export grain in this period despite the famine, because it brought higher prices abroad than within India.

Industrial capitalism was complicit in very high levels of violence and exploitation through its integration with colonialism. The economies of colonies were often operated through a **concession** system, by which a colonial government would grant monopolies to companies operating out of Europe, the United States, or Japan. Such monopolies were not the kind of free markets that Adam Smith and other capitalist thinkers had imagined, but instead restricted free labor and the development of a free labor market. Nevertheless, they were highly profitable and thus often pursued by alliances of colonial administrations and industrial corporations. Because the concessionary companies had a monopoly, and because colonial subjects had few rights and no votes, these regimes were often highly violent and abusive toward their workers. Perhaps the most brutal example was the Congo "Free State," which from 1885 to 1908 was run as King Leopold of Belgium's personal rubber-gathering corporation. Entire communities were press-ganged into collecting rubber day in and day out. As a result, a large portion of the population died from disease, malnutrition, overwork, and sometimes execution. In 1904, British diplomat Roger Casement reported on the economic exploitation:

> [A] fleet of steamers … navigate the main river and its principal affluents at fixed intervals. A railway, excellently constructed in view of the difficulties to be encountered, now connects the ocean ports with Stanley Pool… [Yet] … A careful investigation of the conditions of native life around (Lake Mantumba) confirmed the truth of the statements made to me—that the great decrease in population, the dirty and ill-kept towns, and the complete absence of goats, sheep, or fowls—once very plentiful in this country—were to be attributed above all else to the continued effort made during many years to compel the natives to work india-rubber… Two cases (of mutilation) came to my actual notice while I was in the lake district. One, a young man, both of whose hands had been beaten off with the butt ends of rifles against a tree; the other a young lad of 11 or 12 years of age, whose right hand was cut off at the wrist… In both these cases the Government soldiers had been accompanied by white officers whose

names were given to me. Of six natives (one a girl, three little boys, one youth, and one old woman) who had been mutilated in this way during the rubber regime, all except one were dead at the date of my visit.

As Casement's report makes clear, the colony had been set up for resource extraction, with steamboats and railroads ready to take away the products harvested by forced labor under the most brutal of regimes. Perhaps this was an extreme case of colonial rapacity, but it was also representative of the distorted form of capitalism that was often implemented in the colonies.

Capitalism and the family

Capitalism brought with it a particular concept of what constituted the family, one with which we are generally familiar today. For most societies in the past, the family was defined by connections between large, extended groups of kin who were reliant upon each other either through formal rules of obligation or informal customs. Beginning in the late eighteenth century, however, the strengthening of capitalism helped to contribute to the idea of the **nuclear family**, headed by a single man, married to a woman, and their children. The nuclear family had the advantage of allowing the head of the household—usually a man—to legally monopolize his capital (money, land, etc.) and to pass it on only to his direct descendants rather than to share it with more distant relatives. It was, in many ways, the representation of the capitalist doctrine of individual wealth in the form of the family.

Within the nuclear family, men were generally expected to work to raise capital or receive a wage, and women were generally expected to work only at home. Of course, this wasn't realistic for most of the working classes, who needed two incomes to support their families. Thus, to be able to keep one's wife from working outside the home was, to many men in capitalist societies, a sign of having entered the bourgeoisie or the upper classes.

The principle of the wage-earning father and the domestic mother was reinforced over time by both laws that defined property rights and moral ideas about what was respectable. But underneath the surface, many people lived different lives. Women continued to work outside of the home, not only because they had to, but sometimes out of choice. Nor was the nuclear family as rigid in practice as it was in theory. Families also often took in or adopted their cousins and more distant relatives. Married or not, plenty of men and women had children with multiple partners. If one were to look deeper, same-sex relationships also existed in capitalist societies.

Economically, however, the laws that defined nuclear family operated to preserve capital within a line of direct descent, passed most often from father to children, thus allowing wealthy families to protect their money and possessions. In many regions of the world, such arrangements were novel and strange. A more communal sense of family and inheritance still survived. But the laws regulating the nuclear family frequently spread with the expansion of empires, and gained ground in many parts of the world. In some West African societies, for example, property had historically passed through the female line, so that men would pass on some of their possessions to their sister's children, as well as to their own. This tended to stabilize larger families and tie them together. By the early twentieth century, however, many men in this region of the world were adopting the nuclear family model and passing on their property and money only to their own, biological children.

Socialism

By 1850, industrial capitalism seemed to be conquering the world. Just at the moment, however, a number of alternatives emerged from within the very societies working hardest to spread it. The most powerful of these critiques proved to be the doctrine of socialism, which proposed to eliminate social classes and hierarchies and promised to improve the lives of workers. The emergence of this socialist critique was a long and convoluted road, and it was never widely implemented in the period before the First World War, but it nevertheless plays an important role in the history of the long nineteenth century.

Capitalism's discontents

As capitalism became the dominant economic system around the world, it transformed peasants, artisans, and farmers into wage-workers. Not all were happy with these changes, and opposition to capitalism was as swift as its rise and spread. Sometimes, this opposition seemed to be merely a set of complaints about specific working conditions and wages. Sometimes it took the form of resistance to the monetary system and wage-earning lifestyle as a whole. It's difficult to see the full picture of this opposition to industrial capitalism in the historical record because a lot of it took the form of individual actions that aren't obvious or large scale. Workers who felt like their wages were insufficient or who were suffering from diseases caused by poor working conditions would usually resort to small-scale protests. Often these included choosing to work slow, avoiding hard tasks, sabotaging their machines in difficult-to-detect ways, or stealing from their employers.

Over time, however, opposition to capitalist wage labor and its abuses became more highly organized. Because of Britain's early industrialization, some of the first organized incidents of resistance occurred in Britain, where workers who could no longer grow their own food protested the rising food prices and low wages as early as the 1720s. Other protests came from farmers who had lost their land and artisans whose livelihoods had been replaced by factory machinery. Blaming industrialization for their troubles, these groups attacked threshing machines and machine looms. Assuming the name **luddites**, some workers continued to smash machines and protest industrialization into the 1810s. Other protests were aimed at free trade laws that kept the price of grain high, leading to famine in parts of Ireland and Scotland and increasing to poverty in England.

Gradually, however the protests began to assume a new tone in which employers, rather than machines, were seen as the source of problems. Workers learned to combine their efforts through **trade and labor unions**, organizations that brought together people in similar occupations for joint action. In Britain and elsewhere, laws were passed to restrict these unions, but they weren't entirely successful. In 1818, the first really effective workers' union, the General Union of Trades (GUT), was established in the City of Manchester. Its leaders tried to bring together workers in many trades and in other cities—including shipbuilders and silk weavers in London. Although the GUT was suppressed soon after, it became a model for others that soon followed.

As capitalism stretched into new areas, unions began to pop up in response all around the world. In southern Africa, Zulu men who washed clothes organized themselves into the Washerman's Guild beginning in the 1860s. In India, a loosely affiliated set of organizations led a series of rebellions and strikes, often supported by unemployed weavers. Railway workers, of whom there were 400,000 in India during the 1860s, were especially well organized. Their strikes were often incited by violence from European overseers, including the frequent, casual beating and sometimes murder of workers for "insolence."

Employers and their government allies responded to unions and strikes through a variety of strategies, but divide-and-conquer was perhaps the most effective. For example, in order to head off unions in India, the British exploited and widened preexisting social divisions among the many hereditary occupation groups, or **castes**, of the colony. In the United States, employers and the government tried to stop the organization of unions by exploiting racial and ethnic divisions. When one group of workers went on strike, members of a different ethnicity were brought. For example, Slavic immigrants were often pitted against African Americans and Latinos. Nevertheless, unions steadily gained strength in the late nineteenth-century United States, striking against big businesses such as steel mills, mines, and machinery companies. Employers resorted to force to suppress the strikes, sometimes leading to violent clashes. Perhaps the most famous was the Homestead Strike at the Carnegie Steel factory in Pennsylvania, where private security opened fire upon the strikers and their families, leading to a pitched battle that was settled in the company's favor only with the support of the U.S. Army.

As this example illustrates, governments tended to side more with employers than with strikers. This association meant that strikes and opponents of capitalism sometimes became antigovernment rebellions. This kind of rebellion became more common in the early years of the twentieth century. The 1905 Russian Revolution is a case in point. It emerged from the fertile ground of long-standing poverty of rural peasants, who earned so little money that they could not buy food, pay taxes, or purchase land to improve their situation. The peasants made common cause with the growing urban working class. Many of the new factories in which they worked had terrible conditions including shifts longer than 12 hours, fines for mistakes, and the lowest wages in Europe. The workers began to organize in the last years of the nineteenth century, and by 1902, a number of strikes began at factories around the country. They enlisted peasants and student support. The result was a near civil war that left thousands of workers killed or imprisoned before the government regained power.

A not dissimilar pattern brought about open conflict in 1910 in Mexico, where the government of Porfirio Diáz was similarly promoting industrialization but doing little to help the rural peasantry laboring on big haciendas. More than 95 percent of Mexico was owned by a wealthy 5 percent of the population, while workers labored in perpetual debt. When dissenters like Emiliano Zapata and Pancho Villa raised the flag of rebellion against the hacienda system, peasants and workers flocked to their banners. Their movement set off a civil war. Despite conflicts between moderate constitutionalists and radicals, these rebels eventually overthrew Diáz, and put in place a number of reforms meant to help workers and peasants.

The emergence of the socialist critique

While the 1905 Russian Revolution and the 1910 Mexican Revolution were outpourings of anger and frustration, they were also manifestations of a philosophical and ideological alternative to capitalism in the form of socialism. **Socialism** can be described as an economic theory of organization that places the control over assets— factories, markets, and capital—in the collective hands of the workers rather than in the hands of individual owners.

Socialism was a reaction to industrialization, classical liberalism, and capitalism. While each of these ideas promised to free people—from hard labor and slavery, from political oppression by dictators and monarchs, and from economic want— nineteenth-century workers rarely felt these benefits. Detractors complained that these transformations had freed only the middle classes while leaving laborers and the poor in a new kind of servitude, paid tiny wages for hours and hours of long work. Through socialism, these critics of capitalism promised not only to redistribute wealth from the middle classes to the workers and peasants, but also to free them from the oppression of the industrial system.

Just as capitalism emerged from Enlightenment ideas about freedom, modern socialism was largely the product of the Enlightenment philosophy of egalitarianism. Eighteenth-century philosophers, especially the French thinker Jean-Jacques

Rousseau, believed that a perfect egalitarian future could come from people giving up their individual property rights to the collective community. In the 1790s, Gracchus Babeuf built on this argument by observing that the French Revolution hadn't brought wealth to the poor. Calling for a more radical revolution, Babeuf led an ultimately unsuccessful rebellion against the government in the name of equality and collectivity.

As socialist ideas made their way to Britain, they became more closely suited for the terrible conditions of the Industrial Revolution. Nineteenth-century British socialists witnessed the horrors of the factory system first-hand. Some, like Robert Owen, were factory owners who tried to create better and more egalitarian conditions for their workers. Owen managed a cotton mill at Lanark, in southern Scotland, in the early 1800s. He was shocked by the conditions he found, and poured money into social programs including decent housing, schools for workers' children, and a reasonable wage plan. While these projects restricted the profits Owen and his partners made, they also increased worker productivity. New Lanark attracted a great deal of attention, and stimulated socialist thinkers, although Owen himself never really embraced socialism and did not turn his factory over to his workers.

Socialism continued to gain adherents in the early decades of the nineteenth century. By 1848, as we have seen, socialists who were allied with social liberals and nationalist rose up in rebellion against monarchies and conservative governments across Europe. They were rapid suppressed, and initially socialists were dispirited by the failure of this uprising. Yet through these rebellions, a new force emerged to guide the next phase of socialist thought and action. This was the collaboration of the two German socialists Karl Marx and Friedrich Engels who together founded the **Marxist critique** of international industrial capitalism. Marx and Engels were the first socialists to use the term **communism,** by which they meant that they believed workers' rights could be protected only by a government that abolished private property entirely. In 1848, they published their critique of capitalism in a book known as *The Communist Manifesto.* This work was among the first to recognize the global nature of the capitalist world economy, writing in 1848:

> The bourgeoisie, by the rapid improvement of all instruments of production, by the immensely facilitated means of communication, draws all, even the most barbarian, nations into civilization. The cheap prices of its commodities are the heavy artillery with which it batters down all Chinese walls…. It compels all nations, on pain of extinction, to adopt the bourgeois mode of production; it compels them to introduce what it calls civilization into their midst, i.e., to become bourgeois themselves. In one word, it creates a world after its own image.[6]

As students of history, Marx and Engels believed that the engine that drove historical change was struggle between the social classes. From this basis, he predicted that the next great change would come from the proletariat (workers) overthrowing the bourgeoisie (owners). They argued that industrialism enslaved workers, who did not profit from their own work under this system but rather lost their share of any profits to owners and investors. Marx and Engels believed this situation could not last, and they anticipated that workers would eventually achieve greater control over the economy and enjoy its benefits. Yet they did not believe this would happen peacefully. While they supported movements to negotiate for better working conditions and shorter working days, they also believed that revolution—and not negotiation—would ultimately be necessary. In *Communist Manifesto,* for example, the pair wrote that "the proletariat have nothing to lose but their chains. They have a world to win."

Marxism quickly became a dominant stream of socialist thought. However, rival theories continued to emerge. One important philosophical socialist strand was **anarchism**, which unlike Marxism did not call for government control of the means of production. Rather, anarchist thinkers like Michael Bakunin believed that the state was unnecessary to ensure worker's rights. Bakunin predicted that after a proletarian revolution, governments would eventually wither away entirely. As socialism gained strength in the late nineteenth century, followers of Bakunin and of Marx increasingly clashed with each other even as they fought the forces of capital and the state.

The global anti-capitalist intellectual tradition

A significant cadre of modern capitalism's opponents emerged from societies outside of the industrialized core. Probably one of the most significant of these was Dadhabai Naoroji, a South Asian scholar who was trained in both local and Western education traditions. Naoroji was not necessarily opposed to capitalism in principle, but he argued that British companies and colonial administrators unfairly used capitalism to siphon Indians' wealth into their own profits. In 1880, he wrote:

> It is not the pitiless operations of economic laws, but it is the thoughtless and pitiless action of the British policy; it is the pitiless eating of India's substance in India, and the further pitiless drain in England; in short, it is the pitiless perversion of economic laws by the sad bleeding to which India is subjected, that is destroying India. Why blame poor nature when the fault lies at your own door? Let natural and economic laws have their full and fair day, and India will become another England, with manifold greater benefit to England herself than at present.[7]

Similarly, the first major successful uprisings with deep socialist roots—the 1910 Mexican Revolution and the 1917 Russian Revolution—occurred in states outside of the industrial and capitalist core. In Mexico, the socialist forces were led by revolutionary leaders like Emiliano Zapata, who drew supporters from the hacienda and plantation workers and built them into an army. Zapata was frequently disappointed by his fellow rebel leaders, many of whom espoused liberal and democratic ideas but who failed to turn land over to rural workers. In 1911, he set out his socialist ideas in a document known as the *Plan de Ayala,* which espoused the Enlightenment moral ideals of "Reform, Liberty, Justice, and Law" and in which he called for the wealthy to turn land over to communities and workers.

> In virtue of the fact that the immense majority of Mexican pueblos and citizens are owners of no more than the land they walk on, suffering the horrors of poverty without being able to improve their social condition in any way or to dedicate themselves to Industry or Agriculture, because lands, timber, and water are monopolized in a few hands, for this cause there will be expropriated the third part of those monopolies from the powerful proprietors of them, with prior indemnization, in order that the pueblos and citizens of Mexico may obtain ejidos, colonies, and foundations for pueblos, or fields for sowing or laboring, and the Mexicans' lack of prosperity and well-being may improve in all and for all.[8]

The Mexican Revolution proved that socialism was a potent force for change. But for most of the world, however, the long nineteenth century was a period of capitalist ascendancy. Throughout the long nineteenth century, socialism remained mostly a whisper. It would only come into global focus with the Russian Revolution in 1917.

Figure 5.5 Emiliano Zapata and revolutionary fighters, 1914.

Key terms

anarchism [172]
bank [146]
bonds [154]
bourgeoisie [151]
bubble [154]
capital [145]
capitalism [145]
castes [169]
communism [171]
concession [166]
consumer [154]
core states [154]
free labor [152]
free markets [152]
gentlemanly capitalism [160]
gold standard [157]
industrial capitalism [154]
industrious revolution [148]
invisible hand [152]
laissez-faire [153]
luddites [169]
market [146]
Marxist Critique [171]
nuclear family [167]
oligarchy [157]
periphery [154]
profit motive [146X]
proletariat [151]
regulation [147]
social class [162]
socialism [170]
stocks [154]
trade and labor unions [169]
utilitarianism [153]
utopian [144]
wage earner [154]

Further readings

Socialism was created and debated by many important intellectuals in this period.
Their writings can be found in *Socialist Thought: A Documentary History*, edited by

Albert Fried and Ronald Sanders, Revised Edition (New York: Columbia University Press, 1992).

Among the most important theorists of political and economics in the era was Rosa Luxemburg, whose *The Accumulation of Capital* (Eastford: Martino, 2015), translated by Agnes Schwarzschild, is a critique of both capitalism and the work of Karl Marx.

Michel Beaud, *A History of Capitalism, 1500–2000*, New Edition (New York: Monthly Review Press, 2001) is Tom Dickman and Anny Lefebvre's excellent translation of an accessible, classic French history of capitalism.

Paul Bowles, *Capitalism* (Harlow: Pearson, 2012) contains an excellent discussion of the supporters and detractors of capitalism, both in the modern period (1750–1914) and since.

Interlude 3: Memorializing Marx

Some of the most visible public markers of history in the modern world are statues and murals that depict great figures from the past. Such memorials, usually placed in prominent public places, are meant to display the history and values of a community. Most celebrate great leaders—generals, presidents, and statesmen—or religious figures like saints and popes. Often, these men (and they are usually men) are placed on horseback, in grand style, with swords in their hands or at their hips.

Yet one of the most widely memorialized figures in the twentieth-century world was not a military man, king, or president, but rather a stout German economist and philosopher with wild hair, who often wore rumpled suits and was more at home in a newspaper office or a university hall than a battlefield or parliament. Karl Marx's fame came not from military victories or dynastic rule, but rather his complex and sometimes arcane theories of history, society, and economics. In some of the most influential writings and speeches in human history, Marx interpreted human history as a struggle between social and economic classes and predicted a revolution that would create a classless, egalitarian society. It is for this philosophy, and especially the theory behind communism, that his image became a common feature of statues and murals in many parts of the world.

During his life, Marx was a highly regarded but controversial figure. It was after his death that he was elevated to the status of a hero. In 1917, his followers seized power from the Romanov rulers of the Russian Empire, and created the Union of Soviet Socialist Republics (USSR). They introduced the world's first national communist economic system. In the decades that followed communist states sprang up in many parts of the world—especially in Eastern Europe after the Second World War and in the Caribbean, Latin America, Asia, and Africa following the struggles for decolonization of the 1950s–1980s. China, the world's most populous nation (and largest economy), remains at least nominally communist today. In these countries, statues and memorials to Marx became common features on the streets and in public squares and buildings.

As communist governments began to fall in the 1980s, however, such memorials became controversial. Many of the leaders of the movements that brought about these new regimes sought to destroy them. Others, however, wanted them preserved both as a memory of the communist era and because some still supported communist ideals. Even in Moscow, capital of Russia—and once of the communist Union of Soviet Socialist Republics—there were calls for the removal of monuments to Marx. Marxism has largely been replaced in Russia today with a growing sense of nationalism, and Marx was not Russian but rather German. Ideas have been floated, therefore, to replace Marx with a Russian historical figure.

One of the largest remaining statues to Marx is a bust of his head in the German city of Chemnitz. This bust was raised in 1971 by the communist government of East Germany, a satellite of the USSR. Chemnitz was even renamed Karl-Marx-Stadt during this period. For years, parades and festivities were held with the bust as a backdrop, and it became an important meeting place and symbol of the city. Following the reunification of Germany under a noncommunist government in 1990, however, new members of the Chemnitz regional government proposed that it be destroyed. Instead, it was turned into an attraction for tourists that would help bring money to businesses in the city. This was an incredibly ironic fate of a Marxist monument!

Figure 5.6 Karl Marx monument in Chemnitz.

Figure 5.7 Mural, Coit Tower. Artist John Langley Howard, at right center, is crumpling a newspaper and reaching for Marx's *Das Kapital*.

In Hungary as well, conservative politicians in 2014 demanded the removal of a statue of Marx in the entrance hall to a university. The university, which had been called Karl Marx University of Economics during the communist period in Hungary's past, had changed its name but had not removed the statue. In fact, members of the university faculty continue to defend the statue on the ground that Marx's work continues to be very influential in sociology, economics, and political science.

In the United States, Karl Marx featured in murals painted during the Great Depression. Many of the painters of that period were unemployed and politically radicalized by the poverty they saw around them. They put memorials to Marx and his publications in such public sites as Coit Tower in San Francisco, where an artist is shown reaching for Marx's book, *Capital*. Over the years, there have been calls for this mural, also, to be altered or removed, but the city has resisted these demands.

As communism has faded in many parts of the world, images of Marx have also faded in importance. A few are still highly visited by tourists and admirers, however. For example, Karl Marx's London house is one of the top tourist attractions for visitors from China. In fact, Chinese citizens wishing to visit the United Kingdom often tell their government they wish to do so in order to visit sites associated with Marx. This may or may not be merely an excuse to tour a foreign country!

The controversies over Marxist memorials that erupted in the 1990s and still occur today show the continued presence of the past in our daily lives. Sites dedicated to history are places where people fight over meaning in the contemporary world.

While Marx is dead and gone, his legacy lives on in the ideals of socialism—and more specifically communism—which continues to be controversial in many parts of the world today. Nor is Marx the only figure whose memorials are controversial. Other statues and places of memory that represent nationhood, ethnicity, and gender continue to be sites of contestation in societies around the world. These include statues of colonial figures like Cecil Rhodes in Africa and Confederate Civil War soldiers in the United States. Recently, movements to remove both have become sites of protest, counterprotest, and violence. Despite depicting events that took place over a hundred years ago, they still have meaning in contemporary societies, demonstrating the way that history is something living and public and contested in our world.

6

Explaining the World

Revolutionary change doesn't always come from the barrel of a gun. Sometimes, it comes through a microscope. Charles Darwin's formulation of the Theory of Evolution through Natural Selection was one such revolution. Not entirely accepted at the time of its publication, by the end of the long nineteenth century it had become the pre-eminent scientific discovery of its age. Darwin's work would not have been possible without the decades of science and Enlightenment thought that preceded it, and these provided the bases of future efforts to understand changes in ourselves and the environment around us, and to feed our growing population. While still not fully realized, today Darwin's theory provides the basis for disease eradication, nutritional sciences, ecological projects, and our understanding of human relationships with our global environment.

after describing

    Darwin's theory was just one of a welter of new, scientific ideas about our world that emerged over the long nineteenth century. It was part of the wider development of the earth and life sciences, a set of innovations in intellectual thought that were equally significant as the liberal and religious developments described in the previous chapter. To study these groundbreaking ideas, we need to introduce some additional key terms. Some of the words introduced in this chapter apply to the study of the earth and its materials. These include **geology, stratigraphy,** and **radiometric dating**. However, most of the new terms in this chapter relate to the life sciences and their social impact, especially evolutionary theory. These include the twin theories of **monogenesis** and **polygenesis** as well as terms used for classifying species and understanding concepts in reproduction such as **taxonomy** and **heredity**. Several terms relate specifically to Charles Darwin's Theory of Evolution through Natural Selection including the concepts of **evolution** and **natural selection** themselves. We will also look at the ways in which these ideas were used in society through such concepts as **Social Darwinism, racism,** and **eugenics.**

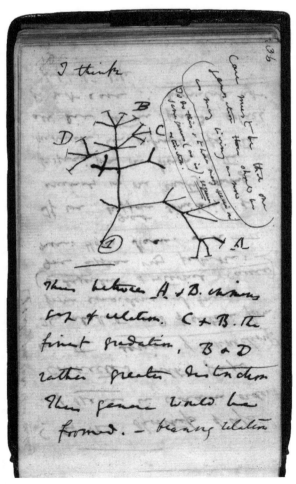

Figure 6.1 Page from Charles Darwin's notebooks, c.July 1837. One of the most important sketches of all time—Darwin's proposed "Tree of Life"—depicts how species (1) might evolve over time into multiple viable descendant species (A, B, C, and D) and multiple nonviable dead ends.

By the end of this chapter you should be able to:

- Summarize major advances in the life and earth sciences over the course of the long nineteenth century.
- Distinguish between the monogenesis and polygenesis theories of human origins popular in the nineteenth century.
- Explain the major arguments put forward by Charles Darwin in his Theory of Evolution through Natural Selection.
- Interpret the nineteenth-century application of Darwinian evolutionary theory in scientific and social contexts, including its misuse in racial theory.
- Compare and contrast notions of biological race as a way of dividing the world with civilizational and technological models presented in other chapters.

Explaining the world and all within it

The Enlightenment project was a wide attempt to understand the world and all that lived in it. One product of this effort was the earth and biological sciences, which became widespread academic fields for the first time in this period. Nineteenth-century scientists made many of the most important conceptual breakthroughs in the history of science, beginning with innovations in the field of geology and culminating in the evolutionary theories of Charles Darwin and Gregor Mendel, which form the basis for our understanding of all life on this planet today. However, science was also misused by proponents of nationalism, colonialism, and exploration, giving rise to the theoretical division of the human species into biological "races," an idea with enormous and detrimental consequences.

The birth of the earth sciences

Geology—the study of the substances of which the planet earth is composed of and the processes by which they moved and transformed—was one of the cornerstones of scientific development in the nineteenth century. Scientists' emphasis on geology was a product of several trends. One was the growth of industrial mining and resource exploitation, which inspired scholars such as the German Abraham Werner to try to understand how deposits of valuable minerals could be more easily identified and located. Capitalism played a role in this research, as companies and states sponsored research in order increase their income from mining. By the mid-nineteenth century, many governments also began to fund geological mapping and surveying in order to help promote mineral exploitation, both at home and in overseas colonies.

The result of all of this research and surveying was the growing awareness that the earth was formed of many different layers of rock and minerals. Two great theories emerged to explain the how these layers had formed. One of these, called Neptunism, was based on Christian readings of the great flood detailed in the Old Testament. Neptunists believed that this flood had laid the layers down. The other school of thought, known as Plutonism, taught that the earth had once been a molten, burning ball. As it slowly cooled, layers of rock formed.

The debates between Neptunists and Plutonists contributed to a wider argument about the age of the world. Whereas Neptunists thus accepted biblical arguments that the earth was quite young (perhaps as little as 5700 years), Plutonists believed that it was much more ancient. As early as 1749, the French experimenter Georges-Louis Leclerc (Comte de Buffon) began experiments with cooling globes. He argued that the world was not 5500 years old, as the Bible seemed to suggest, but rather as much as 75,000 years old. In the 1830s, British geologists began to approximate the age of rock in different areas by building vast **stratigraphic** charts that detailed the order of layers in different areas. By the early twentieth century, **radiometric dating**—estimating the age of minerals and rocks by measuring radioactivity—led to the estimation of the age of the earth at between two and four million years.

Geologists and scientists in the related field of geography also began to map the surface of the world in an attempt to understand the processes by which it changed. They built this field from the ground up, including creating a vocabulary to use in describing their discoveries. Some of this vocabulary included written

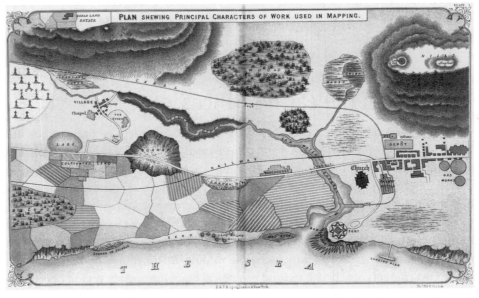

Figure 6.2 One of André's maps showed major topographical and man-made features like hills, churches, farmhouses, a quarry, a mud bank, a river—one of each.

words, but a great deal was visual symbols. Geography required the development of a common set of images, symbols, and ways of drawing the world around them that would be easily recognizable to other surveyors and researchers. The visual vocabulary that nineteenth-century geographers developed was so successful that it is still immediately recognizable to us. In the beginning, however, map-making and charting was so revolutionary that it required the sharing and debating of visual dictionaries. George G. André was a British geologist and draughtsman who made just such a guide in his 1874 *Draughtsman's Handbook*. This was a book full of maps of places that did not exist except in his imagination, but which demonstrated ways of depicting different layers, objects, and sites.

These maps were, in essence, proposals for ways to depict the world around us on paper. The scientific and surveying community was full of such proposals in the eighteenth and nineteenth century, and some—like many of the ones shown by André —were accepted as useful and became almost universally adopted. They helped advance our understanding of the planet just as much as written texts of the era.

The birth of the biological sciences

Earth sciences like geographers developed alongside allied scientists working in the field of biology in the nineteenth century. Indeed, biologists' understanding of the history of life on earth and the processes of evolution owes much to the fossils and data dug up and analyzed by earth scientists. Yet it was contemporary life that most fascinated the first modern biologists, known at the time as natural philosophers. Most were Europeans, and they were driven by the European encounter with the many new species, often described by explorers and colonizers who were driven by the nineteenth-century obsession with ordering and describing all things. The German natural philosopher Alexander von Humboldt, for example, travelled much of the world. His descriptions of species and environments in the Americas was one of the foundational texts of biology. Carolus Linnaeus was another important scholar. His research was funded by the king of Sweden, who lacked a global empire but still wanted to profit from European "discoveries." Linnaeus received a stipend to study plant and animal species, and ended up developing a **taxonomy**, or organization chart, of all species and their relationship to each other. We still use a version of this taxonomy today. Linnaeus and those who followed him gave every species a Latin name, and then organized them into larger groups by shared characteristics ascending from individual species through larger genera, families, orders, classes, and phyla to the vast kingdoms such as plants, animals, bacteria, and fungi.

While Linnaeus organized life into categories, other natural philosophers grappled with the question of what life actually is. They were assisted by tools like microscopes that had been developed by earlier generations of tinkerers and experimenters. In the

1750s and 1760s, Lazzaro Spallanzani in Italy and John Needham in Scotland used the microscope to study whether microorganisms could generate spontaneously. Because a system of scientific publication and correspondence existed in Europe by this time, a wide group of biological researchers were able to read their arguments in journals and letters.

The argument about the origins of microorganisms continued into the 1860s, when the French scientist Louis Pasteur demonstrated that microbes did not spontaneously generate but rather proliferated through reproduction. Pasteur's work was driven in part by the needs of French wine-makers, sheep-herders, and businesspeople who were searching for ways to protect animals against disease and to stop bacteria that spoiled their products. Nor was this the only scientific work prompted by the capitalist drive to produce goods and bring them to market in better condition. The Austrian monk Gregor Mendel made an important contribution to agriculture when trying to raise the best peas to feed his fellow monks. He bred different plants with each other, and measured the resulting hybrids. As a result of his research, he argued for the first time that one could predict certain traits in a descendant by looking at its parents. This research formed the framework for modern genetics. But it began as an exercise in crop improvement.

The Theory of Evolution through Natural Selection

In the early nineteenth century, a number of trends came together to demonstrate that the species living on earth had replaced earlier ones, and also that species tended to become modified over time. Perhaps most importantly, fossil evidence was accumulating that showed that some plants and animals that had existed in earlier times were now extinct. One geologist, William Smith, was even able to demonstrate that different examples of the same species could be found in layers of rock in different areas, but that had been laid down in the same period. Meanwhile, Thomas Malthus's work on human populations suggested that competition for food and other resources may have helped to drive this process of change.

In response, a number of biologists took on the question of why species changed over time. In France at the beginning of the century, Jean Baptiste Lamarck first described these changes as **evolution**. Lamarck argued that evolution occurred when individuals sought ways to overcome a challenge or take advantage of an opportunity. Over the course of an individuals' life, he suggested, it could change its structure and shape by using or not using different organs. For example, giraffes had slowly stretched their necks by constantly straining to reach leaves on tall trees. Lamarck then suggested that these changes would become **hereditary**, or passed on to offspring.

Lamarck's theory of change within an individuals' lifetime would be definitively disproven by Gregor Mendel's experiments 50 years later. In between, however, a much more significant theory was posited, one that would change our understanding of life on earth forever. Its author was Charles Darwin, a trained clergyman with a penchant for studying the natural sciences, who was engaged as a naturalist on a voyage to South America in 1831. As with many other intellectuals of the time, it was his exposure to several different parts of the world that helped him develop his Theory of Evolution through Natural Selection.

Darwin's global experiences gave him three key insights. First, he saw that the flora and fauna in different parts of the world were very different and often uniquely suited for the environment in which they lived. Second, he was exposed to the fossilized remains of long-dead animals, several of which he unearthed in South America. For example, he excavated the body of a megatherium, a giant and extinct sloth. Yet he noted that this creature, which no longer existed, bore a startling resemblance to the sloths that still lived in the region.

Perhaps Darwin's most important insight, however, derived from samples of different species of animals that he gathered from the Galapagos Islands, a small and isolated archipelago off the coast of Ecuador. He discovered something fascinating about the birds of the islands. As in other parts of the world, the Galapagos Islands had birds that specialized in many different ways of foraging for food. Some had big beaks for cracking nuts, others long beaks for tearing into cactus fruit, while still others had thin, sharp beaks for picking insects out of their hiding places. In most parts of the world, widely different species occupied each of these specialities. Yet in the Galapagos Islands, birds of all specialities were types of finches, seemingly related to a species common in nearby South America. Darwin concluded that the Galapagos finches descended from a small group of birds that had arrived on the island on driftwood or been carried by the wind, and these birds had evolved over time to take advantage of the many different food sources on the island.

Upon his return to Britain, Darwin used his notes and observations to develop a theory of how living things might change over time. The work that he eventually published had several main points. Darwin argued that species changed over time, and that many different species might descend from a common set of ancestors. He contended these changes probably occurred very slowly through **natural selection.** He postulated that small changes cropped up in individuals within a species frequently. Some of these variations were detrimental, and led to the death of the individual. Most were probably unimportant. Some changes, however, presented an individual with advantages that gave it a higher probability of surviving and reproducing. In making this point, Darwin was building on an idea coined by Malthus, called "survival of the fittest," which stated that individuals best suited to their environment were more likely to survive and pass on their traits. Finally, he argued individuals passed on these variations to their descendants, in the process gradually creating new species.

Darwin kept his theory secret for a decade. One reason for his hesitation to publish was that he recognized that some Christian authorities would see his work as an attack on established doctrine, which stated that God had created the earth in perfection, with all of the species in it already established. He had already witnessed a similar 1844 book called *Vestiges of the Natural History of Creation* come under heavy attack from religious leaders. Eventually, however, he came to believe that the evidence he had collected was too important to ignore. Thus he finally published it in a book called *On the Origin of Species by Means of Natural Selection, or the Preservation of Favoured Races in the Struggle for Life* in 1859.

Darwin's description of the mechanism for evolution was not immediately accepted, but it gradually gained the backing of important scholars, especially as evidence that supported his arguments began to pour in from other researchers. By the early twentieth century, it was recognized as probably the most important work in modern biological science ever published, an honor it still carries today.

The specter of race

Much of the work in biology and evolution in this era was related to plants, animals, and microorganisms. However, among the important contributions of these scholars was the recognition that humans were part of the natural world and hence also experienced biological processes. This was not an entirely new idea, but within the biological sciences it took on a particular importance in several ways. One of these was the development of the idea that humans were a species themselves (labeled *Homo Sapiens* by Linnaeus), but that we were made up of a number of different "races."

Modern notions of race, most of which originated in Europe or with European colonial settlers, depended largely upon the category of skin color. While other physical characteristics were not entirely ignored, nineteenth-century racial theorists came to define people by the color of their skin as "negroid," "asiatic," "mongoloid," or "caucasian." This one easily observable trait made it simple to sort the world into groups, although exactly how to make the division was highly debated throughout this period.

A related debate about human origins dominated the study of race in the early years of the nineteenth century: did humans all evolve from a single set of ape ancestors (a theory known as **monogenesis**) or from several different ones (**polygenesis**). Immanuel Kant, a proponent of monogenesis, argued for the historical unity of humans. However, he incorrectly assumed that our ancestors evolved in Europe, and that migration to other regions led to three non-European races: red (Americas), black (Africa), and yellow (Asia). Polygenesists, who believed that the races did not have common ancestors, tended to believe that humans' differences were the result of very different evolutionary pathways in different parts of the world. As a result, they

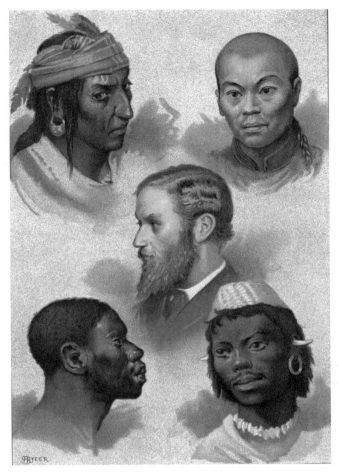

Figure 6.3 Image from the mid-nineteenth century depicting the argument that all humans belonged to one of five races, which is based on Johann Friedrich Blumenbach's analysis of human skulls. This work was foundational to modern race theories that drove policy in many countries.

tended to hold stronger beliefs in white supremacy than in monogenists, although both exhibited racist thought and actions.

Polygenesis finally declined in the late nineteenth century with the broad acceptance of Darwin's Theory of Evolution through Natural Selection. Yet his work did not kill racial theory altogether. On the contrary, it may have unintentionally strengthened the strains of **racism** emerging in Europe in the late nineteenth century by emphasizing survival of the fittest. Racism was on the rise for a number of reasons. Most importantly, race was a useful concept for those Europeans who sought to justify the Atlantic slave trade, colonialism, and overseas settlement. Arguing that there were different races, and that they had different attributes, legitimated the conquest of other peoples. Racism also mobilized the language of science to justify and explain the eradication of populations in regions being settled by Europeans. The decline of the Native American population as well as the hunting and extermination of indigenous Australians and the Khoisan of South Africa could all be legitimized through the survival of the fittest concept. Similarly, British massacres of South Asians in the wake of the Indian Rebellion of 1857 could be explained as a necessary step for disciplining a lower race.

Although it may seem to cut against the idea of individual liberties and political participation, this conceptualization of race was very much in keeping with Enlightenment project. Scottish philosopher David Hume, otherwise known for his work on capitalism, was a leading proponent of the idea that Europeans (or, as he wrote, people of "white complextion [sic]") were superior to others. He especially argued that "negroes" were inferior. Other important Enlightenment thinkers who contributed to the concept of race included German philosopher Immanuel Kant and the father of anthropology, Johann Friedrich Blumenbach.

Scientific notions of race also coexisted happily with nationalism, so that by the era of the New Imperialism Britons, Germans, and other Europeans could argue that their national "races" were proving their evolutionary virility by expanding into new territories while prohibiting inferior individuals from reproducing.

By the early twentieth century, scientific racism had become entangled with nationalism in the practice of **eugenics**. This was described as the science of "racial health." Eugenicists, many of them based in Britain, Germany, and the United States, argued that their own societies should actively control reproduction to promote health, energy, and intelligence. For example, Sir Francis Galton (a relative of Charles Darwin) misused Darwin's Theory of Natural Selection to argue that the societies could become better if the "best" individuals were favored to have children. Galton and other eugenicists called for the sterilization of groups and individuals that did not meet their exacting standards—not only members of "inferior" races but also disabled people and even the poor. They also called for racial purity, believing that reproduction between people of different races weakened a society. Ironically, eugenics was becoming popular at about the same time as Gregor Mendel was showing that cross-breeding different strains of plants could produce very beneficial attributes, evidence that directly contradicted eugenic thought.

Eugenicists were among those who used pseudoscience to legitimize segregation and discrimination in this era. In the nineteenth century, Asian and African subjects of European empires were often physically separated from their white rulers. Similarly, African Americans and indigenous peoples were often segregated from European Americans. The justification for this discrimination was the supposition that Europeans were not only cleaner but also more prone to diseases than other, "inferior" peoples. There was, in reality, no science at all behind this argument. It was merely a justification for a policy that allowed the ruling classes to reserve superior land and living situations for themselves and to justify the boundary of race that served their needs.

Reactions to the new biology

The biological sciences represented a field of great innovation in the period preceding the First World War. Looking back on these advances, it is difficult not to see them as transformative of both our human understanding of the world and our experience in it. However, as with many other areas of innovation, the discoveries of early biologists were controversial and not always well understood in their era.

The scientists

Even scientists themselves often missed the incredible scope of the project in which they were engaged. Their writing tells us that they generally saw themselves as laboring on specific questions rather than on building a revolution in understanding life. This is true, for example, of demographers Thomas Malthus in England and Hong Liangji in China. Malthus, even after his 1798 *Essay on the Principle of Population*, saw his main contribution as being in the field of economics, in terms of figuring out the price of food and the cost of raising families. Liangji, whose work five years earlier had predicted a coming famine in China, focused his energies on warning the Qing government of the problems he accurately estimated. Both men were passionate, but neither saw themselves as helping to create a new field of study.

In a similar way, Gregor Mendel didn't know that he was on his way to becoming the father of modern genetics. An Augustinian monk, Mendel was actually quite modest, and worked in near isolation. His vocation gave him a chance to quietly contemplate and then experiment with the plants that the monastery grew for their food. Early in his experiments, he turned to working with the common pea, which had the advantage of growing rapidly. Thus Mendel could grow several generations of plants quite quickly, and note which traits were passed on from parent plants to their offspring. His findings, which he published in a scholarly journal, were enormously significant. Yet few people paid attention to them for several decades, and Mendel himself gave up on his experiments in his old age and focused instead on running the monastery.

By contrast, the theories of the origins of life developed by Louis Pasteur and others in the mid-nineteenth century received rapid attention, partly because they were immediately applicable. Pasteur's discoveries of the way that microbes such as bacteria developed and how they could be killed were put to use by the agricultural industry very rapidly. Within a few decades, the beer and milk industries across the industrialized world had adopted **pasteurization**—the process of rapidly heating products to kill microbes. His research was also applied to vaccinations and to the sterilization of surgeon's hands and medical instruments. Pasteur, an ardent Christian, felt that these discoveries were a way of understanding the shape of the universe, and that they should not threaten anyone's conviction in God.

Charles Darwin, as well, was an ardent Christian who did not feel that his discoveries interfered with a belief in God, although he feared that others might see them as antireligious. This fear delayed his publication of *On the Origin of Species*. Unlike many of his contemporaries, Darwin had a sense of the enormity of the subject he was studying and of the implications his own research. Yet he often wrote of himself as a mere mechanic, stating: "My mind seems to have become a kind of machine for grinding general laws out of large collections of facts."

Popular responses to Darwin's Theory of Evolution

Although he personally preferred to focus on developing specific conclusions drawn directly from evidence, Charles Darwin could not avoid the fact that his findings did not fit well with existing explanations about life and humanity, especially religious understandings. Specifically, the Theory of Evolution through Natural Selection was difficult to reconcile with the worldview of evangelical Protestantism that was so important in Darwin's Britain. Scientists in many industrialized societies who embraced evolutionary theory often found themselves at odds with religion, especially those who worked in universities with connections to evangelical sects. Geologist Alexander Winchell discovered this to his detriment in 1878, when he lost his position at Vanderbilt University in Tennessee for teaching Darwinian theory.

Yet many Christians had no problem with evolutionary theory. In Denmark, some Lutheran theologians with a long history of questioning biblical texts saw no contradiction between their faith and evidence of evolution. Evangelist Henry Drummond in Scotland tried to reconcile the two in his 1883 book *Natural Law in the Spiritual World*. Edward Lewis, who taught at the (Protestant) American College in Beirut, responded to Muslim students' demands for the latest scientific knowledge by speaking to them about evolutionary theory, and encountered few problems.

Of course, not all evangelicals accepted Darwin's work. Lewis, like Winchell before him, eventually found himself dismissed by his university. Biblical literalists rose to oppose the argument that evolution occurred at all, contending instead that all species on earth had all been created and placed on earth by God in their current form. Darwin's arguments that humans, too, had evolved over time—published in his second book *The Descent of Man*—were especially controversial. A leading critic of this theory was Charles Hodge, the principal (President) of Princeton University.

His book *What Is Darwinism?* argued that this theory of evolution was entirely incompatible with Christian faith.

Darwin was somewhat baffled by religious figures' opposition to evidence of evolution, wondering why "we can allow satellites, planets, suns, universe... to be governed by laws, but the smallest insect, we wish to be created at once by special act." In *On the Origin of Species,* he wrote:

> There is grandeur in this view of life, with its several powers, having been originally breathed by the Creator into a few forms or into one; and that, whilst this planet has gone cycling on according to the fixed law of gravity, from so simple a beginning endless forms the most beautiful and most wonderful have been, and are being, evolved.[1]

But Darwin could not control how others used his theories, and as we have seen, some of the ways in which they were applied were deeply divisive rather than grand. For example, there was the work of Herbert Spencer, who applied evolutionary theory to human social interaction in the last two decades of the nineteenth century. Spencer was a particular proponent of the idea of the "survival of the fittest," arguing that some races were superior to others because they were more "fit." Leaping over the polygenesis/monogenesis debate, Spencer argued that some races were really earlier stages of evolution that had been surpassed by "modern" (white) humans. The body of theory to which he contributed, known as **Social Darwinism**, quickly found expression in modern racism. Nor was it merely theoretical. Spencer's work and others like it were cited in policy debates like the Chinese Exclusion Acts, which limited immigration from Asia to the United States and many Latin American countries. They were also cited to justify colonialism. Biologist Alfred Russel Wallace, for example, famously argued thus:

> The intellectual and moral, as well as the physical qualities of the European are superior; the same power and capacity which have made him rise in a few centuries from the condition of a wandering savage ... to his present state of cultural advance ... enable him when in contact with savage man to conquer in the struggle for existence and to increase at his expense.[2]

Social Darwinism was even used to legitimize widespread atrocities and disasters including colonial massacres and the decline of Native American and Polynesian populations, which some European settlers argued was a natural expression of their inferiority. Finally, it was expressed in eugenic policies aimed at sterilizing or limiting reproduction by particular groups, whether people with disabilities, ethnic minorities, or just the poor.

Would Darwin himself have supported Social Darwinism? There is absolutely no evidence he would have. While Darwin showed that species changed over time and even gave way to new species, he did not express a belief that some species (or human communities) were "superior" to others. Rather, Darwin believed that the human species, like all others, responded to changing environmental conditions in diverse ways rather than in pursuit of a particular outcome or goal. While some species, and even some individuals in a species, might be well suited to certain environments, there was no such thing as a "superior" example overall.

Key terms

eugenics [190]
evolution [186]
geology [183]
heredity [186]
monogenesis [188]
natural selection [187]
pasteurization [191]
polygenesis [188]
radiometric dating [184]
racism [189]
Social Darwinism [193]
stratigraphy [184]
taxonomy [185]

Further readings

The connection between racism and misconceptions of science is exceptionally well described in John P. Jackson and Nadine M. Weidman, *Race, Racism, and Science: Social Impact and Interaction* (New Brunswick: Rutgers University Press, 2005).

Darwin's life story is intertwined with his development of the Theory of Evolution through Natural Selection in Eugene Byrne and Simon Gurr's *Darwin: A Graphic Biography* (New York: Smithsonian Books, 2013).

7

Changing Environments

Darwin's Theory of Evolution through Natural Selection was a theory about change in nature, and just about any inhabitant of the nineteenth-century world could look out and see the natural world changing around them. For some, the biggest changes were the result movement to a new location, as this was a period of immense human migration. For others, change was occurring because of human activity in the natural world in which they lived. The Industrial Revolution and global capitalism, in particular, dramatically increased the human impact on the environment. Its legacy is still evident—and ongoing—today.

Understanding nineteenth-century environmental change requires a scientific vocabulary. We introduce a number of useful new terms in this chapter. Some of these terms have to do with the modernization of human use of the environment, including **monoculture farming**, **deforestation**, and **conservationism**. A few important labels—**climatology** and the **El Niño-Southern Oscillation**—apply specifically to our understanding of the weather.

By the end of this chapter you should be able to:

- Describe major patterns of global human and food crop movements in the long nineteenth century.
- Identify key trends in environmental change over the course of the long nineteenth century.
- Connect the growth of empire and nationalism in the nineteenth century to human migration, demographic shifts.
- Explain ways in which demographic and environmental changes in this period triggered transformations in social and cultural behavior.

Figure 7.1 Indian migrant laborers, South Africa. The demand for labor on South African mines and fields was high in the nineteenth century, and the British Empire made it easy to recruit impoverished laborers (or draft political prisoners) from the Indian subcontinent.

Fruition of the Columbian Exchange

The promise of the modern age was that people would bring nature under human control for the first time. The exchange of animal and plant species from one continent to another provided many populations with a wider range of foods than ever before. Railroads and shipping offered the potential to move food from farms to cities to feed the masses. Nationalism assured territory for every people on which to settle, domesticate, and cultivate. There was hope that capitalism would rationalize markets and make resources available around the world, and even that science would defeat disease and tame nature. Modernity thus created the expectation that humans would be ascendant over nature!

In reality, the modern era brought environmental confusion and, sometimes, catastrophe. Famines seemed to get worse, rather than better. Starvation drove millions to migrate, while nationalism bred racism and anti-immigrant sentiment in the regions to which they moved. Nor could global capitalism solve these famines—indeed, it seemed to make them worse. Industrialization contributed to pollution that affected living conditions in cities and countryside. Science failed to defeat disease, while modern warfare caused massive suffering. The progress promised by the Enlightenment seemed at times like a poisoned chalice—great potential turned to great suffering.

In the midst of all this turmoil, the greatest movement of people and things in human history achieved its height. The Columbian Exchange was the flow of humans, plants, and animals back and forth between the Americas, Eurasia, and Africa that had begun in the fifteenth century. Now, 400 years later, its full effect reached deep into societies around the world as new waves of migrants alongside locals and transnational companies intensified agricultural and industrial production around the world.

Movements of species

By the mid-nineteenth century, the fruits of the Columbian Exchange were evident almost everywhere. Its impact was most dramatic in the Americas, where Eurasian crops—especially wheat and rye—spread westward with settlers across the continent. Large areas of both North and South America were being actively transformed from wild grasslands into vast grain-fields, making these regions breadbaskets for both local cities and global consumers. Other grasslands were turned over to massive herds of cattle imported from Eurasia as vast ranches crisscrossed the land with barbed wire.

In Africa, it was crops from the Americas that caused the greatest transformation. The most significant of these was maize corn that originated in Meso-America.

This crop, which grew extremely well in the summer-rainfall climates of much of the trunk of Africa and along the West African coast, yielded an enormous number of calories compared to many existing local staples. These calories helped to create a population boom in the region just as the Atlantic slave trade, which had long constrained African populations, was coming to an end. Ground maize meal became a staple among the Akan of West Africa—as the fermented mush known as *kenkey*. Made into porridge, it became the staple of southern and East Africa in the nineteenth century. This new foodstuff contributed to a rapid population growth that resulted in social and political transformations in some regions. In southern Africa, for example, population growth due to the introduction of maize may have caused fights over water and land that pitted communities against each other. One result, in the 1810s, was the formation of larger and larger states, a trend that culminated in the founding of the Zulu Kingdom by Shaka kaSenzagakula. King Shaka was able to successfully manage the violence caused by this competition by forming large social and military regiments made up of youth from many different communities, and to create a massive state that survived until the new imperialism of the 1870s.

In Europe, the potato was the American crop that had the biggest impact. Potatoes could be grown on marginal, sandy soil that could not support other crops, and also survived in quite cold climates. Their addition to the European diet added many calories to people living in these areas, especially in regions like Ireland. By the nineteenth century, perhaps as much as 40 percent of the Irish population subsisted only on potatoes and milk. As it turns out, this was a reasonably healthy diet since potatoes provided all of the nutrients needed by a person except sufficient protein and vitamins A and D, which milk contributed. As a result, by the 1820s, mortality rates were on the decline in Ireland. The potato was also rapidly becoming the key carbohydrate across Scandinavia, Central Europe, and Russia.

In China, it was the sweet potato that allowed the opening of new land to cultivation. Like potatoes, sweet potatoes can grow in difficult and nutrient-poor soil. Thus they could be cultivated in the mountains in the interior of southern China, which had long been forested and wild. In the late eighteenth century, impoverished farmers had begun to move to these mountains in search of land, and their numbers increased after 1800. Most of the diet of these upland-dwellers came to be based on sweet potatoes. Maize, also, was adopted by Chinese farmers, in the lowlands, although it did not surpass the existing staple grains of rice and wheat.

Movement of peoples

The movement of foods to new areas helped to contribute to a population boom across the long nineteenth century. Between 1750 and 1914, the global population more than doubled, surpassing a billion people for the first time in human history around the middle of the nineteenth century. By the time the First World War began, about 1.8 billion humans were alive. Eurasia had by far the majority of this population—well over a billion in Asia, with an additional almost 400 million in Europe. About 150 million humans lived in Africa, a population still ravaged by the long-term impact of the Atlantic slave trade, and about 200 million in the Americas. The population of Oceania and the southern Pacific Ocean region remained under 10 million.

This rising global population was the subject of an increasing number of philosophical and scientific studies over the course of this era. In 1793, the Chinese intellectual Hong Liangji began to record the effects of population growth in southern China. He wrote a number of essays predicting eventual famine if family sizes were not somehow restricted. Another important scholar of demographics was the Englishman Thomas Malthus, who similarly predicted in 1798 that populations could not continually rise. Malthus forecasted that rising populations would eventually be curbed by limitations in food, by disease, and by changing human behaviors. He accepted that populations rose when land and resources became available, as in the settlement of the Americas by Europeans (and Africans) and the arrival of American crops in Eurasia and Africa. However, he believed that these increases in population would always be limited by positive checks (rising mortality rate) and preventative checks (lower birth rate). Because he was in Europe rather than in China, Malthus' work was taken seriously by Enlightenment scholars while Hong Liangji remained unknown outside of China. But Hong may have been the better scholar. Malthus in fact failed to understand the degree to which innovation and the movement of peoples and crops could lead to long-term sustained population growth.

Even as the movement of food species helped to contribute to global population growth, demographic shifts were also being driven by a massive increase in human immigration in this period. The migrants included large numbers of both free migrants as well as enslaved individuals and indentured laborers. In some cases, migrants traveled through government-sponsored programs meant to attract or push labor into areas that were producing raw materials to feed the factories of the Industrial Revolution. In other cases, they paid their own way, hoping to escape poverty and discrimination or looking for new opportunities. One of the main causes of mass migration was simply population growth. The population of Europe, for example, rose from 188 million in 1800 to almost 400 million in 1900, without the addition of much new farmland. While food supplies were generally sufficient, except in famine years, jobs and housing were all in short supply. It was this kind of "push" factor that especially stimulated migration to Australia and North America.

Not all migrants moved voluntarily, although it is difficult to sort out involuntary migrants from those who chose to move. This is especially true because the two categories overlap, especially in times and places of chaos and violence, where families fleeing disaster intermingled on ships with others who had become indentured or prisoners because of their debt. Nevertheless, some mass cases of involuntary migration stand apart in this era.

The Atlantic slave system was one of these. By the mid-eighteenth century, the slave trade was just reaching its peak. Between 1750 and 1800 alone, four million enslaved Africans were transported across the Atlantic at a rate of almost 100,000 a year. Partly because the population of West Africa had already been devastated by centuries of the trade, most of these captives came from the west coast of Central Africa. The largest percentage was disembarked in the Caribbean, where they would be forced to labor on sugar plantations, although almost as many ended their journey in Brazil. The abolition of the Atlantic slave trade by most European countries and the United States in the early nineteenth century slowed but did not end this trade. Clandestine human smuggling merely replaced the legal trade in enslaved Africans. Almost as many captives—approximately three and a half million—were transported in the 50 years after 1800 as in the 50 years before. However, abolition did cause the patterns of this trade to shift. In order to avoid antislavery squadrons based in West Africa, slavers moved south and even around the Cape of Good Hope to Southeast Africa, and the vast majority of captives were disembarked in Brazil and Cuba, where the trade remained legal until the 1860s, rather than British and French colonies or the United states, where it was illegal. The trade only really ended in the mid-nineteenth century when insurance companies, aggravated by losing money due to the actions of antislavery squadrons, finally refused to underwrite slaving voyages.

Prisoners—both citizens and colonial subjects—formed another large body of migrants in this period. This category comprised a diverse group that included convicted criminals, poor debtors, and political prisoners. Britain was one of the largest transporters of convicts, most of whom were sent to Australia and Tasmania. Meanwhile, convicts from Britain's South Asian colonies were conveyed to the Andaman Islands. French convicts were sent to penal colonies such as New Caledonia and French Guiana. By both their presence and their labor, convicts were tools for enlarging the boundaries of empire. Many were transported to dangerous or contested frontiers. Beginning in the nineteenth century, for example, Russia shipped thousands of prisoners to the Pacific edge of Siberia while Japan sent theirs to the northern island of Hokkaido, just across the Le Perouse strait from the Russian prison labor camps. These two groups, living and laboring in horrible conditions, were used to develop the frontier between the two countries.

Despite the large number of involuntarily transported people, however, the majority of nineteenth-century emigrants moved to a new location at least partly through their own choice, whether fleeing a desperate situation or hoping for a better life, or both. Three great circuits characterized voluntary global migration patterns during the nineteenth century. The first crossed the Atlantic Ocean. After about 1850, most transatlantic migrants were Europeans, and the majority—65 percent of these—went to the United States. Brazil, Argentina, and Cuba, and Canada also received large numbers of immigrants. In the middle decades of the century, the largest single community within this network was poor migrants from the British Isles, including Ireland. The Irish potato famine of 1846–1847, as a single event, prompted one of the largest mass migrations in human history, mostly to the United States.

After the 1880s, transatlantic steamships began to bring large numbers of poor families from central and eastern Europe. Some of these were from groups experiencing familiar push factors of poverty and hunger. By and large, however, food production in Europe (and from colonies abroad) had caught up by this period, and hunger was not as acute. Instead, many immigrants were minority populations persecuted in their homeland. These included Jewish communities fleeing religious persecution in Russian territory. They and other eastern Europeans—such as Slavs and Poles—were not always welcome in their new home because of the rising specter of racism, as we will see.

The Americas also experienced a massive in-migration from across the Pacific Ocean. Approximately two and a half million inhabitants of South, East, and Southeast Asia arrived on the continent between 1850 and the First World War. Some were brought as laborers to the British Caribbean, where it was hoped they would replace slaves freed in the 1835 emancipation. Others were driven by famine and poverty at home and drawn by the opportunity of work building the infrastructure—railroads and roadways—of the U.S. West and coastal South America. Many of these economic migrants were farmers from the poverty-stricken provinces of Guangdong and Fujian. They signed indenture contracts, many of them fraudulent, to work on mines, railroads, and plantations. These migrants faced even worse racism than eastern Europeans. From the 1880s, many American countries—and Australia—even passed laws forbidding migrants from Asia.

Still another large group of Asians migrated along a third circuit from India and China to Southeast Asia. Almost 30 million Indians emigrated along this route during this period. Their travel was defined by the contours of the British Empire, for the imperial government encouraged Indians to become shopkeepers and smallholders or indentured them as laborers at the far reaches of the growing empire. Chinese workers, meanwhile were brought to the islands of Southeast Asia and to Burma by independent companies. Four million migrated to Thailand, a million to the Dutch empire, several million to British Singapore and Burma, and more than two million to the growing French colony in Indochina. Most of these migrants were fleeing revolts, famine, and general overpopulation, and drawn by the hopes of a better life abroad.

In East Asia, growing populations led governments and individuals to open up ecologically marginal regions to habitations. Northeast Asia, was the destination for several million Chinese, Korean, and Japanese settlers in the early twentieth century. In the Mediterranean, several million migrants moved from the packed cities of southern Europe and the Levant to North Africa. Many were French and Spanish

Figure 7.2 An Australian anti-Chinese immigrant cartoon, 1886, titled "The Mongolian Octopus—His Grip on Australia," from *The Bulletin Magazine*, Sydney, Australia, August 21, 1886. Propaganda like this helped to stir up racist anti-Chinese sentiment in the Americas and Australia during this period.

Table 7.1 World population growth (millions) by regions, 1850–1950

	1850 population	1950 population	Average annual growth (%)
Receiving			
Americas	59	325	1.72
North Asia	22	104	1.57
Southeast Asia	42	177	1.45
Sending			
Europe	265	515	0.67
South Asia	230	445	0.66
China	420	520	0.21
Africa	81	205	0.93
World	1200	2500	0.74

Sources: Colin McEvedy and Richard Jones, *Atlas of World Population History* (London: Penguin, 1978).

citizens following pathways of imperial control to Algeria, Tunisia, and Morocco. Still others came to Africa from Lebanon, Syria, Malta, and Italy, looking for new opportunities and hoping to benefit from the advantages that were available to lighter-skinned people under colonialism.

An age of famines

By the mid-nineteenth century, migration had become part of a global economic system harnessed to industrial capitalism. Migration patterns in widely disparate parts of the world provided the labor required to harvest raw materials to keep factories running. Large agricultural regions were turned over to growing individual crops to feed workers, while others produced mineral resources. Growing urban areas were populated by factory workers—immigrants from rural regions and faraway countries—processing these raw materials. Others worked to build the railways and transportation networks to move food, resources, and finished products long distances to and from the industrial cores.

The growth of global capitalism introduced some efficiencies into this system. It made food-producing and resource-rich regions responsive to open markets, meaning that the companies that grew or bought food crops could send them to the highest-paying region of the world. Like many other nineteenth-century ideas, this system seemed to be a pure positive until, late in the nineteenth century, the free market combined with natural disasters to produce a number of famines around the world. These famines resulted in the death by starvation of hundreds of millions of people. Among the largest are shown in Table 7.2.

Nature, of course, played a role in these famines. In each case, shifting rainfall patterns known as the **El Niño-Southern Oscillation** caused several years of drought. The actual culprit was the sun. The global climate, as we now know (and as scientists began to figure out in the late nineteenth century), is intensely affected by energy from the sun, most of which reaches the world around the equator. This energy then drives wind diffusion around the world and defines the patterns by which water condenses into clouds. However, summer weather development happens differently every year, depending partly on the amount of solar energy received into different regions of the world. This in turn shapes wind patterns. In El Niño years, for example, wind patterns reverse their normal direction, causing rain to fall on typically dry Peru but causing a failure of the vital monsoon rains in India, China, and Brazil. This in turn leads to famine in these densely populated regions.

Table 7.2 Famines around the world, late nineteenth century

Place	Year	Mortality estimate
North Africa	1870s	2.2–3.5 million
India	1867–1879	6.1–10.3 million
India	1896–1902	6.1–19 million
China	1876–1879	9.5–20 million
Brazil	1876–1879	0.5–2 million

Source: Niño and the Making of the Third World (New York: Verso, 2002).

The famine of 1876–1878 was perhaps the most significant example of a famine caused by the El Niño-Southern Oscillation. It resulted in a failure of monsoons to bring rains to East and South Asia, which was coupled with devastating drought on the other side of the Indian Ocean in East and North Africa and a knock-on effect in Central and South America. As the rains failed, food crops withered in the fields, and without crops, people starved.

Ironically, we know about the El Niño effect partly because geographers and climatologists were able to observe the droughts of 1876–1878. Gradually, over the next decades, they began to understand the connections between weather patterns in different parts of the world. In fact, the El Niño droughts helped to stimulate the birth of the modern science of **climatology**—the study of weather. Yet this awareness came too late to help the millions who died in the late nineteenth-century famines.

While modern science was too late to help shape a response the famines, modern global capitalism and imperialism were present to play a role. Unfortunately, this role was almost uniformly negative. The global depression that began in 1873 meant that many independent states—including North African states such as Morocco and Latin American countries like Brazil—had little money put away to help their starving populations. China's financial and food reserves had similarly been emptied by the draining of silver that resulted from the opium trade. Meanwhile, the globalization of markets and search for profits that were a feature of industrial capitalism meant that crops grown near a famine region were often sent thousands of miles away to places where food prices were higher rather than to feed starving people nearby.

Things were even worse in colonial possessions affected by El Niño. Imperial officers showed little concern for starving populations. In fact, they often exploited the political disruption caused by droughts. Numerous conquests occurred during periods of famine—including the U.S. intervention in the Philippines, German military action in northern China, Italy's invasion of Ethiopia, and the expansion of the British Empire in southern Africa.

Colonialism was also linked to mass terror and murder outside of famine, of course. Early in the long nineteenth century, indigenous people were hunted and often exterminated by European settlers in southern Africa and Oceania. The aboriginal population of Tasmania, off the coast of Australia, was just one community that was entirely eliminated. In North America, members of indigenous groups such as the Lakota were confined to tiny territories that couldn't possibly sustain them. Ethnic cleansing—to use a modern word—also accompanied nationalism. Over 200,000 ethnic Turks fled nationalist riots in Greece in the 1820s, and a large number of Greeks similarly had to flee the Ottoman Empire. Russian anti-Islamism and expansionism culminated in the expulsion of the majority of the Muslim Tatars during the Crimean War of 1853–1856 and of many Muslims of the Caucasus Mountains about a decade later.

The Industrial Revolution and the natural world

The Industrial Revolution, along with industrial capitalism, provided nineteenth-century societies with means and the motive for more intensive exploitation of the natural environment than ever before in human history. The demand for food to feed workers who were no longer cultivating food themselves stimulated intensive farming of single staple crops over vast areas. The demand for land for agriculture in turn promoted the cutting down of forests, whose trees were in any case needed as raw material for construction and industry. Animal pelts, feathers, oils, and furs were also processed in factories for consumer use. So, too, were mineral resources, including an increasing range of industrial fuels. The result of all of this work was widespread pollution and resource exploitation. Yet, at the same time, some individuals and governments became aware of the need to conserve resources for both economic and societal reasons.

Monoculture farming

Over the course of the nineteenth century, large areas of land were turned over to single crops—both commercial crops like sugar cane and staple foods like wheat. Called **monoculture farming**, this type of agriculture had serious implications. Different plants affect the soil in different ways, extracting certain minerals or adding them to the soil. Mixing crops can hence be an effective strategy for retaining soil fertility, while monoculture farming depletes large areas of key nutrients. Some crops of the industrial age were particularly bad in this respect. Cotton, for example, sucks nitrogen from the ground at a rapid place. Its cultivation in far corners of the world in the nineteenth century proved devastating to the soil of some areas, and it was the need to replace these nutrients that drove (first) the guano rush of mid-century and (later) the industrial development of artificial fertilizers.

Another potential problem with monoculture farming was that it increased the threat posed by crop diseases—and hence famine. Huge numbers of a single plant species planted together made it easy for beetles, fungus, and other pests to spread from one plant to another over wide areas. Moreover, the lack of genetic diversity inherent to industrial monoculture farming meant that disease resistance was lower on these farms. Thus, for example, although Peru has thousands of different species of potato, it was only a few species, and especially the so-called lumper, that made it to Europe. Shen a potato blight hit this crop, it spread rapidly, unimpeded by the resistance that genetic diversity makes possible.

The disease that ultimately hit European potato crops in the 1840s was a mold that had travelled from the Americas, probably in a load of guano. In 1844, Belgians began to report that some potatoes they were growing had dark, moldy spots. By mid-1845, these spots began to appear on potatoes in nearby France and the Netherlands. In September, British officials in Ireland reported that somewhere around 30 percent of the potato crop was failing. This statistic was particularly concerning because, as we have learned, many Irish families subsisted almost entirely on potatoes. The result, for Ireland, was entirely predictable. Starvation stalked the countryside. Peasant farmers, many of them with no access to cash at all, sold everything they had to buy food and then wandered the countryside begging. The British government voted for food relief and built urban soup kitchens, but this strategy was not only insufficient but actually counterproductive, for it meant that farms were abandoned by families who moved to cities in search of food. Greedy speculators, seeking to capitalize on human suffering, bought the land they had temporarily abandoned for almost nothing. They then turned the land from producing food to cash crops, like wool-bearing sheep, extending the food shortages. This was the process that created the years-long Irish famine, which in turn drove massive migration from Ireland to North America and Australia.

Sweet potato monoculture in China was equally problematic. Although sweet potatoes did not succumb to a massive blight in this era, their cultivation did contribute significantly to a series of floods and famines. In the late eighteenth century, much of the mountainous interior of southern China was being actively cultivated to grow

Figure 7.3 "The Ejectment," from *The Illustrated London News,* December 16, 1848. The image shows starving Irish families being evicted from their homes.

sweet potatoes. The process went like this: all of the trees on a mountainside would be cleared, sweet potatoes would be sown, and the crops would suck up nutrients. In a few years, the mountainside could no longer support crops, and had to be abandoned. The farmers would then move on to the next mountain. The first signal that this process was going to cause a crisis was the devastation of mountainside environments. By clearing the trees, the farmers also caused massive erosion. When rains fell, swollen streams would carry loose soil down the mountainside. As a result, rivers—including the massive Huang He—became swollen with soil and water that had once been absorbed and held in place by trees. This caused further devastation in the fertile lowlands. The Huang He flooded numerous times in the eighteenth and nineteenth centuries, leaving millions drowned and vast regions of farmland ruined.

Hunting, fishing, and cutting timber

Monoculture farming was motivated by the need to feed and house the growing global population and provide them with the goods they demanded. This same need also triggered dramatic increases in hunting, fishing, and the clearing of forests over the course of the long nineteenth century.

The expansion of hunting was driven mostly by the expanding middle classes' growing demands for luxury goods. The popularity of fur clothing was the cause of the hunting of beavers, fox, martens, minks, otters, and other fur-bearing animals in the European and North American north. Some fur-bearing animals, like the sea otter, were almost driven to extinction even before 1800. In the nineteenth century, ivory and ostrich feathers became important markers of middle-class status in Europe. Ivory was already in great demand, especially in East Asia but the demand surged to meet Europeans' desire for ivory-keyed pianos and other marks of middle-class status. This increased demand led to huge elephant hunts in Africa, where the elephant became extinct across much of the continent. European demand for ostrich feathers for hats and clothing similarly led to the eradication of the birds from some areas of southern Africa before they were successfully domesticated. In the United States, demand for leather resulted in the massacre of the massive bison herds of the plains. Leather production was the fifth largest industry in the United States in 1850, and millions of bison were killed for their hides, which were turned into both clothing and the belts used to help power industrial machinery. Not all hunting was for such practical outcomes, however. Some hunts were merely for trophies, a practice that expanded in the nineteenth century as, for example, Europeans learned from the Mughal elite to hunt tigers and other rare South Asian animals. Still other big cats and exotic animals were trapped for zoos, the first of which opened in London in 1828, followed by Berlin in 1844.

The great hunts in the oceans, by contrast, were more often aimed at providing mundane but important commodities. For example, the great cod populations of

Figure 7.4 The trophy room of a colonial official's residence in British India.

the North Atlantic were progressively being exploited to feed the enslaved African population of the Americas and Caribbean, and factory workers in Europe. Whales were hunted to near extinction for their fat, which was turned into whale oil for lighting lamps. Their bones were also processed into frames for corsets, thought to increase the beauty of women, and whalers harvested ambergris, a whale secretion that formed the base of perfumes.

Deforestation—the clearing of forests across large regions—also increased dramatically in this period. There were several drivers of deforestation. The timber provided by cutting trees was used for housing and for ships. Clearing forests also helped to expand the amount of land available for cultivation. The growth of a middle class—in Europe, the Americas, and Japan especially—also increased demand for beautiful hardwoods like teak and ebony. Such woods became important trade goods and even helped to drive international policy. Britain's nineteenth-century acquisition of Burma was partly an effort to secure its huge teak forests. Similarly, the expansion in navies and merchant fleets stimulated timber industries in new areas of the world. Again, Britain's efforts to secure western Canada (British Columbia) were mainly an attempt to ensure that they possessed enough straight, tall trees to make masts for the country's warships.

Europe, North Africa, and Asia, with their large populations and demands for farmland, experienced the most rapid large-scale deforestation during this era. Between 1750 and 1850, Europe probably lost about 185 thousand square kilometers of forests, while the (much larger) southern and eastern Asia experienced a similar rate of deforestation, with China leading the way in clearing forests for agricultural land. Indeed, trees became so rare in China in this period that wood theft was made a crime by the Qing Dynasty.

In addition, wood was harvested in North America. European settlers had been clearing forests in the North American interior for well over a century, but the trend peaked after 1850 as the forests of the Pacific northwest and the inland south were harvested. This was also the period in which Southeast Asia and tropical Africa began to first experience massive deforestation. On the islands of Java and Sumatra, especially, clear-cutting for expensive teak and to open land for vast coffee plantations devastated the ancient forests between 1840 and 1870.

Mineral extraction and pollution

Untouched natural environments and low-impact lifestyles were simply not suited for the needs of the Industrial Revolution. Low-intensity farming couldn't possibly produce enough calories to feed cities densely populated by factory workers. Transportation required the taming of rivers and land to the needs of canal-boats and trains. Important minerals had to be dug from deep in the ground, no matter how the mines might impact the surface. Chemical industries also had to get rid of their wastes, and in their ignorance, river and lakes seemed as good a place as any. As a result, the Industrial Revolution was as much about transforming and exploiting nature as it was about changing work habits and lifestyles.

In areas of intense factory development, rivers were channeled to provide a consistent flow of water and, sometimes, power. Waterwheels and later dams were constructed to harvest power from the flowing water while locks and canals channeled it to help move goods. Meanwhile, pipes and sewers drained waste from humans, animals, and factories directly into major rivers. From the mid-nineteenth century, these urban pollutants were joined by agricultural runoff that included large amounts of fertilizers. This pollution slowly turned wild waterways full of wildlife into dead zones. Dams blocked fish from spawning grounds, plants and animals were killed by runoff, amphibians found that rock and concrete provided them no shelter to hide from predators and the sun. From London's Thames to the Merrimack in New England, rivers died.

The extraction and use of fuels and mineral resources also had massive environmental costs. Coal, of course, was one of the prizes of the mining treasure hunt of the eighteenth and nineteenth centuries. Along with whale oil, it was the fuel that drove the early industrial world. Some forms of coal also became sources of carbon for smelting iron. To meet the rising demand, coalfields were located and mined in many parts of the world. Among the largest coal-producing areas was the mid-Atlantic region of the United States. Pennsylvania and West Virginia, especially, became pockmarked with massive coalmines that had increasingly deep shafts sunk underground. But this was just one of many coalfields. By 1911, 66.5 million tons of the substance was being mined around the world every year. Of course the mining and transport of coal had enormous impact on the local environment. Large areas became honeycombed by mineshafts, and sulfuric acid-laden water leached from them, killing animals and plants down-stream.

The burning of all of this coal had even broader repercussions. Areas surrounding the most intensive coal-burning factories and iron smelteries became desert-like wastelands covered in drifts of ash, denuded of their plant and animal life. In cities, the constant burning of coal for heat and factory fuel led to daylong and often deadly smog, like the London "pea-soup" fogs that could persist for weeks. This air pollution heavily affected the growth and development of children and was a leading cause of lung disease in adults.

By the early twentieth century, coal as a fuel was being slowly being overtaken by petroleum oil, the product of ancient creatures and plants transformed by millions of years of pressure into complex hydrocarbons. Petroleum products had been known in ancient times, but were used in only limited quantities before the industrial age. In the mid-nineteenth century, however, technological advances made it possible to use these "oils" to light lamps. The discovery of large deposits of petroleum oils in Pennsylvania in 1859 drove the United States to become the first large adapter of petroleum-fueled lighting. A concurrent rise of the price of whale oil—due to over-fishing—helped drive the switch. Soon, petroleum oils were also being used to fuel stoves. In the 1890s, tinkerers discovered that the oils could drive trains and ships as well, and by the early twentieth century they were the chief fuels for personal transportation devices—the first cars.

The arrival of cars also contributed to the transformation of the landscape, although only slowly before the First World War. The technology needed to produce asphalt was developed in the nineteenth century, and soon roads were being constructed at a faster pace than were railroads. In industrialized cities, automobile exhaust became a deadly contributor to bad air, although it probably wasn't worse for human health than the defecation and urination left behind by the horses that cars replaced.

Alongside construction materials like iron and fuels like coal and petroleum, much of the mining expansion in the nineteenth century was focused upon luxury goods and currency materials like gold and diamonds. In South Africa, diamond mining slowly expanded from a small-scale activity to the massive digging that culminated in the deepest hole in the world—the diamond mine at Kimberley. Not far away, South Africa's massive gold mining industry was similarly transforming the landscape and dumping chemicals in the local ecosystems—largely to feed the

Figure 7.5 Oil wells as far as the eye can see in Los Angeles, California, c.1900.

voracious quest luxury of the middle class. In the early years of the twentieth century, for example, the De Beers diamond company managed to convince many middle-class women in Europe and the Americas that they should marry only those men who gave them diamond rings, thus suddenly and successfully exploding the global demand for diamonds. Not too many years later, this had become a global standard for the middle-class wedding.

The beginnings of modern conservation

Pollution, deforestation, and resource extraction were hallmarks of the modern era, and they rapidly drew the attention of people determined to preserve pristine environments. These early environmentalists were partly spurred by reports and experiences of the rapid impact of deforestation on small islands like Mauritius in the Indian Ocean, colonized by industrialized European societies and rapidly clear-cut. In these small environments, deforestation caused ecological mini-apocalypses in as early as the 1850s, a trend that was only to spread as the century wore on.

In the late eighteenth century, several German principalities began to regulate their forests in an attempt to conserve at least some of their tree cover. Because these were small states with autocratic rulers, they were able to implement the policies for doing so quite quickly. These were not the first forest management strategies. Japan, for example, had centralized management of many forests centuries earlier.

What was new in the case of the German principalities was that their governments implemented their conservation strategies in a very modern way. Their strategies were scientific, utilizing data collected by lumberjacks and government agents. They also drew heavily on the tools of modern capitalism, as the officials in charge used economic calculations to help determine which trees to cut and which to retain. Finally, they were connected to the university system, which began to participate in the training of foresters.

By the late nineteenth century, **conservationism**—the movement to protect natural resources—had become widespread. Some proponents even began to make arguments that resources should be preserved for their beauty rather than for economic or even ecological reasons. Among the leaders of this movement were naturalists in the U.S. West, especially John Muir, who founded the Sierra Club in 1892 to protect the forests of California from clear-cutting. Others who became concerned about these environments included hunters such as U.S. President Theodore Roosevelt, who so enjoyed his hunts in the western states that he created the U.S. national park system in 1906. By the onset of the First World War, proponents of similar park systems had emerged in many parts of Europe, Oceania, and Africa. Their work was not always uncontroversial. Settlers, miners, and others who wished to take advantage of the land for its resources objected to setting it aside. At the same time, individuals and communities who had lived on the land for a long time objected to being moved off of land to make room for "pristine" natural environments.

Modern life and modern death

The changes in human interaction with the environment that characterized the long nineteenth century did not only take the shape of mass migration and industrial production. Human-nature relationships were also expressed as they always had been: in the consumption of food and drink, in reproduction, in disease and medicine. These elements of daily life (and death) were also transformed in the nineteenth century through processes related to industrialization and capitalism.

Birth and death

In the eighteenth century, scientists such as Thomas Malthus and Hong Lingji initiated the first extensive studies of the rise and fall of human populations. They found that they were living in an age of massive population increases spread over much of the world. This huge demographic increase was by and large not the result of reductions in mortality rates, however. The causes and treatment of disease continued to be badly understood. Epidemics tore through societies around the world, often following upon the heels of famines or wars, and often connected to migration. Human-to-human transmission caused measles outbreaks in the United States in 1759, 1772, and 1788. Cholera was one of the greatest killers, leaving over almost two million dead in two of the largest nineteenth-century pandemics, with many smaller outbreaks. Post-famine Egypt experienced a destructive epidemic in 1881. Influenza was even more devastating as it often affected the young and healthy. An 1889 pandemic beginning in Saint Petersburg, Russia, soon spread around the world killing over a million people. This was merely a foreshadowing of the 1918 global epidemic that would kill approximately 75 million people at the conclusion of the First World War.

Admittedly, there were a number of practical advances in the field of medicine. For example, smallpox immunization strategies helped to decrease the rate of infection for that disease globally during the long nineteenth century. While basic immunization techniques had been in practice in Africa, China, and India for at least a century, it was Englishman Edward Jenner who first conducted scientific vaccination trials in 1796. Jenner demonstrated that the less dangerous cowpox organism could be used to stimulate immunity to smallpox, and soon vaccinations using cowpox were in use in Europe, North Africa, the Americas, and Japan. Yet immunization rates overall remained low, and as late as the 1870s a smallpox epidemic could kill more than 180,000 people.

Meanwhile, the agricultural revolution and global capitalism were promoting high rates of noncommunicable disease. Tobacco, once restricted to infrequent use in North America, was on its way to becoming a global killer. Both snuff and tobacco smoke seem to have contributed to increasing rates of cancer in Europe and Asia in this period. At the same time, cheap opium from South Asia, given to children to keep them quiet and well-behaved, contributed to infant mortality rates in Europe in the mid-nineteenth century, and probably elsewhere as well.

Nor was there a decrease in mortality rates due to war. Eighteenth-century revolutionary wars and even the Napoleonic Wars had resulted in limited civilian casualties. However, nineteenth-century campaigns of colonial conquest such as the Anglo-Zulu War of 1879, the Anglo-Sudan conflicts, and Russian expansion in Central Asia caused widespread death both through conflict itself as well as by the destruction of infrastructure and crops that accompanied it. The mechanization of weaponry and the increasing size of armies also contributed to higher death tolls in the nineteenth century. Internal conflicts were especially long and destructive. An estimated 20 million people died during the Taiping Rebellion in China, and at least three-fourths of a million—mostly combatants—perished during the U.S. Civil War.

So if mortality rates were not falling rapidly, how could the global population be rising so quickly? Simply put, it was more births rather than fewer deaths that led to population increase. This snowballing global birth rate was largely a result of natural growth together with the increased production of food. The addition of new crops such as sweet potatoes in China, potatoes in Europe, wheat in North America, and maize in Africa provided plenty of calories for populations to grow. Thus through most of the nineteenth century, populations grew almost everywhere

Toward the end of the century, however, birth rates in some urban areas began to level off and even to decrease. The main reason for this plateau effect seems to be that factory workers calculated the value of children differently from farmers. For agricultural families, more children generally meant more workers to bring in the crop. For factory workers and the middle class, however, children were an added expense but contributed little much to a family's income. This was especially true as child labor and school attendance laws came into effect in societies like the United States and Great Britain, late in the nineteenth century.

However, while families might plan to have fewer children, actually reducing birth rates was a more complex process. Bourgeois morality, with its stated aversion to "sexual excess," helped to promote abstinence in some people. But sex—as throughout human history—remained a major feature of life. Rather than a reduction in sex, therefore, the decline of family size among some urban communities was a product of various forms of birth control. The most controversial, even in the nineteenth century, was abortion. Abortion rates rose rapidly in this period, especially in Europe and the Americas. In Berlin, as many as a quarter of working-class pregnancies may have ended in abortions by the 1890s, while in St. Petersburg, Russia, the number of apportions appears to have increased by a factor of 10 over the course the nineteenth century. In China and India as well, abortion rates climbed. Other forms of birth control were even more common. Industry and chemistry combined to create the modern condom and diaphragm in the nineteenth century, and although some men saw these as cutting against their masculinity there is significant evidence that women, especially, promoted their use or used them in secret.

Feast and famine

Eating, of course, was also an important a part of life in this era, but the way people ate was changing, if slowly at first. Urbanization and factory work was beginning to remove many people from their connections with the land, and as it did so consumption of food changed as well. In many industrialized societies, the advent of wage labor was linked to the development of mass grocery stores, the expansion of restaurants and cafeterias, and the beginning of a market for semiprepared preserved foods like canned meals and soup packets. The working-class factory worker diet that resulted was often quite poor, with few fresh fruits and vegetables. Even babies saw a worsening of their diet in some cases. With working-class women increasingly employed, alternatives to mother's milk had to be found for babies. Industrialization and science provided answers: glass bottles, rubber nipples, and "scientifically" designed formulae mixing animal milks, sweeteners, and other ingredients. Unfortunately, many of these formulae were not healthy at all, and their introduction contributed to the diseases suffered by children already facing the dangers of unhealthy air, child labor, and lack of sunshine.

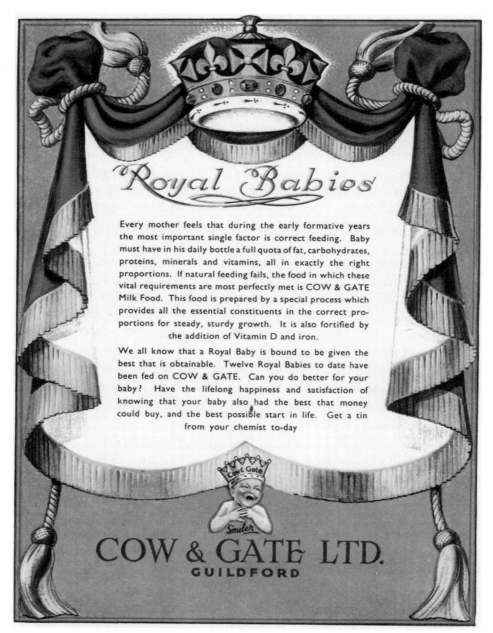

Figure 7.6 Advertisement for Cow & Gate baby milk powder, 1951.

Of course, even worse problems afflicted areas affected by famines. As we have seen, the combination of natural and man-made factors created desperate famines in the 1870s, especially. A British observer in India, Lt. Colonel Ronald Osborne, described the famine there:

> The corpses of the dead were strewn along the cross-country roads. Mothers sold their children for a single scanty meal. Husbands flung their wives into ponds, to escape the torment of seeing them perish by the lingering agonies of death.[1]

Osborne had no doubt who was to blame. He pointed to the colonial administration, which had turned land historically employed for food production over to cash crops, and who pretended the famine they had helped to cause did not exist. "Amid these scenes of death," he wrote, "the Government of India kept its serenity and cheerfulness unimpaired. The journals of the Northwest were persuaded into silence. Strict orders were given to civilians under no circumstances to countenance the pretence of the natives that they were dying of hunger." The Qing Dynasty in China evinced a similar lack of concern for its own citizens during famine there. Of course, the starving did not take such lack of concern lying down: from peasant uprisings in India to the Boxer movement in China, famine played a large role in rebellions against authorities in this era.

Toward the other end of the socioeconomic spectrum, the emerging bourgeoisie spent this era creating not only their sense of heightened personal morality but also the table manners and diet by which they might prove their rising status. Many sought to emulate the very wealthy, who dined in grand style. In the 1870s, such great chefs as Auguste Escoffier in France began to standardize culinary education and menus as well as table settings. They also proposed a cuisine pecking order. Of course, French cuisine was at the top, and therefore the wealthy ate multicourse menus of richly sauced French-style cuisine. The middle classes tried to emulate these experiences, and many were soon purchasing obscure cutlery like snail forks and caviar spoons.

Migration played an enormous role in food experiences in this period as well. Both immigrants and the societies that received them had to adjust to the new cuisines being brought into their regions, sometimes in interesting ways. For example, many of the Italians who moved to the East Coast of the United States in the late nineteenth century brought a southern Italian diet based largely on corn-meal with just a small amount of (more expensive) sauces. As their wealth improved in their new country, they shifted to the higher-status foods of Italy—especially wheat pasta—and also increased the amount of sauce in their dishes. These changes to an American style of heavily sauced pastas was quite unknown in Italy.

The Chinese global migration also resulted in new culinary styles. In the western areas of North America, Chinese immigrants took on roles of preparing food for mining companies and railroad company cafeterias. In the city of Mexicali, Mexico, they developed a unique style of cuisine that adapted to local ingredients and palates. In Singapore, southern Chinese migrants' dishes remained almost unchanged, but came to coexist with a wide range of Indian and Malaysian dishes. In San Francisco, United States, the largest expatriate Chinese community in the Americas developed many of the staples of Chinese American cooking. European American ingredients like broccoli replaced Chinese greens, and Chinese American chefs invented new dishes like chop suey, which mixed meat, vegetables, and noodles for easy one-bowl consumption. There are many legends about the origins chop suey—such as that a Chinese cook invented it after-hours for drunken miners—but they cannot be confirmed.

Altered states

Migration patterns and industrialization affected consumables that weren't foodstuffs. In particular, patterns in the consumption alcohol and other drugs responded to the movement of people and changing social and cultural patterns of the era.

Beer was the great drink of the Industrial Revolution, and several of the major types of beers emerged and spread around the world in this period. Science also played an enormous role in this process. Calorie-rich porters meant to provide energy to factory workers were developed in London in the early eighteenth century. A notoriously tricky product, their production depended on thermometers, hydrometers, and massive steam kettles that were widely available for the first time. India Pale Ale (IPA) was also a product of this age. Its development was partly a result of empire, for IPAs were in high demand in India especially. Reputedly, they could survive the long journey from Britain to India better than most porters and stouts, but it's likely that they were really just refreshing and better suited to a hot climate. By the early twentieth century, IPAs were joined by other lighter styles of beer, especially German pilsners and lagers. The global popularity of this style was stimulated by German Protestant missionaries who set up breweries wherever they established themselves. A number continue to be produced today including Tsingtao beer (China) and Windhoek lager (Namibia, formerly German Southwest Africa).

Wine, also, spread around the world with Europeans. French vintners followed their army into Algeria and, even in that Muslim-majority country, began to produce large amounts of wine in the mid-nineteenth century. French, Spanish, and Italian immigrants set up wine industries in almost all of the Mediterranean climate regions of the world including in California, Chile, Australia, and southern Africa. This wine colonization turned out to be fortuitous for Europe. When the phylloxera insect plague spread through European vineyards in the late nineteenth century, North American grapes were available to save them. Because the insects came from North America, many grapes in California were already resistant. However, they were generally seen as inferior for wine production. Fortunately, science came to the rescue. By the end of the century, vintners had learned to mix North American and European vines to create hybrids that were both phylloxera resistant and appealed to European palates!

Alcohol was not the only major intoxicant of the era, for this was also the period that gave us cheap opium and cocaine. The development of inexpensive processed opium in 1818 created a generation of drug addicts, from opium smokers in China to consumers of laudanum and other "calming medicines" in Europe and the Americas. We have already seen the ways in which the global opium market broke down Qing Dynasty's social and economic system in China, but it was also prescribed in bourgeois societies around the world as a way to make children better-mannered and more polite. Meanwhile, the alkaloidization of the Peruvian plant coca, first discovered by German scientists in 1860, led to a product marketed for the opposite effect from opium. Scientists and leaders around the world argued that cocaine was excellent for promoting vigor and energy, as well as for its anesthetic properties.

Of course, not everyone embraced alcohol and drugs. Temperance movements of the nineteenth century, many based on the foundations of evangelical Protestantism, pushed for their criminalization not only because of their addictive properties but also because of the violence and misbehavior that resulted from their abuse. Similarly, Chinese reformers attacked opium consumption. The results of the two movements were quite distinct, however. Whereas middle-class European and Euro-American Temperance movements were able to influence laws regarding alcohol in the United States and Europe, these same governments used their power to put down reformers in China who tried to halt the negative impact of the profitable opium trade on their society. This difference is typical of an era in which capitalism, industry, and race shaped distinct outcomes for people around the world.

Key terms

climatology [204]
conservationism [212]
deforestation [208]
El Niño-Southern Oscillation [203]
monoculture farming [205]

Further readings

Mike Davis's *Late Victorian Holocausts: El Niño and the Making of the Third World* (New York: Verso, 2002) was the book that broke the story on the human contributions to nineteenth-century global famine.

Madeleine's Children, by Sue Peabody (New York: Oxford University Press, 2017), tells the story of a family torn apart and fighting to be free across the late eighteenth and nineteenth century Indian Ocean world.

There are now many histories of global migration, but Patrick Manning's *Migration in World History* (New York: Routledge, 2005) remains one of the best. Chapter 8 covers the eighteenth and nineteenth centuries.

Epilogue: The Origins of the First World War

Historian Heather Streets-Salter tells the story of a very modern event that occurred during the First World War, in the British colony of Singapore. In February 1915, barely six months into the conflict, a group of Indian soldiers mutinied against the British authorities in the colony. They were influenced by anti-British propaganda spread by German prisoners-of-war, as well as a sense of religious unity with the Muslim Ottoman Empire, since both states were ranged against Britain and its allies, but their own growing awareness of their Indian "national" identity also played a role. But the revolt was put down not only by British industrial might but also by forces of its allies—Russia and Japan—quickly called to the spot. Even China, technically neutral, assisted by asking Chinese Singaporean civilians to remain calm.

The Singapore uprising and its suppression is an oft-ignored episode of the First World War, which broke out in August 1914 and came to a conclusion over four years later. It is ignored in part because it does not fit in with the principal narrative of the war as an unexpected conflict between great, imperial, industrialized states that had not faced each other in an all-out war for several decades. In fact, however, the First World War was truly global in that it not only drew in the great powers, but involved the participation, in various ways, of people around the world. Fought across Europe, in parts of Africa and Asia, and in naval confrontations in all of the major oceans, it also drove the U.S. invasion of Haiti and influenced events in China and mainland Latin America. Of course, this was not the first transcontinental conflict of the long nineteenth century—the 164-year period covered in this book began with Seven Years War, which had also spread across oceans and continents. But the First World War was global in a new way, its participants ranging from the European powers like France, Britain, Germany, Russia, Italy, the Ottoman Empire, and the Austro-Hungarian Empire on which we typically lavish attention, but also their the Asian, African, and Caribbean colonies and ultimately Japan, the United States, China, and many Latin American states as well. Beyond the level of the state, it also shifted local economic and cultural dynamics in regions that were not even officially involved in the conflict.

In this series, we treat the First World War as a threshold event—the conclusion of the long nineteenth century and the beginning the era in which we lived today. This conflict heralded changes and ushered in a new and highly unbalanced era in human history that included the Second World War and the Cold War period. But the 1914–1918 conflict was also the apex of the many transformations that occurred in the century-and-a-half that preceded its outbreak. In this epilogue, we will look at some of the connections between the themes described in the chapters of this book and the causes and events of the First World War.

Nationalism and imperialism

The First World War drew on popular political sentiment to a greater degree than any previous major conflict in global history. The two greatest political forces of the time, nationalism and imperialism, were both central to popular sentiment in favor of war. The ambassadors and generals who rushed to war did so by calling upon the national patriotism of the people, in particular. Germany and Italy, both still relatively new states, longed for a struggle that would prove that they were as great as the older powers. France still smarted from a defeat in the 1870–1871 Franco-Prussian war, and its patriots hungered to reclaim provinces lost to Prussia. Russia's pan-Slavic nationalism drove that country to support its Slavic neighbor Serbia, while Austro-Hungary attacked Serbia partly in an effort to control the ethnic nationalisms among Serbs, Czechs, and other minorities within its own borders. Of course, the leaders of the major powers often underestimated the nationalist hunger that would take the opportunity of war to emerge from minorities and subject peoples within their states. Arab and Armenian nationalism in the Ottoman Empire is just one example; the Indian nationalism of troops who rebelled against the British in Singapore is yet another.

Imperialism was the other potent political force behind the rush to the battlefronts in 1914. For example, the nationalist leaders of the Ottoman Empire hoped to reclaim their lost empire in the Balkans. Britain, France, and Russia, in return, each hoped to claim a slice of the Ottoman Empire. Britain and France claimed sections of the Mediterranean coast and Arabian interior, while Russia hoped to force the Dardanelles Straits open in order to dominate trade in the eastern Mediterranean. Britain and France also plotted to gain new territories that included the four German colonies in Africa. Even non-European powers used the war to build empire. Japan claimed German territories in the Pacific, while the United States occupied Haiti in 1917.

Empires also contributed to the war in terms of strategic materials and manpower. Indeed, it can be said that Britain and France could hardly have won the war without the aid of their colonies and possessions. Britain mobilized 2.5 million colonial soldiers and laborers, of whom 1.2 million Indian troops formed the largest contribution. France mobilized 475,000 colonial soldiers, of whom 335,000 were

Figure E.1 A patriotic French journal from 1915 showing a wounded soldier clutching the French flag, entitled "Love for the Flag," in *Le Petit Journal,* July 11, 1915.

African. Other colonial subjects were drafted as munitions and agricultural laborers to replace French soldiers fighting at the front. Often, these soldiers and workers were treated quite badly. The French had a policy called *encadrement*, for example, which isolated Africans from the local population. Indian soldiers faced harsher discipline than British troops did, including physical punishment like whipping. Such treatment did not stop them from contributing to the ultimate victory which Britain and France shared.

Industrialization and militarization

By the 1910s, industrialization had transformed transport, work, leisure, daily life, and even arts and literature in many regions of the world. In some societies, industrialization had so thoroughly pervaded daily life and the way people thought that it formed an important part of their national and individual identities.

One of the areas where the Industrial Revolution had a great impact in these societies was by promoting militarization. As we have seen, industry gave the armies of European states, Japan, and the United States huge military advantages over smaller, nonindustrialized states and societies. Other states—like China and Egypt—had attempted to similarly modernize their armies and navies, but because they lacked the industrial economic infrastructure, they did not succeed in this period.

Yet this military and economic power came at a great cost. In order to prepare for future wars, the industrialized states continually built up vast armies of men and huge stockpiles of munitions. Moreover, they planned for their wars by calculating, using the mathematics of the industrial capitalism, how they would be able to move these men and materials to the front lines. What this meant was that the general staff of each of the great states created a timetable of mobilizations and railroad movements that—once embarked upon—could not be stopped. As a result, when conflict threatened to break out in 1914, the states of Europe collectively rushed to implement their industrial and transportation timetables with hardly a look back, and could not stop them from unfolding into open warfare.

Once the industrialized powers' armies met, however, they found a war they had not expected. Because none of these countries had experienced extended conflict against other industrialized power in decades or more, during which time military technology had changed dramatically, they had no idea what machine guns and cannon could really do. They imagined they could roll over each other as easily as they had defeated the nonindustrialized societies in other parts of the world. Instead, they found offensive operations and fast movement just about impossible. Machine guns could rake advancing forces, artillery could break up formations of men miles from the front. Most ominous of all was chemical gas—a product of the second Industrial Revolution's emphasis on chemistry—of which war poet Wilfred Own famously wrote:

> Gas! Gas! Quick, boys!—An ecstasy of fumbling,
> Fitting the clumsy helmets just in time;
> But someone still was yelling out and stumbling,
> And flound'ring like a man in fire or lime…
> Dim, through the misty panes and thick green light,
> As under a green sea, I saw him drowning.
> In all my dreams, before my helpless sight,

He plunges at me, guttering, choking, drowning.
If in some smothering dreams you too could pace
Behind the wagon that we flung him in,
And watch the white eyes writhing in his face,
His hanging face, like a devil's sick of sin;
If you could hear, at every jolt, the blood
Come gargling from the froth-corrupted lungs,
Obscene as cancer, bitter as the cud
Of vile, incurable sores on innocent tongues,

Capitalism

As late as 1913, just prior to the outbreak of the war, proponents of capitalism had argued that the explosion of international trade and the links between banks in different countries would make war impossible. They contended that investment and commerce had so interlinked economies in different countries that they could not afford to go to war with each other, or they would mutually destroy the economic foundations on which their states were built.

In reality, however, economic rivalries were already contributing to the bad feelings between rival "great powers." Britain and Germany, especially, competed with each other to sell their goods on global markets and to dominate shipping around the world. France, meanwhile, resented Germany because it controlled the coal-producing provinces of Alsace and Lorraine. Russia resented the fact that the Ottoman Empire could block vital trade routes into the Mediterranean. These economic resentments may not have been leading causes of the war, but they certainly contributed to it.

Perhaps more importantly, the language and ideas of international economic collaboration faded as soon as nationalist sentiment was stirred up in May and June 1914. From the moment the war started, bankers and industrialists were among the biggest supporters of national war efforts across Europe. In some cases, they had hopes for material gains. Investors in arms and munitions companies, shipbuilding corporations, and other businesspeople saw the war as potentially very profitable. Most, however, merely believed that a short war leading to victory would be good for their country.

Race and morality

The long nineteenth century was supposedly an era of progress toward more enlightened and moral modern civilization. Supposedly, these values should have halted the most destructive war in modern memory. Instead, modernity in its moral, intellectual, and philosophical guises helped to bring it to fruition. Some states merely manufactured moral arguments to explain their decisions to go to war. Britain, for example, justified its decision to enter the war on the basis of alleged atrocities on the part of Germany, including the supposed murder or rape of children and nuns in Belgium. These allegations were later disproven. Broader moral arguments were also mobilized by the great powers. When the United States entered the war in 1917, President Woodrow Wilson argued that its purpose was to "make the world safe for democracy."

Pseudoscientific racialized arguments were similarly mobilized to justify many states' involvement in the war. Eugenicists were breaking new ground, for example, as the war began. In the United States, Madison Grant was preparing to publish his book *The Passing of the Great Race* in which he would argue a scientific basis for discrimination against Native Americans and African Americans and the exclusion of Asians. Admittedly, major challenges were arising to race theory as a few scientists began to amass evidence that the very concept of race was flawed. Yet, by this time, racism was deeply engrained in the dominant culture of modernity, and it played a role in the war development of the First World War. Racialized depictions of potential enemies, for example, helped convince the populations of the major belligerent powers to go to war—the cruel German, the feeble Frenchman, and the barbaric Turk, for example.

At the same time, the idea of "survival of the fittest" found an odd expression in military tactics. Officers and philosophers, especially in France, came to believe that victorious societies proved their fitness through élan—energy and vigorousness. This concept was of course adapted from the Theory of Evolution through Natural Selection. Yet it was incredibly unsuited for industrialized warfare. In pursuit of élan, French generals drove their troops to always be on the attack in the early days of the war. This meant that they charged machine gun emplacements and defensive fortifications, leading to massive casualties.

In fact, the combination of scientific research and industrialization had created a new kind of war, although few acknowledged it in 1914. Research into human biology set the stage for the development of poison gases, an important weapon in this conflict. The development of petroleum fuels also allowed machinery to be moved to and from the front lines quickly. By 1914, U.S. oil fields were producing 300 million barrels of oil a day, and the belligerents were striving to catch up. One thing that had not caught up was medical science, which remained woefully unprepared for the horrors of the war.

Questioning the war and modernity

As we can see, First World War was a crescendo of all of the cultural, political, and economic development of a global modernity across the long nineteenth century.

It quite easy to see this modern war in universal terms—a conflict that drew in people from around the world and created a shared set of experiences. In fact, the war—like modernity itself—took on many different flavors, all of them modern but nevertheless quite different. Taken as a whole, moreover, these experiences undermined confidence in modernity at the moment in which it seemed to have become ubiquitous. These sentiments and experiences help to reinforce the idea of multiple modernities even at these final moments of the long nineteenth century.

In the first place, the war experience was a great shock for many people, especially soldiers. Many came from rural areas, often those whose integration into the mainstream of the modern world was far from complete. Whether Siberian recruits fighting for Russia, American farm-hands from the U.S. West, or sepoys from the mountains of Kashmir, many soldiers came from places where industrial machines and modern weaponry were still strange, and where family ties were more important than even the call of the nation. Many of these soldiers, initially often willing to serve, eventually found conditions too foul to continue willingly. French troops refused orders to go into the meatgrinder of combat in 1917. African and Asian troops protested their treatment at the hands of racist officers and joined widespread mutinies. Russian soldiers and sailors reacted to the suffering of modern combat by supporting revolution at home.

The Russian revolution was evidence of the power of the socialist flavor of modern thought, a reaction to capitalism. From the beginning, European socialists tended to be among the few within their societies to oppose the war. They argued that combat would only result in the deaths of millions of workers without advancing their interests. Many socialist organizations, like the Socialist Party of France and the Social Democratic Party of Germany, actively protested against the coming of the war.

Leading socialists blamed capitalism for the outbreak of the war and called for a proletarian revolution to end it. Perhaps the most important of these was the Russian communist Leon Trotsky, who began to write about this subject in as early as November 1914. Trotsky argued that the First World War was the result of capitalist economic growth in each country. He argued that the banks and industries of these countries had reached their limits within each state, and were now competing for global control. Thus the war, he argued, was really an attempt by the wealthy of each country to control the economy of the whole world. Trotsky predicted that the war would bring an end to both the nation-state system and the global capitalist economy. In the end, of course, he was wrong. Nevertheless, the deprivations and horrors of the war did create the opportunity for socialists to seize power in at least one large country—Russia—in 1917.

The war also brought into question the moral values of modernity. Some scholars have argued that the war involved the destruction of everything that Europeans (especially) had been taught to hold sacred: humanism, Enlightenment values, and rationalism. In fact, many individuals and groups who were against the war argued early on that it contravened the values—both secular and religious—that they held most dear. Pacifists and conscientious objectors included Christian moralists in Germany and Britain. In British-ruled Ireland, Catholic religious leaders joined the protests against the war. Other objectors were socialists, many of whom who argued that the real enemy was the ruling class. Their opposition to the war often included moral claims against the fighting. For example, Russian socialist Valentin Bulgakov's stated in his appeal that "the common enemy… is the beast within us."

In the colonies, as well, the values of modernity promoted by the "civilizing mission" were brought into question by the war. Submarine warfare disrupted the economic cycle of raw materials for finished products on which the economies of colonies were now based. This caused massive suffering for many, especially women, trying to survive in the colonial possessions. The supposed organizational superiority of Europeans was disproven by these failures. Meanwhile, soldiers returned home having seen Europeans killing each other, and often having fired upon Europeans. These veterans, in some cases, were among the first generation of modern Africans and Asians to start organizing for the end of empire and colonies.

Most of these facts were unrecognized in 1914, however. Pacifists quickly found themselves overwhelmed by the nationalist, pro-war sentiment and moral outrage that inexorably drove the world toward this watershed event. The war was therefore seen mostly as the culmination of modernity. By the very horrors, however, the next four years would help to begin the century-long process of tearing that modernity apart.

Notes

Introduction: The Construction of Modernity

1 William Gqoba, "The Cause of the Cattle-Killing at the Nongqause Period," translated by A. C. Jordan in *Towards an African Literature: The Emergence of Literary Form in Xhosa* (Berkeley: University of California Press, 1973), 111–112.

2 Faith and Question

1 S. Augustus Mitchell, *A System of Modern Geography for the Use of Schools and Academies* (Philadelphia: T.H. Butler, 1881).
2 Andrew Reed and James Matheson, *A Narrative of the Visit to the American Churches by the Deputation from the Congregational Union of England and Wales* (London: Jackson and Walford, 1838).
3 Italics added. Jean-Jacques Rousseau, *On the Social Contract*, in *Basic Political Writings*, translated by Donald A. Cress (Indianapolis, 1988), vol. 1, 146.
4 Sarah Stickney Ellis, *The Women of England: Their Social Duties, and Domestic Habits* (London Printing, 1843).
5 Florence Hartley, *The Ladies' Book of Etiquette, and Manual of Politeness*, 1860.
6 Ruth Smythers, "Instruction and Advice for the Young Bride," *The Madison Institute Newsletter*, 1994.
7 Edward Carpenter, *Homogenic Love and Its Place in a Free Society*, 1894.
8 Op. Cit. McVay 27.

3 Nationalism and the Nation-State

1 Voltaire, *The Philosophical Dictionary*, Selected and Translated by H. I. Woolf (New York: Knopf, 1924).

4 Industrialization

1 William Wordsworth, "The world is too much with us; late and soon," 1806.

2   *Boston Evening Globe*, January 16, 1919.
3   Parliamentary Papers of Great Britain, 1842, vol. VXI, cited in *Internet World History Sourcebook*. http://www.fordham.edu/halsall/mod/1842womenminers.asp.

5 Capitalism and Socialism

1   Adam Smith, *An Inquiry into the Nature and Causes of the Wealth of Nations*, 1776, Electronic Classic Series Publication, http://www2.hn.psu.edu/faculty/jmanis/adam-smith/wealth-nations.pdf, 362.
2   David Hume, *Of the Independence of Parliament*, 1742. Brochure, available online at https://ebooks.adelaide.edu.au/h/hume/david/of-the-independency-of-parliament/.
3   Jean-Baptiste Say, *Catechism of Political Economy*,(Paris, 1817), reprinted 1970, 37, 41, 118.
4   Thomas Paine, *The Rights of Man,* 1791.
5   Cecil Frances Alexander, *Hymns Ancient and Modern* (London: William Clowes & Sons, 1904), hymn 573, 1848.
6   Karl Marx and Frederick Engels, *Manifest of the Communist Party* (1848, 2004 English edition), available online at http://ocw.nd.edu/political-science/the-rise-and-fall-of-world-communism/readings/Manifesto.pdf, 16.
7   Dadabhai Naoroji, "Memorandum No. 2 on the Moral Poverty in India and Native Thoughts on the Present British Indian Policy," November 16, 1880, in *Voices of Indian Freedom Movement*, edited by J. C. Johari (New Delhi: Akashdeep Publishing, 1883), 100.
8   "Plan de Ayala," in John Womack, *Zapata and the Mexican Revolution* (New York: Knopf, 1969), 402.

6 Explaining the World

1   Charles Darwin, *On the Origin of Species by Means of Natural Selection, or the Preservation of Favoured Races in the Struggle for Life* (London: John Murry, 1859), Chapter XIV. The phrase "by the Creator" may not have appeared in the first edition.
2   Alfred R. Wallace, "The Origins of Human Races and the Antiquity of Man Deduced from the Theory of Natural Selection," *Journal of the Anthropological Society of London,* 1864.

7 Changing Environments

1   R. Osborne, "India Under Lord Lytton," *Contemporary Review* (December 1879), 564.

Glossary

acculturation— a process by which one community comes to associate with cultural traits or social patterns of another group

agnosticism— the view that the existence of God is unknowable

anarchism— the concept that humans should be able to produce societies that provide rough equality of opportunity, but without large-scale institutions

assembly line— a system of production by which specialized workers produce small parts of complicated products that move from worker to worker, gradually reaching completion.

bank— financial institution that accepts deposits and uses these funds to extend credit for profit

bonds— loans made by individuals to state or private organizations in return for the promise of repayment with interest

bourgeoisie— the "middle class" of professionals and business owners who had capital to invest and whose morals, aspirations, and needs were central to the development of modern types of economics, politics, and culture

bubble— excessive investment in a product or enterprise in return for the promise of large profits, often fraudulently, that bursts, producing extensive losses for investors

capital— money, land, or labor available for investment in projects or products

capitalism— the philosophy in support of an economic system in which markets of all sorts are free and largely unregulated and assets are generally in the hands of private individuals or groups of individuals

castes— a class system, found in a number of societies in particular periods, that is relatively rigid and provides little opportunity for social mobility. Membership in castes may or may not be related to occupation, race, ethnicity, or religion.

civilizing mission— the argument, largely held by European and Euro-American settler societies, that they had a duty and a right to "civilize" subject peoples through colonial rule and cultural transformation

classical liberalism— a commitment to fundamental liberties including freedom to choose one's religion, to speak, to assemble, to a free press, and ultimately, to the right to aspire to a life of freedom with aspirations to advance in society as well as support for free trade, individual property rights, and open markets.

climatology— the modern scientific study of weather and climate

colonialism— the ideas, policies, and actions by which imperial citizens rule over the subjects of empires

colony— a colonial possession held by an empire as a nonsovereign subject

commodity replacement— the substitution of one set of goods (usually imported) for another (usually produced domestically)

communism— an economic system in which the means of production are in the hands of the state as a representative for the workers

conservationism— the movement to protect natural resources

consumer— within capitalism, a way of viewing people based on their role as purchasers of goods and materials

core states— states, in economic models of the nineteenth century, that are industrialized and have extensive commercial networks with states or societies that provide raw materials and consume investment and finished products

creole nationalism— the ideology of nationalism as exhibited by settler communities politically alienated from the metropole

cultures of imperialism— set of ideas and doctrines in support of empire, normally found in imperial metropoles

defensive modernization— the reformation, industrialization, and modernization of a state or society in order to resist possible occupation or subjugation by other states

deforestation— the clearing of forested areas by human action

deindustrialization— the process by which productivity and industrial activity is reduced in a region or industry

dependency— an economic relationship in which one state or population produces raw materials and consumes finished products processed by another, creating an inequality in income and wealth

El Niño-Southern Oscillation— the irregular series of climatic changes characterized by unusually warm water off the Pacific coast of South America that causes a reversal of Pacific wind patterns and hence drought in large parts of Asia.

empire— a collection of states and societies, in which one polity exerts control and sovereign authority over others held in an unequal relationship

enclosure— the process by which individually owned or communally owned farming lands were combined and transferred into private ownership for the production of cash-earning agricultural or animal products.

Enlightenment, the— a body of intellectual and philosophical transformations, global in origin but centered in northwest Europe, that raised questions about authority, humanity, and challenged understandings of the physical, theological, sociopolitical, and economic systems of the world. Three core ideas of the Enlightenment were a belief in progress and an emphasis on reason and individual liberties.

ethnicity— the identification of a group by association with a shared culture, language history, and background.

ethnic nationalism— the form of nationalism associated with the idea of the nation as a product of a shared heritage, language, faith, and birth.

eugenics— the pseudoscientific pursuit of "racial health" and quest for "racial purity" that justified sterilization, segregation, and oppression

evangelism— broadly, the spreading of a gospel by personal witness or preaching, but specifically a movement within Protestantism that stressed individual spirituality, personal redemption, obedience to God, and the duty to teach these ideas to others.

evolution— in the context of living organisms, the process by which change occurs and species diversify

factories— a building or site where raw materials are processed into finished products

first-wave feminism— the first advocates for equality and rights for women to use modern ideas and organizational structures

free labor— the argument that individuals should be able to sell their labor on a free market to the highest bidder

free markets— the doctrine of an unregulated market in which goods, labor, and capital can be bought and sold by the highest bidder

fundamentalism— religious movements that call for a return to basic and original ideals

gentlemanly capitalism— a system, particularly related to the British Empire, in which financiers aspiring to the upper classes support imperial projects

geology— the science of the earth and its components

gold standard— a system by which the value of a currency is defined in terms of an amount of gold

gunboat diplomacy— an aggressive foreign policy supported by the use or threat of military force

heredity— the transmission of physical or mental characteristics genetically from one generation to another

imperialism— the ideas and actions by which a society creates and maintains an empires

inculturation— the gradual acquisition of characteristics and norms of a culture by an individual or group

indirect rule— a strategy by which a colonial government co-opts local leaders to support them or work with the colonial state.

industrial capitalism— a phase of capitalism in which finance was closely connected to the needs of industry, and which became powerful on a global scale in the nineteenth century

industrious revolution— the global expansion of trade and middle-class demand for goods that stimulated production of manufactured products in the period leading up to the nineteenth century

informal imperialism— a situation in modern imperialism in which a state is not formally a colony but nevertheless is in fact ruled by another

invisible hand— the Enlightenment argument that the prices of goods and services would naturally find their balance in an unregulated market

laissez-faire— a type of capitalism that calls for a complete lack of regulation

luddites— protesters, many of whom had lost their jobs due to industrialization, who destroyed machinery in the nineteenth century

market— in the context of capitalism, the exchange of goods and labor

Marxist critique— an attack on industrial capitalism for the oppression of workers and concentration of wealth in the hands of a wealthy minority. Marxists called instead for a socialist system that would provide greater equality and put the means of production in the hands of workers.

metropole— the sovereign state or society within an empire

millenarian— a religious or spiritual movement focused on apocalyptic change

missionaries— religious evangelists, often sent overseas to convert foreign populations

monoculture farming— the farming of a single crop over a large area

monogenesis— the theory, sustained by evidence, of the evolution of ancestral humans from a single hominid population

nation— the community of people identified by culture or ethnicity

nationalism— the ideology by which the leaders and proponents of the nation argue that the nation should govern its own state

nation-state— the legal, sovereign political unit that is ideally an expression of the nation

natural selection— the observation that evolutionary change occurs through many small changes that in some cases present individuals with a higher probability of surviving and reproducing.

new imperialism— a term used to describe the late nineteenth-century period in which industrialized societies of the world developed cultures of imperialism and used increased capital and new technology to conquer almost all of Africa and much of Southeast Asia and the Pacific

nihilism— a belief characterized by the rejection of all religious and moral principles

nuclear family— the family as defined as mother, father, and children

oligarchy— a powerful group of wealthy families or corporations that possesses some political authority or influence

pasteurization— the process of applying heat to destroy pathogens, usually in food or drink

paternalism— the attitude that one is, or should act like, a father figure toward others, whether children, women, ethnic minorities, subject peoples, etc.

periphery— in the context of industrial capitalism, states or regions that produce raw materials and consume finished products

polygenesis— the now disproven theory that different human populations evolved independently from hominid ancestors

primitivism— a view or approach that exalts and values something perceived as uncomplicated and simple, and hence pure

profit motive— financial gain as the incentive for labor or economic activity

proletariat— the class of workers who have nothing to sell except their own labor

racism— the impression and institutionalized system of oppression by which people are sorted into races, which are then ascribed traits and placed within a hierarchy

radiometric dating— a system of estimating the age of minerals and rocks by measuring radioactivity

realism— a school of art that called for representing the world as it actually was perceived by the artist

reformism— an approach to change that calls for institutional changes or progressive improvements

regulation— intervention by a body in an activity, usually applied to government intervention in the way that business or other economic activities are run

romanticism— an artistic genre of the nineteenth century that focused on heroic deeds, great epics, and emotional experiences. Associated with nationalism in some cases, it was also frequently a rejection of industrialization.

secondary imperialism— the expansion or empire-building undertaken by former colonial possessions, particularly in the Americas

secularism— a doctrine in support of the separation of religion from the political and social spheres of decision-making and daily life

segregation of tasks— a production system in which many individual workers each specialize in one or more tasks that together make up a whole process

social class— the ordering of society into groups, often hierarchical, by social and economic status

Social Contract— the belief that a contract should exist that spells out the obligations of different groups of citizens and sovereign rulers toward each other, and their rights

Social Darwinism— The misapplication of the theory of natural selection to that groups of people, especially grouped as "races", as a way to justify a hierarchical social order

social sciences— professions that study human societies, their relationships to each other and the world around them

socialism— an economic system of collectivity in which the means of production are in the hands of workers or their representatives

stocks— equal parts expressing ownership in banks, mills, factories, or corporations

stratigraphy— the branch of geology concerned with the order and relative position of the layers of earth and rock that make up the planet.

syncretism— the organic amalgamation of faiths or cultures

synthetic— man-made

taxonomy— the systematic classifaction of something, including living organisms

trade and labor unions— a labor collective that negotiates on behalf of workers

travelogue— books written by travelers, recording their journeys and experiences among other cultures and societies

utilitarianism— a philosophy that calls for absolute rationalism in decision-making

utopia— the concept of a perfect place or society, often expressed in nineteenth-century philosophy as the objective of a particular system of thought, economics, or politics

wage earner— a person who works for a fixed or regular payment in the employ of someone else, a corporation, or a government

Index